studio voices

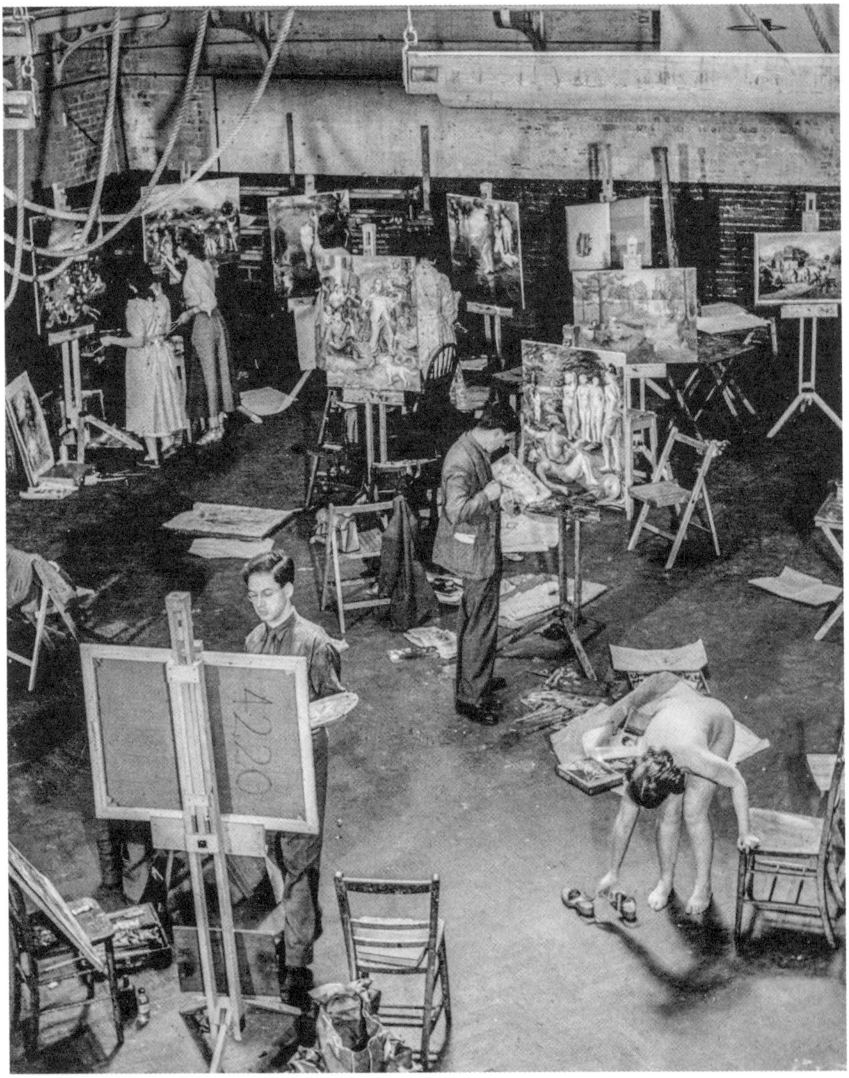
4220

studio voices

art and life in twentieth-century britain

michael bird

LUND
HUMPHRIES

First published in 2018 by Lund Humphries in association with the British Library

Lund Humphries
Office 3, Book House
261A City Road
London EC1V 1JX
UK

www.lundhumphries.com

ISBN: 978–1–84822–230–4

A Cataloguing-in-Publication record for this book is available from the British Library

Set in Adobe Garamond Pro and Akzidenz Grotesk
Printed in China

FRONTISPIECE: Students and life model in the gymnasium at Chelsea School of Art, 1962. Photographer unknown.

FRONT COVER: Phyllida Barlow in her studio in Finsbury Park, London, 1971. Photograph by John Malcolm Couzins.

BACK COVER: David Nash working on *Forms that Grow in the Night*, Llwyn Gell Workshops, Blaenau Ffestiniog, *c.*2007. Photograph by Ian Parker.

And there's childhood, there's art school, there's love, marriage and children, there's cabaret and theatre, there's films, there's assemblages, there's constructions, and installations. There's rituals. There's myself, today, talking.

Bruce Lacey[1]

Contents

Acknowledgements 9

Foreword by Cathy Courtney 11

Introduction: The Kitchen Sink Too 15

1 Home is Where We Start From: Children and Parents 29

2 This is What I Want to Do: First Steps in Art 53

3 The Sound of Bombs Falling: A Century of War 77

4 Self-propelled People: Going to Art School 99

5 Strange Calm and Turbulence: On Painting 127

6 It Has Substance: On Sculpture 153

7 The Strength of an Idea: Conceptual and Performance Art 179

8 The Work Completes: Being an Artist 201

Short Biographies 211

Notes 227

Image Credits 244

Index 245

Acknowledgements

This book is based on research I undertook as National Life Stories Goodison Fellow in 2016–17. I especially thank Rob Perks, director of National Life Stories, and the oral history staff at the British Library, who have cheerfully provided all manner of practical assistance, and Cathy Courtney, founder and project director of Artists' Lives, for her encouragement and guidance throughout. I am grateful to the Authors' Foundation for additional support that enabled me to continue to work on the book beyond the Goodison Fellowship's 12-month timeframe.

For their help in allowing access to Artists' Lives recordings that are not in the public domain, and providing photographs and information, I thank Georgia Adams, Rob Airey at the Wilhelmina Barns-Graham Trust, Phyllida Barlow, Polly Bielecka and the team at Pangolin London, Paul Caro, Oona Connell, Amie Conway at Flowers Gallery, Liz Counsell at Annely Juda Fine Art, Catharine Feiler, Katharine Heron, Susanna Heron, Tess Jaray, Andrew Lambirth, Matthew McDonald at the New Art Centre, Sarah Marchant, Jessica Ramsay at Waddington Custot, Julian Rothenstein, Richard Selby at the Redfern Gallery, and Ferriel Waddington. The Lund Humphries team have done a brilliant job in keeping this book on track, and it has been a pleasure to work with them again. Thank you Lucy Myers, Sarah Thorowgood, Tom Furness, Victoria Lyle and Lucie Ewin.

Foreword

In 2016 Michael Bird was appointed a Goodison Fellow, with a brief to work with recordings generated by the Artists' Lives oral history project run by National Life Stories at the British Library. He was already familiar with parts of the NLS collection, having listened to the life story recordings of figures such as Lynn Chadwick and Sandra Blow, and had quoted from their testimonies in monographs about them.

Michael approached his 12-month fellowship with two main aims. The first was achieved in 2017: an exhibition of the Ingram Collection at The Lightbox in Woking shaped by the inclusion of edited extracts from the Artists' Lives recordings, which illuminated the paintings and sculptures on display. The second and more major task, in terms of man-hours and navigation, was to compose this book, using the NLS recordings to tell the tale of the development of British art in the twentieth century.

I am pleased to say that Artists' Lives did what I had always hoped it would do. It confounded Michael's initial assumption of what that story would be. When he excavated the summaries of the recordings and chose likely sections to listen to, looking for the thread he expected to find, the thread kept snapping and sheering off in other directions.

One of the prime motivations of starting Artists' Lives was to create a platform where artists could tell their stories in their own way and in their own words. Not instead of other recordings and texts, but in addition to them. This was in part because of an awareness of the discrepancy between the language and concerns of artists and their way of telling their stories compared to that of art historians and other commentators. I think it was 15 years into the project before an artist mentioned even so soft a term as 'modernism', yet they were perfectly articulate and able to express exactly what they wished to pin down.

Another motive was to take the making of art out of the art-world bubble and to set it alongside everyday life: the buying of potatoes, the catching of buses, the paying of bills, visits to hospitals, births, deaths and marriages. Artists' Lives is rare in the sense that it is run not within a specialist art department but alongside other oral history projects that cover a wide spectrum of professions and industries. Whoever the subject, the recordings follow the life-story methodology pioneered by the oral and social historian Professor Paul Thompson. So the artists, like everyone else taking part, discuss wide-ranging aspects of their lives; for example, family background and childhood, politics, food, religion, sex education, clothes, friendships, morals, money, property and all manner of unforeseen topics, as well as an unusually detailed account of their creative lives.

Artists' Lives was begun in 1990, with Eileen Agar as its first contributor, closely followed by Michael Rothenstein, born in 1899 and 1908 respectively, both of whom are quoted in this book. At the time of writing, there are almost 400 Artists' Lives recordings, most around 20 hours in length, many considerably longer. Michael has chosen to concentrate mainly on the recordings made in the first half of the project's nearly 30 years' duration to date. These artists are among those who lived through the era when the shock of abstraction first challenged the primacy of figuration, when the overriding foreign influence shifted from France to America, and when art education underwent a series of revolutions. In many respects, this is already a world that younger generations find hard to calibrate. The richness of the first-hand accounts yielded by the recordings is a way of experiencing the period in a direct and compelling way.

Artists' Lives recordings are unusually detailed, together creating an ocean of shifting perspectives, sometimes affirmative, sometimes contradictory. When I think of Michael starting out on this book, I picture him stepping into the sea with just a small coracle tucked under his arm. Luckily, he is a strong swimmer.

Artists' Lives is run in association with Tate Archive and in close collaboration with the Henry Moore Institute. It is steered by an advisory committee currently composed of: Sir Alan Bowness; Dr Penelope Curtis; Caroline Cuthbert; Adrian Glew; Mel Gooding (Chair); Lisa Le Feuvre; Cornelia Grassi; Professor Lubaina Himid; Richard Morphet, CBE; Clive Phillpot; Dr Andrew Wilson; and Dr Jon Wood.

Many of the open recordings are online, where further details about the project and the work of National Life Stories can be found. For Artists' Lives see www.bl.uk/nls/artists. Whole life story summaries can be word searched via the British Library's Sound and Moving Image Catalogue http://sami.bl.uk. Many NLS recordings are also available for access online at British Library Sounds https://sounds.bl.uk. The Oral History Society's website, www.ohs.org.uk, is recommended for anyone seeking more information about oral history in Britain.

Cathy Courtney
Project Director, Artists' Lives

Introduction

The Kitchen Sink Too

If you want to find out what it was really like to live in a certain place at a certain time, to play a particular role in the society of those days, listen carefully to the people who were there. Never forget that opinions and interpretations can only be as subtle or as valid as the first-hand accounts they are based on. Or that, if these accounts were composed in writing rather than spoken aloud, they are likely to be shaped by textual conventions (sentence structure, punctuation, beginnings, middles and ends) as much as by the pressure of witness. This, very broadly, is where oral history comes in.

And the people whose spoken testimony historians record? For Jules Michelet, who researched his *History of the French Revolution* in the 1840s, while that seismic era was still in living memory, it was 'peasants, townsfolk, old men, women, even children', whose stories (as well as stories passed on to them by their parents) 'you can hear if you enter of an evening into a village tavern; which you may gather if, finding on the road a passer-by at rest, you begin to converse with him'.[2] In London, a few years later, the journalist Henry Mayhew, founding editor of *Punch* magazine turned ardent social researcher, was interviewing 'jugglers, conjurors, sword-swallowers', 'scavengers, night men, flushermen, chimney-sweeps' – people engaged in all manner of marginal yet often essential urban occupations. He would collate and publish their accounts of their lives and livelihoods in a compendious survey, *London Labour and the London Poor*. Mayhew trawled the tenements and backyards of working-class London, transcribing his interviews with the aid of a stenographer. It's not impossible that he edited or enhanced the transcripts; but pointing a camera – at that time an extraordinary new tool of social reportage – also involved editorial choices, and not even the camera was capable of capturing the daily experience of poverty with the immediacy of the life stories Mayhew recorded verbatim, on the spot. When we tune in to those myriad voices – the girl who makes glass eyes for dolls and people, the sunken-cheeked professional whistler, the Punch and Judy man – the catch-all, monolithic category 'the poor', so sanctimoniously touted by Victorian moralists and politicians, atomises as we read.

What about other categories of people – artists, for example? Even in ancient and medieval times, when the most accomplished artists were generally seen as journeymen rather than geniuses, you might assume that this social group was never among the silent oppressed, the crossing-sweepers and cigar-end-finders of the age. Artists' works, sometimes their writings too, survive them; admirers preserve anecdotes about their habits and sayings. And yet, if you think of the nineteenth-century Londoners we can still 'hear', thanks to Mayhew's respect for what Roland Barthes would call 'the grain of the voice',[3] these otherwise forgotten speakers are more audibly present in their Victorian moment than eminent artist contemporaries of theirs, like Dante Gabriel Rossetti or William Morris, whose lives are comprehensively documented but whose intimate verbal quirks are lost to history.

There's a sense, too, in which the significance of artists' work, unlike the tricks of the monkey-trainer's trade, tends to be considered too weighty a matter to be left to artists themselves to expound. This, in turn, leads to a state of historiographical affairs in which artists can sometimes resemble the excluded, overlooked, disempowered groups on which oral historians typically focus.[4] Waiting on the studio threshold, eager to take possession of the artist's story, to tell us what it all means, there is often a more or less well-qualified interpreter. And, no matter how sympathetic or perceptive the critical interpretation, for the artist it is a form of substitute representation that can arouse mixed feelings or worse. There is also usually an element of proxy creativity on the part of the interpreter, as with the professional literary critic or academic for whom, in W.H. Auden's words, 'a poem is not a work of art by somebody else; it is his own discovered document.'[5]

On being told that the great art historian Ernst Gombrich felt uncomfortable visiting artists' studios, the painter Derrick Greaves remarked that, 'it's different for painters.'

> I think painters are rougher than that. They're more – they're bruisers, compared to most critics. And their impulse, their starting point, is in life,

> I think, most painters. And the work of the studio is also a rougher world – it's a rough and tough world where you're engaged with the *most* difficult thing, to translate that thing that attracts you, moves you in a life situation, with all its rough edges and all its subjectivity – to translate that and refine it in the studio, in your own terms, so that it holds that vital ingredient of the liveliness that you've been excited by in real life.[6]

What we have here is one minute, three seconds of Greaves speaking – a brief but telling extract from the many hours of interview he recorded for the Artists' Lives project between July 1999 and June 2000, at the age of 72. This book contains extracts from around 40 such interviews – a total of some ten hours of artists' talking about their lives and work, transcribed with all the 'vital ingredients' of informal, un-tidied-up speech. These ten hours are a minuscule sample lifted out of the vast, still-growing oral-history archive that is Artists' Lives. Inaugurated in April 1990 with an interview with the nonagenarian surrealist painter Eileen Agar, it forms part of the UK's National Life Stories collection, held at the British Library in London and gradually being made available online.[7]

Artists' Lives interviews are different from the interviews usually encountered in the art-world media. They are life-story conversations, ranging not only through creative practice and professional achievements, but also through childhood memories, family life, relationships and unexpected, incidental epiphanies of self-awareness, whether or not these have a demonstrable bearing on art. The artists don't sound like 'bruisers', any more than Greaves himself does, but they don't talk like critics or art historians either; it's the difference between turning the glossy pages of a cookbook and how it feels to have your hands in the mixing bowl. Art is described and discussed, for sure, but there is also space in these interviews for 'every kind of food and drink, every kind of utensil and implement, the usual plain furniture, and even the baby's nappies on the line. Everything but the kitchen sink? The kitchen sink too.'[8]

I'm quoting some familiar lines from a 1954 review by David Sylvester of the work of Derrick Greaves and three other young painters, Jack Smith, Edward Middleditch and John Bratby, who would subsequently, thanks to the critic's way with words, be known as the Kitchen Sink School. As an interpreter of post-war British and European painting and sculpture, Sylvester was one of the best, identifying a particular kind of scarified realism that was then very much in the air. He was an early advocate of Francis Bacon, in whose space-framed interiors all manner of violence and violation seem to be taking place. But babies' nappies and Belfast sinks? Sylvester writes as if he can't imagine how such obdurately quotidian objects could earn a place in art. Thinking of paintings like Smith's *Mother Bathing a Child* (1953), in which a grey-faced woman sponges down a toddler who stands bleakly naked in a scullery sink, he sounds disconcerted to find that, 'There is nothing to hint that the man about the house is an artist or anything but a very ordinary bloke [. . .] in every case it is clearly a kitchen in which ordinary people cook their ordinary food, and doubtless live their ordinary lives.'[9]

Greaves and Smith loathed being labelled Kitchen Sink artists; in their later careers, this memorable journalist's tag became a ball and chain. Even in the 1950s, claimed Smith, 'It was a misrepresentation of my attitude and intention to consider it social realist. If I had lived in a palace, I would have painted the chandeliers.'[10] There was a further irony in that, unknown to either critic or audience, all the 'ordinary blokes' with whom Smith had shared a bomb-damaged house in Earl's Court in the early 1950s were in fact artists:

> I just turned to the environment in which I lived at that time, which was a house which was occupied totally by artists, as it happened, artists who had been at college and left, or were still there. And, so I started to paint the interiors of that house, things left on tables, not set-up still lifes, just milk bottles and things that had been left there. And there was my brother and his wife living in the basement at that time, and they had a child, and I watched the child walking and things like that, and the child being bathed in the sink, because that's where – there wasn't a bathroom downstairs. And so that's where I got those ideas from.[11]

Did the artist nurse a grievance against a critic who had so misrepresented his motives? Not at all, it turns out. In Smith's recollection of another brush with Sylvester, four years later, the writer and the ordinary bloke appear as one and the same person:

> [Sylvester] was someone who wanted to produce an article that he was enthusiastic about, but he wanted it to be so well written that practically it became a work of writing, an art in its own right. And he was very good at it, I think. I liked him very much. I mean he really did care about what he was writing. When he was writing for the Matthiesen Gallery, I was living in Putney and so was he at that time. He arrived one morning about eight o'clock, knocking on the door. I opened the door and there was this,

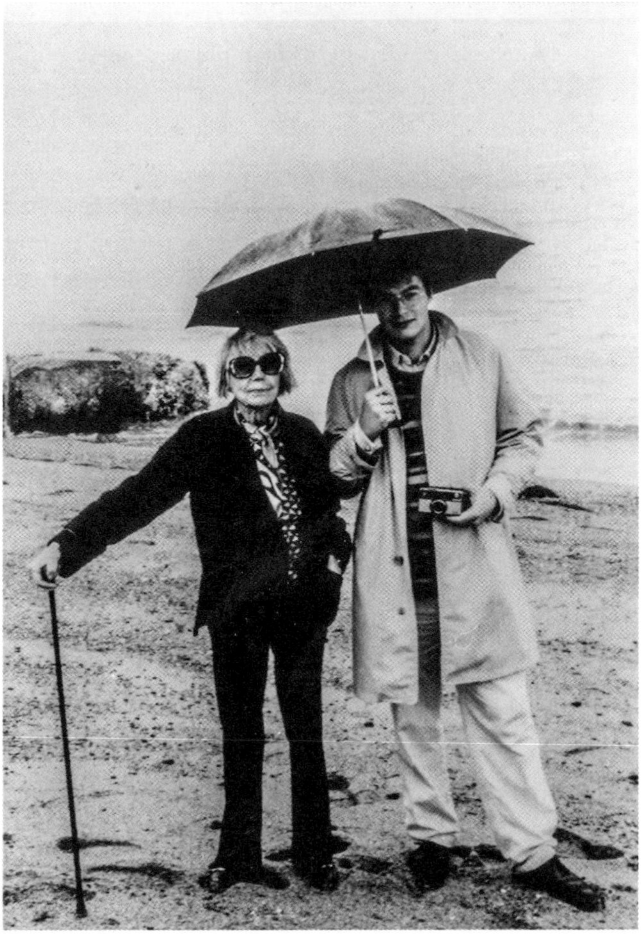

Eileen Agar on the beach at Swanage with her biographer Andrew Lambirth, during the filming of the television documentary *The Colour of Dreams*, 1989. Photograph by Steve Garvey.

this haggard-looking – I mean haggard, he was a pretty heavy man, tough-looking, but, he was kind of green [*laughs*]. A pale green. With huge bags under his eyes, worse than mine. And, he said, 'I've done the article, I want you to look at it.' He said, 'I've been up all night writing it.' I said, 'It looks like it.'[12]

In artists' experience, the studio and the kitchen sink are never wholly separate: 'One wants some kind of quotidian life in the painting,'[13] Frank Auerbach reflects. Listen to Phyllida Barlow describing how it felt attempting to keep up her practice as a sculptor while bringing up five children:

> trying to find that chink in all that – that stuff, of being a mother, being concerned about children, relating to their ways of growing up, and the difficulties *they* might be having, of the challenges they might be having, and then finding those chinks where exploring, making and relating to sculpture, and not relating to sculpture, could be part of that.[14]

It seems clear that these two kinds of 'relating' are themselves closely interrelated, although explaining their interrelatedness in rational terms is less straightforward. That's why it is essential, in transcribing and reading these interviews, to retain and respond to their imperfections as text – the stopping, starting, doubling-back as speakers try to give shape to the stuff of memory for which we can't always find a workable equivalent in words.

The twin convictions that artists' lives are in some ways different from other people's and that they are worth recording for posterity animate the first ever full-scale art history book, Giorgio Vasari's *Lives of the Most Excellent Architects, Painters and Sculptors,* published in Florence in 1550. Much of Vasari's information came from conversations and gossip, perhaps augmented by more formal interviews. The Vasari Tapes, if they existed, would be a Renaissance prototype of Artists' Lives. At the time he was writing, the idea that artists other than the ancient Greeks were worthy of memorialisation still felt audacious and new. Even his classical antecedents were at best patchy and episodic. Almost two thousand years previously, Herodotus had referred in passing in his *Histories* to the architect Rhoikos, the jeweller Theodoros and other such masters of their trade. Much later, in the first century CE, the aristocratic Roman author Pliny the Elder presented artists as people whose words, as well as their works, should be preserved.

Pliny gives an account of an 'amusing exchange' between the painters Protogenes and Apelles – a hand-me-down and probably apocryphal story, to which he adds drama, dialogue and a brief glimpse of Protogenes' workplace–home. Determined to inspect his rival's paintings at first hand, Apelles has sailed to Rhodes, where he 'made at once for his fellow artist's studio':

> but [Protogenes] was not at home. An old woman was looking after a large board resting on an easel. She announced that Protogenes was not in and asked who was looking for him. Apelles said, 'This person,' as he took up a brush and painted an extremely fine line in colour across the board. On Protogenes' return the old woman showed him what Apelles had done. The story goes that, after a close inspection of the line, Protogenes said that the visitor had been Apelles, since such a line could not be the work of anyone else.[15]

There is something about this scene that tells us we're in the world of artists, rather than critics or connoisseurs. Maybe it's the faintly tense blend of rivalry and recognition; or the way we would very much like to know the precise intonation of 'This person'. Friendly, camp or cool? Imagine the words variously spoken by Marcel Duchamp, David Hockney or Lucian Freud. Vasari seems to have read these little stories almost like shooting scripts. While working on the *Lives*, he spent a whole summer covering the walls of his house in Arezzo with frescoes based on Pliny's tales.

The first edition of the *Lives* contains 133 artist biographies, in which Vasari repeatedly makes clear the oral nature of his sources. Individual Lives often open with the words, 'It is said', 'It is also told', or 'I once heard tell'; the narrative is pushed along with phrases like, 'he himself told me'. And since, unlike Herodotus or Pliny, Vasari was himself an artist, he describes his near-contemporaries (Michelangelo is the only living artist to have a full biography in the first set of *Lives*) as fellow professionals and human beings rather than legendary figures. He never sets the art apart from the life. 'It was said' of the Florentine artist Fra Filippo Lippi, for example, that he was:

> so lustful that he would give anything to enjoy a woman he wanted if he thought he could have his way; and if he couldn't buy what he wanted, then he would cool his passion by painting her portrait and reasoning with himself. His lust was so violent that when it took hold of him he could never concentrate on his work. And because of this, one time or other when he was doing something for Cosimo de' Medici in Cosimo's house, Cosimo had him locked in so that he wouldn't wander away and waste time. After he had been confined for a few days, Fra Filippo's amorous or rather his animal desires drove him one night to seize a pair of scissors, make a rope from his bed-sheets and escape through a window to pursue his own pleasures for

> days on end. When Cosimo discovered that he was gone, he searched for him and eventually got him back to work. And after that he always allowed him to come and go as he liked, having regretted the way he had shut him up before and realizing how dangerous it was for such a madman to be confined.[16]

Like Pliny's rival painters, the figure of the artist that Vasari evokes feels very familiar: a man (almost always a man at this date[17]) driven by ungovernable urges ('animal desires') and inspirationally improvisational ('seize a pair of scissors') yet capable of steady productive labour ('back to work'). In later academic art history, by contrast, when connoisseurship and archival research take the place of hearsay and anecdotal relish, there's a distinct flop in energy levels, in sheer creative restlessness. Here's how the American art historian Bernard Berenson characterised Filippo Lippi in *The Italian Painters of the Renaissance*, published in 1930 and long considered a definitive account of the work of many artists previously covered by Vasari:

> Fra Filippo's strongest impulse was not toward the pre-eminently artistic one of re-creation, but rather toward expression, and within that field, toward the expression of the pleasant, genial, spiritually comfortable feelings of ordinary life. His real place is with the genre painters; only his genre was of the soul, as that of others – of Benozzo Gozzoli, for example – was of the body. Hence a sin of his own, scarcely less pernicious than that of the naturalists, and cloying to boot – expression at any cost.[18]

Once again, Lippi is a man of 'impulse' and 'pernicious' tendencies, although the 'sin' of which Berenson accuses him is very different from sex addiction. Compare the two Lippis, and you immediately feel that Vasari's is much more of an artist than Berenson's. The bed-sheet tale may have no obvious bearing on painting, yet in broader terms it's about motivation, energy, invention and the desire to do and make. Cut this out of the story, and you have the art-historian's artist, categorised and trimmed to fit. Not only this, but it's easy to imagine Berenson's mid-century readers feeling similarly put down, anxious that their aesthetic sensibilities might not be fine enough, their knowledge of Renaissance art too narrow or their manners too unpolished to understand what was so wrong with 'expression at any cost'. Snobbery, you can't help reflecting, finds more fertile soil in intellectual life than either in the studio or around the kitchen sink. This is part of what Greaves meant by his 'bruisers' metaphor.

As regards the difference between the artist's and the critic's point of view, 'I try to respect people's opinion,' says the sculptor David Nash:

> because in the cultural sphere one is working in freedom, and it's very important that people feel free and courageous enough to really say what their experience is, because there isn't any law, it isn't like – this isn't in the social sphere, there isn't a law. But all the time there are academics and intellectuals seemingly trying to create law around art, which is I guess a great debate, and artists feel imprisoned by it and push the boundaries down again. As these walls get built up, inevitably they get pushed down again, and art moves on, it's all part of how it works.[19]

When Nash goes on to talk about the artist's 'impulse', his terminology is closer to the 'animal' dimension of Vasari's Lippi than to Berenson's concern to put the Renaissance master in his 'real place':

> I think the whole impulse of art and artists finding themselves, or the human being finding themselves making art, and they are part of this whole activity of making art, is very like being part of the earth in terms of soil, and one can analyse the soil and find all of the different minerals that are in there and the different bacterias and the different fungi, and the earthworms and the bugs, and one tends to think of all these things as separate, but really it's one organism, just one living being, this mantle of topsoil around the planet Earth is like one being. And art is like that, and I'm just like a microbe among many others, and there's a symbiosis, you know, it all works, and we all have to be there.[20]

As one way of approaching the Artists' Lives interviews, the nitrogen cycle is not such a fanciful analogy: you can think of daily life – the sink, the nappies, the whole existential journey without maps – as the topsoil; the 'activity of making' as the growth process; and the atmosphere as the realm in which art exists outside the artist's immediate environment. As Nash puts it, at any rate, everything feeds into everything else.

*

Voices convey much more than the words actually spoken: the rhythms and timbres of thought and emotion, the traces of social class and educational background, geographical and temporal features, and always an element of drama – breaking silence, reliving events, including the listener in a personal arena. Listening is also a more intimate experience than looking or reading. Watching a filmed interview on screen, we tend to objectify the person; when we listen to a voice in isolation, the speaker is inside our head and the images, when they come, play out in the cinema of imagination. But still the only way in which audio recordings can reach an ordinary printed page is via transcripts, in which the grain of the speaking voice has to be aurally imagined though it is effectively absent. The Marxist historian and tireless advocate of 'history from below' Raphael Samuel warned of the numerous 'perils of the transcript':

> The spoken word can very easily be mutilated when it is taken down and transferred to the printed page [. . .] People do not usually speak in paragraphs, and what they have to say does not usually follow an ordered sequence of comma, semi-colon, and full stop; yet very often this is the way in which their speech is reproduced.[21]

Still worse:

> The decadence of transcription may become extreme if the writer, not content with mutilating a text, by cuts and rearrangements, then attempts to weave it together again with interpolated words of his own. Thus, the very process by which speech is made to sound consecutive is also bound, in some degree, to violate its original integrity.[22]

'Decadence', 'mutilating', 'violate': this is the writer as rapist, having his way with history. Samuel urged the transcribers of oral testimony not to purge grammatical idiosyncrasies but to use 'artistry' in an attempt 'to convey in words the quality of the original speech'.[23] To illustrate this point, he compared two published transcripts of interviews with elderly Suffolk farm labourers, the first by literary writer Ronald Blythe, the second by oral history pioneer and folklorist George Ewart Evans. Blythe's interviewee begins informatively enough: 'There were seven children at home and father's wages had been reduced to 10 shillings a week.' But Evans's, though apparently less articulate, is immediately present as a man who has something to say, whatever that something turns out to be. 'It's like this: those young 'uns years ago, I said, well – it's like digging a hole, I said . . .' Here, Samuel observes, 'Syntax is difficult, but

A note about interviews and transcripts

There are summaries, giving varying levels of detail, of most Artists' Lives interviews. Full transcripts have so far been made of a smaller proportion. Where possible, I have used existing transcripts, silently correcting errors in the spelling of names and minor typos, and making small changes to punctuation where I felt that these would convey the rhythm of the speaking voice or the flow of a particular train of thought more clearly. Ellipses in the extracts are within square brackets and are used to indicate a separation of words taken from a single recording. An ellipsis at the start of a new paragraph indicates a different part of the transcript or recording (not necessarily in the sequence in which it occurs in the original recording). The interview time or transcript page reference for each separate section is detailed in the notes. All the recordings contain at least two voices: that of the subject and that of the interviewer. I have not included interviewers' questions and comments; the name of the interviewer for each recording can be found in the first reference to that recording in the notes. Where I comment on what artists are saying, I usually refer to the speaker – even those who have died since their interview was recorded – in the present tense. All but five of the interviews from which I have quoted are available online at sounds.bl.uk.

I

Home is Where We Start From

Children and Parents

If it is true, as Picasso claimed, that every child is an artist, then the creative vocation begins early. The child psychotherapist Donald Winnicott defined creativity as 'the retention throughout life of something that belongs properly to infant experience: the ability to create the world'.[1] Compared with other groups of adult oral history subjects, artists seem to connect particularly readily with their childhood selves, finding the words more naturally for how they felt at the time.

Everyone's earliest memories are theirs alone – unique, vivid, timeless. Yet running through the childhood recollections in this chapter are certain broader historical processes. In the pre-First World War memories of Eileen Agar and Michael Rothenstein, the childhood worlds of French governesses and Cotswold wildflower meadows sound almost too remote to be within reach of the living voice (and indeed, both artists died not long after they were interviewed in the early 1990s). The changes that register in artists' experiences of becoming parents themselves feel similarly far-reaching. Both women and men testify to conflicts in trying to reconcile a desire to continue their own creative work with their new, parallel creative careers as mothers and fathers. It's a question of both personality and when you happen to be born: Reg Butler might have been no more likely to attend his daughter's birth or change her nappy in the enlightened 1980s than he was in the benighted early 1960s. But it's hard to imagine many men of Butler's generation talking like David Nash, as he relives the moment he first became a father: 'I guess a lot of parents feel this, that you become the parents of all children [. . .] and one respects the human being in a deeper way.'[2]

One made one's own life: Michael Rothenstein and Eileen Agar

Michael Rothenstein (1908–93) was the fourth and youngest child of a successful artist, William Rothenstein,[3] who would later become principal of the Royal College of Art and receive a knighthood. His mother, Alice, was herself an artist's daughter and had been an actress before her marriage. Michael was educated at home, in the hamlet of Far Oakridge near Stroud, where he showed precocious artistic talent, producing vast numbers of drawings that his parents lovingly preserved. Incapacitated in his 20s by a severe type of thyroid disease,

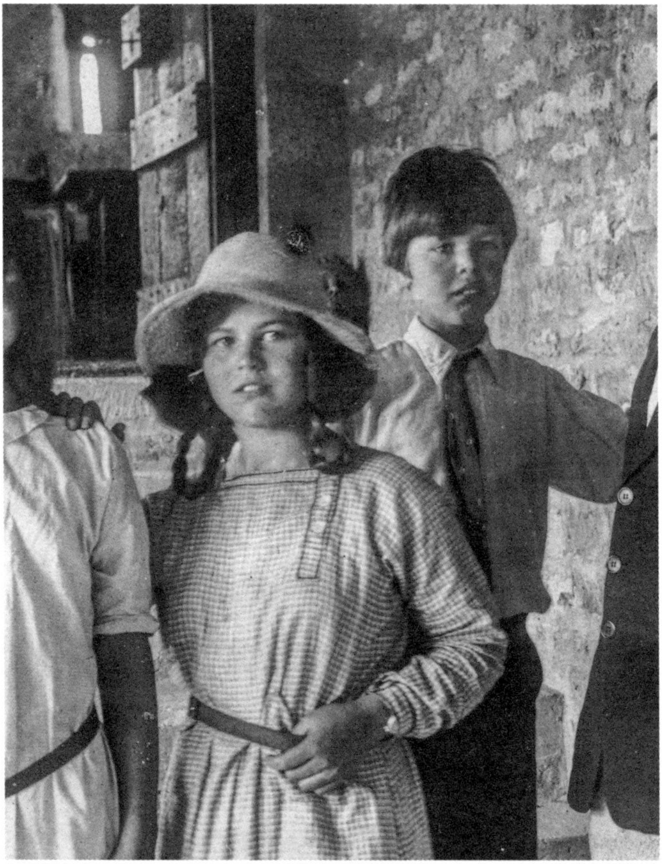

Michael Rothenstein with his sisters Rachel and Betty in the family home at Far Oakridge, near Stroud, *c.*1918. Photographer unknown.

Rothenstein later made a reputation with the topographical watercolours he contributed to the wartime project 'Recording Britain', and for his visually bold and technically inventive prints. His early years would always seem to him 'wonderful, really, such an extraordinary childhood'. Though he would later reject his father's example of the artist 'as a man who trafficked in highly cultural relationships, with highly cultured people, with letters, with books' ('I grew to absolutely hate it'),[4] Rothenstein speaks with the measured fluency and literary intonation of a true heir of Edwardian high culture.

> I spent a lot of time with my two sisters, who were only a little older than I was. Not much with my brother, John,[5] who was eight years older than I was. He was away at public school, Bedales, and later at Oxford, so it was much later I got to know John a bit. But my two sisters were intimates, so it gave one a strange sort of isolation. Socially insulated from other children, because, really, there weren't other children around. And socially insulated also, because my parents were so much older than I was, and my father seemed to live in a rather grand world, which encompassed his own very wide range of interests, literary as well as artistic. So one made one's own life. And it was really very intense. That Stroud Valley was most marvellous at that time. Our house was on a ridge of hill, overlooking the valley. And it was very wild. One could walk through the fields, almost deafened by the natural sounds – the birds, the sawing of the grasshoppers in the grass. It was a continual symphony of sound. Wonderful. Wonderful. The Cotswolds could be windy, and the combination of the creature sounds, and the bird sounds, and the wind through the trees, was something so extraordinary. It's a world of sound which, of course, has vanished, because there are no grasshoppers now [. . .] The fields have lost their voice.
>
> And the butterflies. I think they must have influenced me greatly as a child, because wherever there were flowers, there were butterflies. And I used to visit a rather grand house, at Cirencester, where there were long flower borders, and in the summer, on a warm day, the air shivered with the cloud of butterflies – red admirals, tortoiseshell, brimstone. It was glittering, you cannot imagine how beautiful it was [. . .] I remember walking down the valley one morning, early, and there was a particular tree, and the tree was completely surrounded by green hairstreak butterflies. They made a second coating of brilliantly vibrating leaves. Those things were so marvellous, and they affected me greatly.

> [The house] stood up very high. And three floors, and then there was a yard. And my father converted the barn, the original barn of the farmhouse, across this yard, into his studio. And again, it was rather severe, rather bare, and all the things my father liked. He was very much a collector, as well as an originator, and it was full of interesting things, the house, that is, that he'd collected – Indian miniatures, sculpture, drawings and paintings by friends, by people he'd met in Paris. So it was really packed with interesting things. But from my viewpoint, it was the Indian miniatures which affected me most strongly. And again, it was this element of violence, strange and dramatic happenings, in this tiny world of the miniature, and always in these very violent colours – black hills, gods and goddesses with purple and deep scarlet faces and arms, extraordinary birds flitting in and out of the branches of black trees, laden with orange fruit. It was an extraordinary world that these miniatures represented. And, although the house was full of the most elegant examples, drawings by Augustus John, for example, beautiful, light, charming caricatures that Max Beerbohm had done of Father and his friends, it was these intense, violent images that I remember, and it was those that have affected my work, really, ever since.[6]
>
> [. . .] Mother was a sort of tigress. In her temperament, she was magnificently primitive. She adored my father, and she had a sort of worship of him. And in that sense, she was wonderfully supportive. In other ways, she was not supportive at all, because she didn't understand so many of his tastes, and so many of his feelings. He was naturally an austere man, and my mother was naturally, naturally a luxury lover.[7]

Rothenstein recalls that his mother 'used to buy me penny drawing books, and then I was given colours and brushes, and along with those gifts, I was given these fat, long boxes, with sets of soldiers in the boxes'.[8]

> I would set to work and make [my toy soldiers] fight in my drawing book. And this must interest me because, you see, that act of attempting to make the subject of my drawing more exciting in some peculiar sense, through drawing it, through painting it, is, I think, something very fundamental to forming one's own kind of images. I wanted to make them more exciting than they appeared, standing in a line along the table. So, they got to work in very bloody battles, in my own images. And whereas, as a child, I was a craven coward when it came to any kind of blood, or any kind of accident,

nothing gave me greater pleasure than drawing the chaps with chopped-off heads spouting, spouting blood! And as a result, the red can, cadmium red, or whatever, was always the first one to be used up in the box. But one had such pleasure. These colours would start going fairly dry, and then you'd get them squelchy with water, and the feel of cobalt blue or cerulean, or black and orange, and pink, it was incredible how joyful it was to work along with these colours, to make them spring around on the paper. So I did create a fairly extensive world of my own, a very private world, in these books, in these penny drawing books.[9]

Eileen Agar (1899–1991) was born in Argentina and spent her first 11 years in a wealthy suburb of Buenos Aires, where her father ran the family business. In 1911 he retired and the family returned to London. Determined to become an artist, Agar studied with the sculptor Leon Underwood[10] at his experimental private school in Brook Green, where her fellow students included Henry Moore, before starting at the Slade School of Fine Art in 1925. Her mature paintings, collages and sculptures, which she exhibited in surrealist exhibitions in London and New York, reflect her belief in the creative primacy of the unconscious ('a feminine type of imagination') and her theory of feminine 'womb-magic'.[11] Interviewed at the age of 91, Agar speaks with the brisk, precision-tooled accent of her class and era, completely unfazed by her deafness.

I don't remember very much about Buenos Aires, except a plague of locusts which descended on the whole countryside, and ate up everything, every little bit of leaf or anything [. . .] and we all used to have to go out with sort of carpet, mats, or something like that, you know, to try and beat them down, because you could see them coming over in thousands, and it was most horrifying, and really disgusting. They were awful creatures. And that was the only thing that was dreadful, because, otherwise, it was a lovely climate. It was very warm, a bit cold in the winter, and all the wealthy Argentinians used to wrap up their children in fur coats, though you didn't really need fur coats, but they wanted to show how grand they were [. . .] In summer, which is December, everything was beautiful, peaches, and you could go into the garden and pick peaches, and nectarines, and anything you wanted.[12]

[. . .] We had an English nanny, who was very severe, and then later on, we had a French governess, because my mother also had a flat in Paris, and

> she insisted we should all speak French, because French was the second language, like it is really today as well. It was in those days, so later on, when we were almost at school, we had a French governess [. . .] My mother was very strict, and she loved children, but she was very strict with us, because she said, if we didn't learn now, how to behave, and all the rest of it, you see, we would never learn [. . .] I remember my mother smacking me because I refused to apologise to my godmother about something that I'd done, and I said, 'No, I won't apologise.' And she smacked with the side of her hairbrush, you see, and that made me absolutely furious, and I don't know what, whether I was rude to her or what. I was very rebellious, anyhow. So I must have started as a – certainly at an early age.[13]
>
> [. . .] I always thought that I was a bit different to other people, but I didn't know why. I just thought that I was a bit different, and I must do something different, and so I was always drawing, and thinking.[14]

My first great love: Josef Herman

Josef Herman (1911–2000) was the eldest of three children in a Jewish family in Warsaw. The Hermans were initially quite prosperous, but after Josef's father inadvertently signed away his shoemaking business to an unscrupulous partner, they lived in worsening poverty. Leaving school at 13, Herman worked as a typesetter and graphic artist before enrolling at Warsaw School of Art and Decoration in 1930. The Nazi persecution of Jews and of anyone deemed leftist in politics or radical in art (Herman qualified on all three counts) forced him into exile in Belgium, from where he escaped via France to Britain. From 1944 to 1955 Herman lived in the colliery village of Ystradgynlais in south Wales, where he converted a derelict factory into a studio and painted the above-ground lives of the miners.

Herman had difficult feelings towards his father but idolised his mother, whose illiteracy didn't prevent her inspiring her son with her 'thinking' and 'poetry':

> As a child we lived mostly in the street, there was no conversation at all. With my mother I had some conversations, because my mother was a very reflective kind of nature, you know. She did a lot of thinking. And if she would have been a little bit literate, probably – there was some poetry in her, you know, but she just couldn't – materials, books, there wasn't the

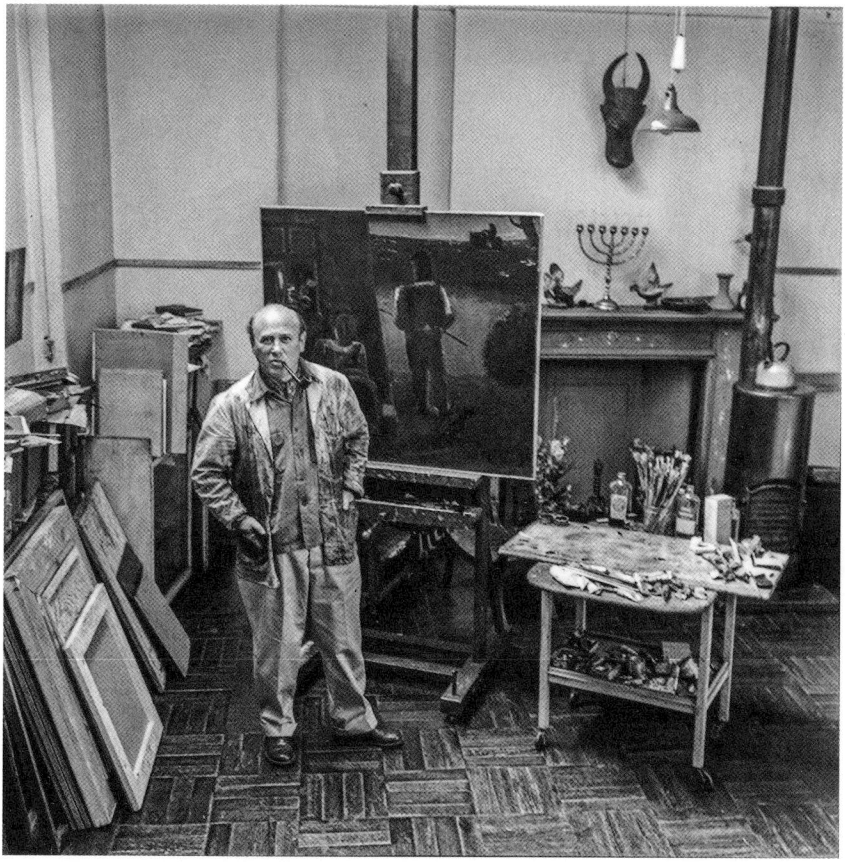

Josef Herman in his studio in west London, 1960. Photograph by Ida Kar.

vocabulary. There was nothing to it. But I remember she was already what I thought an old woman, just about 40, that she learned – she began to learn to read. And I helped her then, reading, and I thought – this was an immense effort. She was a lovely woman, she was really a lovely woman. Not only is it that I was the first son, and therefore she was my first great love of a woman – this is quite natural, this is quite often. But not only this, there was only an objective feeling towards her in her own right.[15]

[. . .] Of course she had to – scrubbing floors for the better families, taking in washing from the better-do families, you know. She always – she was the pillar of the home, there's no question about it. You see, my father

> had days of complete depression when he would do absolutely nothing, and she would treat him as a child. And she would go out and come back with some money – doing all the time. She was always active. And do you know, it's a very funny thing, she never lost her beautiful skin. She had a lovely skin. And her hands have never got swollen, as usually people who do hard work [. . .] I have her photograph somewhere here, which I discovered about a few years ago, the last photograph of her in Warsaw. My God, she was a very attractive woman. She was a very, very beautiful woman, you know. But my love to her was in every respect of the richness of her feeling quality. And so she had no vocabulary to express herself. She would do this sometimes in a gesture. Putting her arm around you. She protected you.[16]

Herman's father, David, was also illiterate, which made it all the easier for his business partner to abscond to America with the money they'd made from supplying boots to the Russian army. David subsequently worked as a cobbler, but, 'If the truth be said,' recalls Josef, 'he wasn't a very good craftsman':

> He very seldom got good work. There were better cobblers in the district than him, you know. But nevertheless he did his best. And do you know, it's a very funny thing, that people with gifts do their best well, and people ungifted who do their best badly, you know. So, he did his best, but it was bad [. . .] He never even understood whether it was bad, or why it was bad. He had no sense of quality whatever. But he was a decent human being.[17]

One day, out of the blue, Herman's great-grandfather turned up: 'nobody recognised him, and he declared himself to be our great-grandfather, my mother's grandfather.'

> Though my mother knew nothing about him, she took him in, and he stayed with us. And the best I remember of him was like old, old man – he kept to children, closer to children than to adults. And practically twice or three times a week he would take me to the old Jewish cemetery. There we would sit, and he would turn a bit philosophic about his life. He would say, 'You know that it's – at the end, I don't know what it was all about.' And I thought from a half-literate person to come such a very profound observation, because we all come to this, sooner or later, to this conclusion. But he was an illiterate old man, you know, but a lovable, a

> lovable character. And the most moving thing which remained with me forever is his death. He used to go late afternoon to bed for a nap, and I was then about four or five, and my mother sent me in to see how the great-grandfather was getting on, because he should have been up. And I went in, touched him. No movement. And then, he used to have very red cheeks, you know, a lovely, kindish face with a beard, you know, and this face was now completely white. So I was frightened, and ran back to my mother and told her this, and she came in. She said, 'You go out. You go out. He's dead.' And this is the first time that I actually witnessed death, and it shook me up terribly.[18]

I'd see the funny side: Michael Sandle and Bruce Lacey

The sculptor Michael Sandle (b.1936) was born in Plymouth, where his father was serving in the Royal Navy; the family then moved to the Isle of Man. Sandle trained in painting and printmaking at the Slade, transferring to sculpture after he heard the art historian Ernst Gombrich lecture on ancient Greek and Egyptian art. He has spent much of his career abroad, teaching in Canada and Germany, where he was Professor of Sculpture at the Academy of Fine Arts in Karlsruhe between 1980 and 1999. Sandle talks about his wartime memories and sculpture in Chapter 3; here he recalls his childhood in a home riven by domestic discord:

> My father was in the navy, Royal Navy for 28 years. He was a taciturn man, often very bad tempered. He was deaf, which probably didn't help. Wasn't a particularly happy man. I didn't see him until I was five because he was posted to Hong Kong. When I say five, it can't be five, it must have been earlier than that, but I remember my mother saying, 'That man is your father.' And there was a man in a cloud of cigarette smoke who I'd never seen before, and that was my father. And my mother was a very tough lady – short, very dynamic, very courageous. I seemed to spend all the time fighting her because she had such a strong will.[19]
>
> [. . .] My mother was the life and soul of the party and she was very popular with children, but she had a sort of other side of her where she could be really rather terrifying and suddenly almost fascist in her behaviour. And one day she was giving a child a party and all the children

> of the moment were there, and there was a table groaning with all sorts of food, jellies and stuff, 'cos she was a very good cook. Then we all were forced to put on paper hats – I used to hate things like this, by the way, but I was there – and my father came home from work and noticed what was going on and thought he would join in. And he went upstairs and got dressed up in her clothes, came down in drag, ostensibly Old Mother Riley. I can remember when he came through the door with her high heels and her dress on, the children froze and were mortified. They were just stunned with embarrassment, and my mother was serving a spoonful of jelly to a child, she sensed it, turned round and the smile from her face, just went from her face and she put on a grimace of pure, naked hatred and she could hardly speak to him, through clenched teeth, 'You stupid bugger.' Now he realised it all had gone horribly wrong, he took off her bonnet, sat down at the end of the table and put his head in his – rested his chin on his hand. He obviously didn't know what to do. And she picked up – there was a pile of ten side plates, and she broke one over his bald head saying, 'You stupid bugger.' Then she picked up another one and said, 'You daft bugger', and she picked up – and she went through the ten plates saying, 'You daft bugger', 'You stupid bugger.' And there were probably 14 traumatised children.[20]

The performance artist and inventor of an anarchic tribe of life-size automata Bruce Lacey (1927–2016) recalls that, when the term 'performance art' first became current in the 1970s, 'it finally explained what I'd been doing all my life'.[21] Lacey grew up in south-east London; after studying painting at the Royal College of Art, he pursued a varied and entirely idiosyncratic career, which included making props for television shows featuring the comedians Spike Milligan and Peter Sellers, and playing George Harrison's gardener in the Beatles' film *Help!* (1965). Lacey constructed his installations, sculptures and automata from all manner of found objects and industrial junk: 'I have collected the discarded objects of society,' he wrote; 'by the juxtaposition of apparently alien objects, they can be given the power to comment.'[22]

> My father was a house painter, but he collected things. They weren't like your high-class antiques, they were like, poor-man's antiques I suppose. And my mother had been a milliner. And they had met at the Catford roller-skating fancy-dress ball one year, where my mother went as a Red Indian,

because she had played a walk-on part in a production of *Hiawatha* at the Albert Hall, so she had this costume from there. And my father decided to go as a circular dinner table, with hoops around him, and he cut a hole in one of his mother's best sheets, and he disguised himself in the middle of the table behind a potted plant – well an imitation one. I imagine he was on roller skates. But he found he couldn't dance with anyone, so he was sitting in the corner looking all miserable, and my mother went over, and she fell in love with his smile, you know.[23]

[. . .] When I was a child and you were in the playground, and children talk about, you know, boast about their parents, I used to say if an aeroplane went overhead, 'My father is a pilot,' and things like that. Yes, one thing about childhood was that my mother was a very gentle woman. She had been a Sunday school teacher, but she somehow or other, she had learnt certain things about ju-jitsu, I mean she was a very spirited woman. In the [Second World] war people queued, and if someone jumped in front of the queue she'd go – only a little woman, get her hand, thumb and finger under his nose, knee in his back, and then lay him on the ground, you know.[24]

[. . .] I used to get caned every day for laughing in class. I'd see the funny side of something. And used to get the alternative, hand or seat, caned on your hand or your seat. I told my mother about this, and what she did, she sewed about four thicknesses of blanket material on the seat of my trousers, so when I went back, up to the teacher, he said, 'Hand or seat?' I'd say, 'Seat.' And of course never felt a thing. But that's where I first learnt acting I suppose. I used to go back and wriggle, and pretend I was in pain.[25]

Lacey's childhood was 'a wonderful time', except that 'one tragic thing happened'. In his retelling of the episode, the full force of the original emotion momentarily returns (the inability of a transcript to convey emotion with anything like the subtlety of the speaking voice is particularly clear here).

My father, my father bought a – gosh – my father bought us this beautiful little ginger kitten, which we called – oh what did we call it now? Twiddles. Twiddles. And I used to go out walking with it. It used to follow me. And we used to go onto the hills. And there was all this bracken. And I used to run about 10 feet away and then lay down with my head close to the ground and I'd, I'd hear her coming towards me, and then like a tiger, and with that scale, come out, you know. And then one Monday, she didn't come home. And then my father found her in the hedge, riddled with gunshot, and we know the local hotel man had been out there shooting. And my father picked up the poor dead animal, took it in, flung it down, he was having dinner, all his guests, and said, 'You shot my bloody cat,' and the man denied it. We sent it off to the vet to have an autopsy; he said he found no gunshot wounds, although you could see all the bullets in it. We found out that the vet was a mate of the hotel man, and so it was all a conspiracy. I know, when my father brought it in, because it was cold, we put it in the oven to try and warm it up to see, to make it – we thought it was going to come alive, but of course it didn't. It was terrible, you know.[26]

It's a tough one: Rosemary Young and Sheila Girling

For Eileen Agar in the 1920s, there seemed to be a clear either/or choice between becoming an artist and being a mother: 'Once you have a child, you're fixed to the child, and you may draw a little something, but that's why I decided I'd never have children. I thought, "You can't do both." Once you have a child, the child comes first, and away goes your art.'[27] Even today, the challenges involved in sustaining an artistic career while also bringing up children are seldom aired in print, though they are often and frankly discussed in Artists' Lives recordings. Rosemary Young and Sheila Girling separately reflect on their experience of trying to balance their own desire to make work with the demands of childcare and wanting to support their male artist partners.

Rosemary Young (b.1930) studied at Camberwell and Wimbledon art schools before enrolling in a four-year sculpture diploma at the Slade in 1949. Her tutor was Reg Butler,[28] at that time being touted as Henry Moore's most promising successor among the younger post-war generation of British sculptors. She and Butler started a relationship; they would later have two children together and eventually marry. In 1955 Young's exhibiting career seemed about to take off with a show at the Hanover Gallery, but she then set her own work aside in order to help Butler with his. Looking back from 1999 at her 20-something self, Young sounds bemused by the gender roles that seemed normal, even unavoidable, just 40 years earlier:

I'm the only person that's ever worked with him [Reg], all the way, all the way through [. . .] I mean, I was in an incredibly privileged position, to be able to be that person. But it became, you know, that was my role. So there was no space to suddenly say, 'I'm going to make a sculpture' [. . .] And anyway, it had gone, it had just disappeared, that and having children – there was no motivation, no energy for it or no nothing. It's extraordinary [. . .] It was as if all the drive that got me to the art school – I mean, I don't know if it's because one's a woman. I mean Reg was pretty scathing about women artists [. . .] Saying that, you know, they had great difficulty in keeping up the motivation, and that you had to be a very, very extraordinary person.[29]

[. . .] And when you think how few there are – there was Barbara Hepworth, Elisabeth Frink. But how happy were they, and you know, how –? They had to stand out from the normal sort of feminine sort of needs, I think. They had to be, they were very exceptional people, and – I don't know about now, like, Rachel Whiteread and all these people. Maybe it's easier now than it used to be. Maybe the business of – that what's expected of you is different. What's expected of women may be different now. But then it seemed to be almost as if, not through any fault of his, he just sucked it away, he drew it out, drew all your energy away from creativity, into being part of a partnership.[30]

[. . .] Because I wasn't married at the time [my daughter was born], I had to go and buy myself a wedding ring [. . .] Anyway, I was called 'Mrs'. But anyway, my daughter started to come in the morning, about four o'clock, five o'clock, and we got into this car, Reg and I, the Jensen, and we went up to London. I think we went through every light and everything, you know, just, great, great speed. And got there [. . .] Cortina was delivered with great ceremony. And in those days you stayed in the hospital six to eight days [. . .] Reg never changed her nappy, either of their [the children's] nappies. And Reg certainly wasn't there when she was born. I think he was outside. Came in pretty quickly afterwards. But I don't think I could have coped with him either [. . .] I don't know that they really wanted fathers in in those days.[31]

[. . .] I couldn't help Reg in the studio to begin with [. . .] That's why it was quite a pressure on me, because I was really the only person that he could work with in the studio. [Reg's work] was going on in the house, and one could if they [the children] cried or something, you could come out. But yes. And desperately sort of needing to help Reg, but not having this same sort of drive. It was all a bit of a bind, you know [. . .] And then my next child was born, Creon, my son, was born in 1960, again in April.

> Then, for Creon we felt that we ought to have somebody, what do you call them? A nurse. So we hired somebody from one of these nanny agencies, who came down just before Creon was born. And dominated us, absolutely scared the wits out of the whole lot of us. And she was only meant to be there for two weeks, but we just couldn't – she insisted on ironing everything and folding everything, and the baby was only meant to be fed at certain times, and we were so frightened of her. Reg said, you know, we can't cope with this, and so he asked her to go after six, five days I think. But it was a sort of Norland nanny or something like that, you know. Then gradually, the children sort of became part of the family.[32]

Sheila Girling (1924–2015) was born in Sutton Coldfield, Birmingham, into an artistic family. As a child she loved botany and science: 'My science teacher very much wanted me to go to Birmingham University and do science, because I was very good at it.' But 'mother said no, if you become a doctor you'll get all different diseases and no, no, no, no, you know, it's a terrible thing. No. Art.'[33] Girling studied at Birmingham School of Art, followed by the Royal Academy Schools in London, where in 1948 she met Anthony Caro. They married while students in 1949; Girling left art school two years later when her first child, Tim, was born.

> It's a tough one really. I mean women haven't been at art that long, you know. I think Tracey Emin, well she's used her body, she's used sex, which is always exciting and people want to go and see it. And she's not married, she's not a mother, so she hasn't any of those handicaps. I think it's terribly hard for a woman to be as successful as a man if she has children. I mean Bridget Riley's never married and never had children, you know. You can be then as focused as a man. And I think women are just as good as men really, I think they have the same abilities. But I do think they have problems, really. I mean you can't escape the fact you have to physically bear the child, and when you have the child you want to feed the child and all these things are so tearing you away. The men go off and the child is there somewhere and they're working all day. But I do think it's hard to be it all really, and I think women have that handicap [. . .] Well now [2009] there's no problem because I'm – my children are grown up and it's their worries now, their children, and of course I adore my grandchildren, but I can send them home when they're tiring. No, there's no problem

> now except that of course I am always the cook and the housekeeper, you know, my husband doesn't do any of that [. . .] I sometimes feel frustrated now when I have to go home and cook a large dinner and Tony's collapsed in a chair watching television. Sometimes I feel slightly – and both my boys cook as well as their wives, which is something that happens nowadays, but it didn't in our day. So I see that they share a lot with their wives, much more than we did in our day.[34]

While Caro's career as a sculptor and teacher flourished, Girling took a long break from painting to bring up their children. From 1960, when Caro began to construct abstract sculptures from metal components, he would turn to her for advice on colour.

> Because Tony was working in the house and in the garage, which was part of the house, I used to choose his colours. He'd got into the steel stuff then, and I would choose his colours and I would paint them by hand, I mean physically paint them [. . .] The baby was in the pram or, you know, be watching you, sitting in a – well mostly in the pram in the garden or staggering around. I mean you'd do it when he was asleep or when he could be put in some place [. . .] I mean, I knew that I couldn't hand my children over to someone to look after them. I didn't want to do that. I mean for me the most important thing really is human life, I felt at that time – well I still do – and I felt I had to give all my creativity to Tony. I thought one of us has got to get there, so it had better be Tony at the moment. And I mean we talked a lot, I gave him a lot of ideas then, you know [. . .] I said look at music, why is music such an abstraction? How can they get into abstraction? And we thought of the timescale in music and he started doing *Early One Morning* [1962] then, going along the whole [metal] pole with intervals. And then we said, you know, you get two different themes blending in music, and he did *Month of May* [1963] then, with different themes going [. . .] I mean, I had lots of ideas that I could give him, and he had lots of ideas to add to it, and we fed each other all the time, you know. We would talk about why we could do this, and no, I didn't ever have any regrets. I didn't feel jealous at all, actually. We felt I wanted children and that was my job really to – it's very hard, I find it's very, very hard for women [. . .] Because children are not just things you can put down and put away, I mean they have a – they're little people, and they're determined to live and they're

going to demand from you. They're amazing, the sort of force of life really. So I was very happy to be then a carer.[35]

In her mid-50s, after a prolonged struggle with creative block, Girling began to paint again and to exhibit regularly.

[Being married to a famous sculptor] has its pluses and minuses. I was nervous first of all to start painting [again] because I knew so much about painting and about art, and I felt nervous about failing, you know, you have to get over that really. I think it's great that we can work together, talk together, live the work together. That's wonderful actually. It's endless sort of – rapport, endless. And I think a lot of it is very hard because I've had to give a lot of time up to Tony, and still do because he doesn't like travelling by himself, and I mean all his shows and whatnot. I learn a lot and I give a lot. It's swings and roundabouts really. I don't think either of us could have done what we've done without the other actually. I mean I don't think I'd have been able to pursue what I've been doing without Tony's constant encouragement and, now let me see what you've done, you know, and that sort of thing. So I think we've both been together moving forward in a way.[36]

The art/life divide: Tess Jaray and Phyllida Barlow

Tess Jaray (b.1937) was born into a Jewish professional family in Vienna. In 1938, the year Austria was annexed by Nazi Germany, Jaray's parents emigrated to England, where they settled in rural Worcestershire. Jaray studied at St Martin's School of Art, moving on to the Slade in 1957. After travel scholarships to Italy and France, she began teaching at Hornsey College of Arts and Crafts in 1964, the same year her first child, Anna, was born. Becoming a mother, 'always seemed to me something I would do', she says, 'although I never really thought about it and then suddenly, one day in my mid-20s, I thought, well you know, let's give it a go.'

And of course none of us really know what it means, otherwise I don't suppose anybody would have children. I had some vague idea that I would devote two years to having children and then get back to my work [*laughs*]. And nobody, nobody corrected me. And I suppose that is how it is. I suppose, like the pain of childbirth, you'd never do it a second time

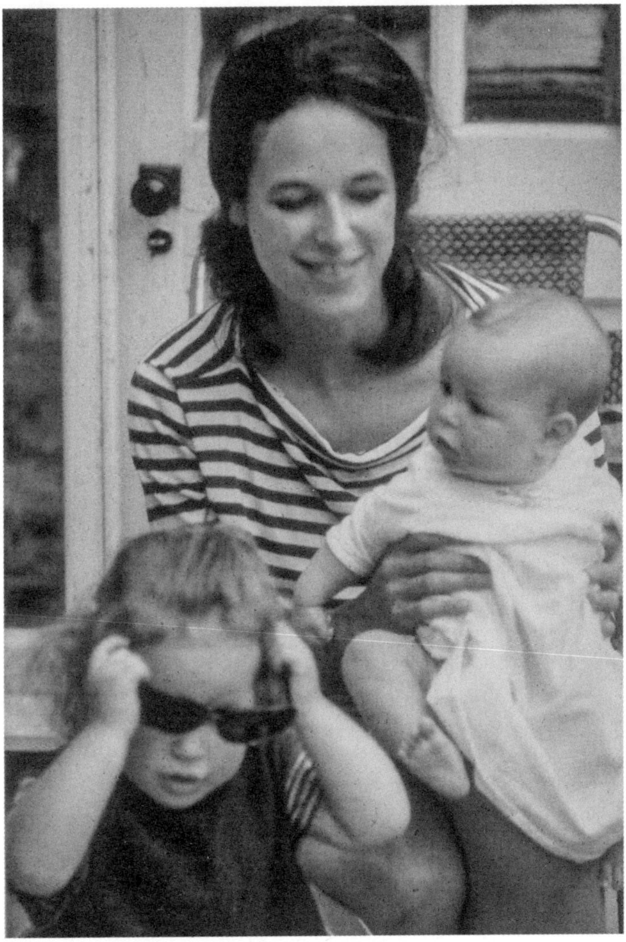

Tess Jaray with her daughters Anna (left) and Georgia, mid-1960s.
Photographer unknown.

if you could remember. You know, we are caught up, we are victims of circumstance and of our own nature.[37]

[. . .] I had a very restricted and quiet life just painting – painting and teaching and bringing up my children. And you know, it's a possible combination, I think, to bring up children if you are a painter, because although everybody says, God! that must be so difficult. And yes, of course it is difficult, but it is difficult no matter what your profession is. And I

> was perfectly aware at the time that, however hard it was and however frustrating, it wasn't as difficult as it would be if I had to have a proper full-time job, nine to six every day, or go and work in a factory. I mean of course there are the disadvantages of – people see you in your studio, and therefore that doesn't count as work, you could be interrupted. And it is also true that I was interrupted continuously by my children, because I was there, and my work could always be interrupted. And indeed that hasn't changed – and I can see it happening in the same way with my grandchildren. Whereas they would never have gone in to interrupt their father. But somehow I am able to accept that. So all those years had been – the action if you like was in my head, it was between myself and my paintings.[38]

Even in the mid-1960s, a decade of radical liberalisation in many ways, the roles of artist and mother of young children were still widely seen as incompatible. Jaray could feel patronised by her male contemporaries:

> I mean not in the literal sense of being patted on the back and, you know, well done dear – but not all that far from it. I think that I did mistake a lot of kindness and encouragement for kindness and encouragement when actually the other students, the male students, simply didn't really see one as a threat, and perhaps there is no real respect as a young artist unless you are seen as a threat as well [. . .] But somehow or other, those were in the days before any kind of feminist awareness. It's very, very hard to throw my mind back. I did start remembering it all rather more when in the late 70s, in 1978 I was part of a group that organised the Hayward Annual, that came to be called the Women's Annual [. . .] I mean that was actually quite interesting, because I had by then become very aware of the various problems of being a woman artist, like everybody else. You know, we'd had ten years of feminist thought and discussion, and I was extremely aware that there were very few women teaching in art schools, very few role models.[39]

In 1976 Jaray, with Liliane Lijn, Kim Lim and Gillian Wise Ciobotaru, put a proposal to the Arts Council for an exhibition of 15 contemporary women artists. The eventual outcome was 'Hayward Annual '78' – the first concerted attempt to stage an exhibition mainly (though not exclusively) of work by women artists in a mainstream cultural institution in Britain. It was, says Jaray, 'one more nail in the coffin of making it possible to have exhibitions of men only.'[40] In its way, it marked a decisive shift: subsequent generations would continue to experience the 'various problems of being a woman artist', but there would now be more (and more visible) role models.

Phyllida Barlow (b.1944) grew up in London and studied at Chelsea College of Art, where she switched from painting to sculpture and was encouraged by her tutor George Fullard to explore 'the awkwardness of how sculpture gets made and things come together that you never expected to come together'.[41] After Chelsea, Barlow studied at the Slade, where she taught sculpture part-time until 2009. Barlow describes making early sculptures out of bales of rags and other discarded commercial or industrial materials and, in the absence of gallery opportunities, exhibiting work between lamp posts in the street, in public parks, even throwing sculptures into the River Thames. Barlow's later career, since about 2010, has been marked by international recognition and high-profile exhibitions, including a show at Tate Britain in 2014 and the 2017 Venice Biennale.

> I regard this time during the mid-70s through to about [19]95 as really an education, you know. It was learning about myself, about myself as in middle age, with a family, husband, with complicated life demands that lots of people have, so nothing – nothing unique or extraordinary about that, but then trying to find that chink in all that – that stuff, of being a mother [. . .] Just the chink where I could get in the studio, and sort of do battle with – is what is in my experience what I wanted to be, as an artist. Who was I, and where was the art/life divide? Did it have a divide, or was the making a continuation of what was happening in my home next door? You know, was it just all one and the same fabric? And in about 1983 I did a talk at Goldsmiths' [. . .] Richard Wentworth[42] asked me if I wanted to come and do a talk, and I thought, 'Oh my God,' you know [. . .] I've got work from the 70s and I've got this – these really strange works that I was doing at night, in the dark – and it was all part of the wondering where I'd put this absolute love of the feel of – of stuff, and how it could become something, but I didn't know what it would become. All I knew was that the handling of it – that was the sort of residue of everything that had led me to sculpture in the first place, was the sense of the physicality of stuff, and that it didn't necessarily have only one way of being, it wasn't necessarily a hundred per cent visual. It was sentient, it was sensory.[43]

The point of it all: Terry Frost and David Nash

Not all first-time fathers were as disengaged as Reg Butler. A generation apart, Terry Frost (1915–2003) and David Nash (b.1945) recall how parenthood affected their art. In 1947, after serving in the commandos including four years as a prisoner of war (see Chapter 3), Frost received an ex-serviceman's grant to study at Camberwell School of Art. In his early 30s, married, with a young child, he found ways of pursuing his studies while pushing the pram in Battersea Park:

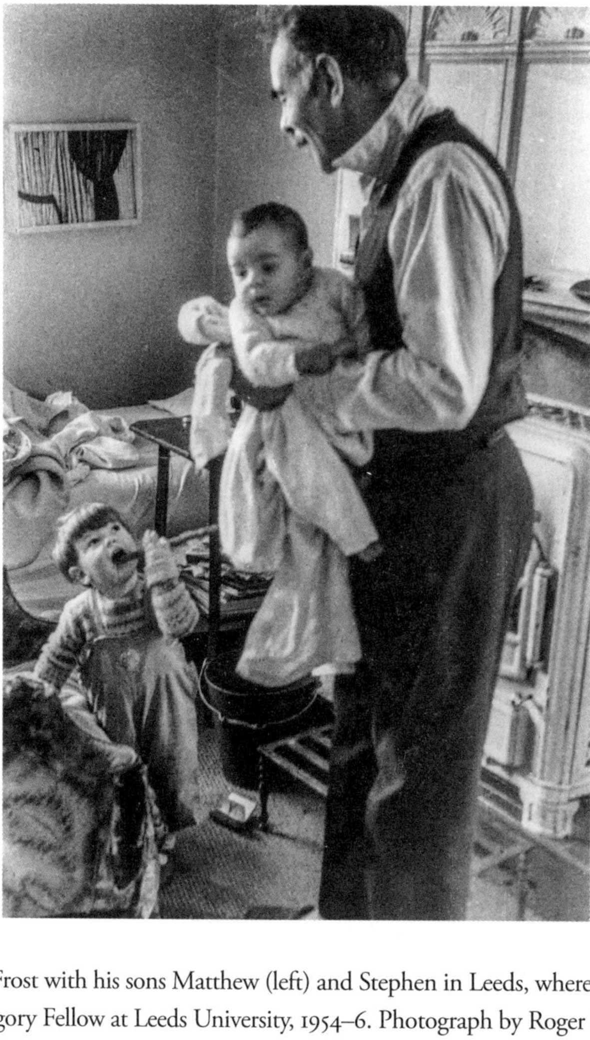

Terry Frost with his sons Matthew (left) and Stephen in Leeds, where Terry was Gregory Fellow at Leeds University, 1954–6. Photograph by Roger Mayne.

> I did paintings of the trees hanging over the water, the lake, and got the reflections and all that, and the swans. And really I was out in the park early every morning because we had Adrian, the first child, who cried like the fury [. . .] And if you are sharing a house and being privileged to have a room in a house where two chaps are living, they don't want that kind of noise, as teachers. I used to be in the park at six o'clock in the morning, wheeling him around to keep him quiet, and if I could get him to sleep, the quicker I could get him to sleep the quicker I could do some drawing. And I learnt all kinds of tricks, because in drawing I used to not only do the drawing but put the colour notes and the tonal notes. And then I thought, well this is a bit silly, doing three drawings to get all these things, so what I did was put some duplicating paper in so that I was able to do my drawing and then make my notes on the one that had come through. I thought that was very good. And, you learn all kinds of things like that.[44]

In the years that followed, when the Frosts were living in St Ives, Terry found work as an assistant to Barbara Hepworth and moved away from the Camberwell style of carefully measured figure painting in subdued tones towards a freer abstract idiom and language of colour that he would develop throughout the rest of his career. He always considered *Walk Along the Quay* (1950) his breakthrough abstract painting; yet the terms in which he describes its genesis are as rooted in daily family life as any work of 1950s' Kitchen Sink realism.

> That child cried for two years, and I had to take him out. Because if you live in St Ives, the houses are so close [in] Downalong [near the harbour], that you wake all the bloody neighbours up, and if they've got a few holiday visitors, they go mad. So I had to take him out. So I had to go down the quay, further away as possible, and he could make a noise like the seagulls, it didn't matter. Now that's why I walked along the quay every morning [. . .] [The canvas] was the same shape as the quay, I mean, you put the lighthouse at the bottom and you walk along the quay to the lighthouse, just like that [. . .] If you walk along a straight line like that [. . .] and you pass all those things on your way, and you come back and do something about it. It isn't like looking at boats on the water from sitting down and having that viewpoint. This is a viewpoint above, from above, and it's a truth, and it is a walk.[45]

David Nash was brought up in Surrey and spent his childhood holidays in Wales; in 1967 he moved permanently to Blaenau Ffestiniog. Nash studied at Kingston College of Art in the 1960s and began to exhibit in the early 1970s. Much of his sculpture is based on large sections of trees, roughly shaped and sometimes charred, sited either indoors or in the landscape. After the birth of his two sons, Nash became intrigued by the educational theories of Rudolf Steiner; in the 1980s he helped to set up a Steiner school in north Wales.

> I missed [William's birth] because it was a very long labour, and the nurses said, 'Go out and get a drink.' And I was just out, and I had actually come back and I was reading a paper in the waiting room when they came out looking for me. So I actually missed the birth with him. I didn't miss the birth with Jack. So when I went into the room there was William wrapped up in this white towel in this perspex, clear perspex cot, looking at me, like looking – 'And where were you then? So that's what you look like.' He was a little toughie right from when he was born, a tremendous will, wilful, and so of course we didn't realise it, we called him William, which is Will I Am. But my priority to change – I could just feel my cogs changing, and my whole priorities. And I guess a lot of parents feel this, that you become the parents of all children, all women become mothers, you know, potential mothers, and one respects the human being in a deeper way, I think. And also when he was growing up and we were playing on the floor, I found that a lot of [the sculpture] I was making was on the floor, my sort of level, eye level, went right down. Then we had Jack in '77, and in preparation for him our little two-room space wasn't going to be big enough so I started quite an ambitious project [. . .] I built a house, which we have since been working on, and since I've been earning quite a bit more money, then I've been able to employ people, so quite a lot of the pretty ghastly bits of carpentry which I did have been taken out and been replaced by something that is a lot more substantial and not so rough. I also realised that – and I had been warned by people in London – 'Be careful of that big building you've got because it could swallow you up in.' Because a lot of people teaching in art schools can afford a mortgage, and they're very skilful with their hands, being sculptors. They buy big houses and they spend all their time doing them up, but because they've got a mortgage it's got to be done up to a certain standard to maintain the value, or increase the value of the house. So in many art schools I went to they would all build a little studio, either in the basement

or down the garden, and I would go and have a look through the window of a shed down the garden, and it would always be full of prams, lawnmowers and bicycles. There was no art going on then, and they were all building their houses.[46]

[. . .] One time I was down at Richard Hughes's[47] place which is on an [Dwyryd] estuary, and his daughter and his grandchild were there. I saw Richard Hughes standing, and I think he was in his place where he wrote, and I could see him through the window, and he was watching his daughter, who was on the lawn, who was unaware of him looking at her, and she was looking at her son playing on the beach, so they were in three different spaces. And I could feel Richard being, he was really woven into life by his longevity, and he was in his 70s then, or early 70s, about 70 years old, and there was his daughter who was probably 35. And she was active, she was a headmistress in Canada, and there was her son who was very young, and he seemed like a strand of rope, a strand of a rope which hadn't been woven in yet, he was like at the front. And I really saw the point of it all.[48]

[. . .] When I had children of my own and seeing them play and how there was nothing between them and the play, there was no anxiety about the history of play and how did what they were playing fit in with the history of playing (I'm making the analogy with an artist, how does my work fit in with the history of art), that you go for it directly, and I've been trying to work intelligently but with that freedom of playing.[49]

2

This is What I Want to Do

First Steps in Art

Is there a point in every artist's life when the 'freedom of playing'[1] David Nash observed in his children becomes a self-aware making of something that could – conceivably, possibly – be called art? It doesn't seem to work in quite that way. More often, the formative influence of childhood toys, pictures on the wall, an art class at school becomes clear only in long-shot retrospect. Eduardo Paolozzi and Kenneth Armitage didn't anticipate, when they were playing with Meccano or improvising from bits of junk, that this would be the start of a lifetime of turning ideas into tangible structures that hold together and stand up. They talk about these toys and activities as if memory were a sculpture in progress. Notice, too, how painters' first memories of art are never purely or even primarily visual: they are also about actions – entering a room, turning the pages of a book – and physical objects. The *mises en scène* in which these artists' early memories are set belong, very largely, to mid-twentieth-century Britain. They predate even the first era of popular children's television in the 1960s, and certainly the Internet age, when the idea of eager self-discovery in a public library has begun to feel strangely anachronistic.

In a wider sense, less immediately to do with making and doing than with personal identity, there does often seem to be a specific moment of recognition, an awareness of what being an artist might mean. For Breon O'Casey this realisation came at nursery school; for Michael Sandle in a local library; for Wilhelmina Barns-Graham in finding a set of artists' hogs-hair brushes mysteriously consigned to her parents' care. Artists who grew up in enlightened middle-class families, like Michael Rothenstein and Patrick Heron, remember their early artworks being admired and treasured by their parents. Other children have to find their own way, through chance encounters and intuitions. 'I knew at the age of 14 that I wanted to be an artist,' says Jack Smith:

> I wanted a different kind of life to what I saw around me. I also came across a book called *Modern French Painters* in the reference library by a man called [R.H.] Wilenski, which was very important to me, it introduced me to modern French painting, Picasso, Braque, Matisse. Made a tremendous impression on me. And I thought, this is what I want to do.[2]

I made things the whole time: Eduardo Paolozzi and Kenneth Armitage

Eduardo Paolozzi (1924–2005) was born in the Edinburgh suburb of Leith. His Italian parents ran a confectionary shop, above which the family lived. Training part-time at Edinburgh College of Art in the 1940s, Paolozzi originally wanted to work in commercial art, but later enrolled at the Slade and began to make sculpture. What interested him most, he said, was 'the golden ability of the artist to achieve a metamorphosis of quite ordinary things into something wonderful and extraordinary'.[3]

In both his sculpture and work on paper, Paolozzi made extensive, idiosyncratic use of collage. In 1946, a decade or so before the official birth of pop art and the associated theorisation of mass media and popular culture, he began to produce paper collages cut from American magazines that had first been brought to Britain by US servicemen during the war. 'One of the great tools in modernism has been collage,' he observes, 'and collage has also been a kind of tool where you can sprinkle the elements, as even in Dada, and that randomness can have as much a meaning as wilful construction [. . .] and the same might be true in sculpture by moving elements around that you get something that's beyond one's deliberate conception.'[4] In the early 1950s he developed a method of pressing fragments of junk into wax sheets, from which he modelled and cast figures in bronze. An inventory of his found materials included: 'Toy frog. Rubber dragon. Toy camera. Assorted wheels and electrical parts [. . .] Model automobiles'.[5]

> I used to like the Meccano magazines very much, but there was – I think occasionally my father would get a cheap offer from a newspaper, and I remember a book I kept reading in a terrified way called *Limehouse Nights*

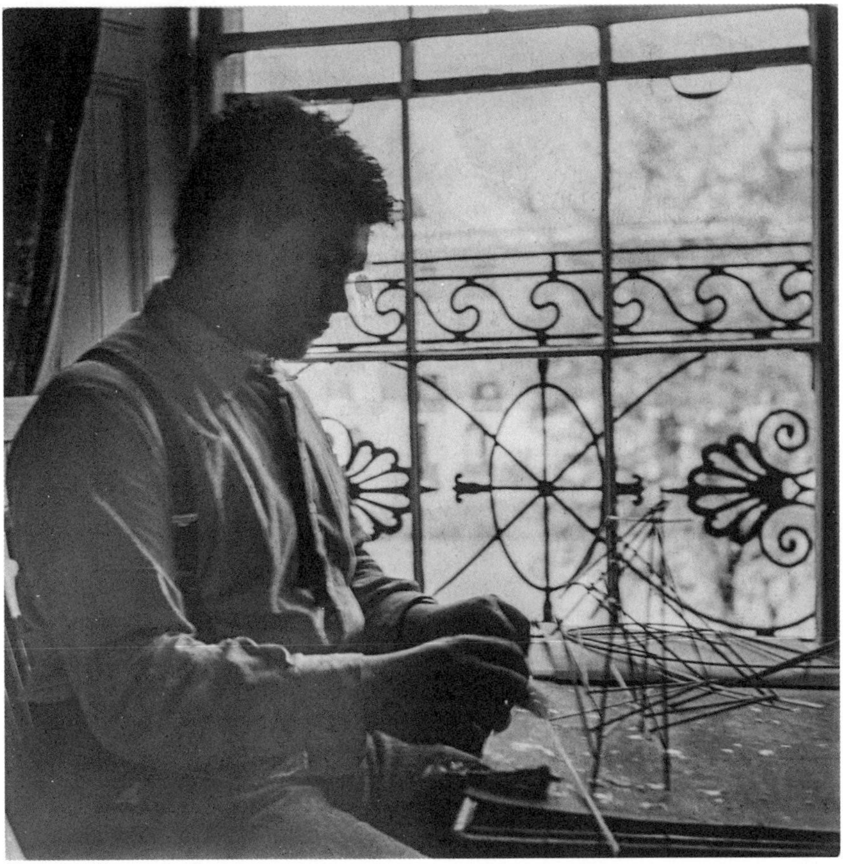

Eduardo Paolozzi working on a balsa wood sculpture at Paultons Square, Chelsea, 1951. Photograph by Nigel Henderson.

by Thomas Burke, which terrified me. And there was a book called *The White Company* by Conan Doyle,[6] I kept reading and re-reading that. But one used to do that then. But there was a lot of pulps around, lots and lots of American pulps, and I think there were things like, now think – I mean even from an early age there was *The Rover* and the *Wizard*, that was the street culture.[7]

[. . .] There was a kind of mahogany box with brass handles which my father gave me, because he used to make radios, and this was some discarded – like bits of a portable radio which he abandoned – but he gave me this wonderful box, and I kept bits and pieces in that. But I remember it had a Trix [construction set] – one of my half crowns I bought, there used to be a kind of cheap Meccano-type of set which I had, called Trix, and the motor, I remember I used to love the motor, electric motor, with a battery, and there were things like that under the bed.[8]

[. . .] I used to draw a lot, because in the shop, not only did we sell ice-cream but we sold chocolates, but good chocolate, and the chocolates would arrive in cardboard boxes and then they were decanted into glass, like glass vases with lids, so there was always a lot of cardboard boxes. There was enough raw material to draw, and I remember drawing on them all the time, but also other people would – at that culture you didn't throw anything away. What was to spare was given to other customers to do the same things, and sometimes people would draw, particularly in winter time people would bring their drawings in, and a lot of the drawings were what might have been called copies, things, football heroes done from newspapers and so on [. . .] Because a lot of the families round this shop were poor, so poor, they were all gas-lit, that to have a radio meant having batteries, which meant that you had to be in employment, but if you were unemployed you had to live in a certain kind of frugal level, which meant that you never threw away a newspaper, it was either used as a tablecloth or some kind of thing for wrapping something up in. I mean that was a time when newspapers were used in fish and chip shops. Nothing was thrown away.[9]

Kenneth Armitage (1916–2002) was born in Leeds, where he attended Leeds College of Art (as had Henry Moore and Barbara Hepworth 15 years earlier). During the Second World War, he served in the Royal Artillery as an instructor in aircraft recognition. His sculpture would almost always be based on the human figure, but the outline contours often echo aircraft silhouettes. In 1946 Armitage became head of sculpture at Bath Academy of Art. The nearby Clifton Suspension Bridge, with its twin towers linked by the slung parabolas of the suspension cables, intrigued him as an example of the integral relationship between structure, form and function – an interest that Armitage traces back to childhood.

Meccano was the thing. Like all boys I thought it was absolutely marvellous, and I made things the whole time. And what I noticed quite small was, sitting in my father's first Austin 7, turning to the right and looking at the mudguard, it described a big arc as you turned round to the right. And

I knew that the wheels underneath, not visible to me, were also turning. But I didn't realise just yet, but I did very soon after, that the wheel on the nearside was turning more than the one on the left. Because if you imagine a car turning in a circle, there is a focal point in the circle, and the wheel that is nearer the focal point must make a sharper turn, because the circle is smaller. And then I found, soon after, that this was achieved by a marvellously simple device on all cars from the beginning, called 'Ackerman Linkage'. Very simply, there is a rod going between the two wheels, mounted on two short arms for the axle carrying the wheels, so that if one wheel turns it pulls a rod and turns the other wheel. But, due to the careful placing of the length of short little arm sticking out, it is so designed that the inside wheel turns a bit more. And so this can then make a perfect circle within the framework of the circles going round the focal point. Now I do remember hearing about that, and trying to make a model of it in Meccano.

But this wasn't my main thing. My main thing was a passion for boats. Very tiny I used to look in shop windows at wind-up boats, mechanical. The tops didn't interest me – the funnels and the superstructure. It was the shape of the hull, which I used to look at with enormous delight, always painted red. I didn't know anything about water dynamic then, but the shape caught my eye. And then my family started going to Filey, and visiting first Filey and Flamborough Head, and I saw for the first time the 'coble', the famous Yorkshire boat [. . .] And this boat really hooked me, I was fascinated with it. To launch it, it had a flat bottom, and it had bilge keels at the lower corners, or 'storkels' as they called it [. . .] And it would be poled out to deeper water, through the breakers, therefore the bows were very deep to go through and over the breakers. And then when it was deep enough they shipped the rudder, which is enormously long. The bows were deep, it was broad in the beam and small in the stern, and for the rudders to be effective they had to extend it well below, to about five or six feet below the bottom of the boat, which was 30 foot long. And so that couldn't be shipped until it was enough into deep water, which must have been quite a job [...] Well this extended right up the coast, and it occupied a lot of my thinking. Meanwhile, my father had sent me to a school to toughen me up.[10]

[. . .] I decided when I was 16 to take up art. I can remember the day [. . .] I had a friend who I used to walk home with from school, and we were both saying, when we were 16, what we were going to do. And that day he said, 'I am going to be an architect', and he did become an architect. And

I said, 'I'm going to be an artist', and I did become an artist. And that was all in, you know, ten minutes, walking – well, quarter of an hour walking home, that day.[11]

Wonderful things: Wilhelmina Barns-Graham and William Gear

Wilhelmina Barns-Graham (1912–2004) was born in St Andrews, Fife, into the Scottish gentry. She sometimes felt that the austere, relatively modest privilege of her upbringing weighed against her as an artist: 'I wasn't born into a working-

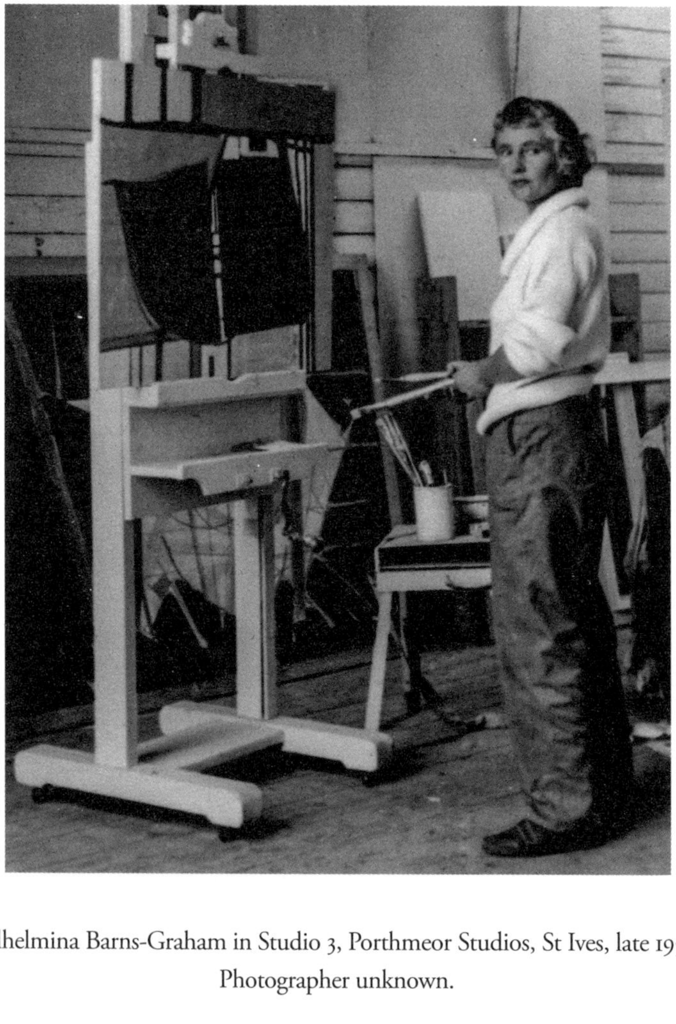

Wilhelmina Barns-Graham in Studio 3, Porthmeor Studios, St Ives, late 1950s. Photographer unknown.

class family [. . .] much to my regret sometimes, because the artist world is mainly out of, not so much the so-called well-to-do people.'[12] She studied at Edinburgh College of Art, then in 1940, unable to take up a travel scholarship to Paris because of the war, went to St Ives, where her fellow Edinburgh student Margaret Mellis, now married to the art critic Adrian Stokes, was living. Here she met Barbara Hepworth, Ben Nicholson and Naum Gabo and became closely involved in the St Ives' mid-century modernist moment. All this was a complete contrast to the world of Barns-Graham's upbringing; yet she dates the first intuition of her artistic vocation to the sight of an artist's equipment in her parents' house, which they had for some reason agreed to store.

> Off their [my parents'] room, there was a big music room there, a wonderful room [in] which my father had a harmonium and my mother a piano, they were very musical and played together. There was a room off it that I was hardly ever allowed into, and it was full of junk, it was Mr Cadogan's things. And my father was in there one day and there was a jar full of big oil brushes. And I remember going up and caressing them, thinking these were the most wonderful things I had ever seen, and my father turned round and said, 'Don't you touch these.' He was perfectly right, he was guardian of these things. And there was another bowl full of great big oil brushes, hog's-hair oil brushes, huge ones, or seemed huge to a child, very clean, some of them were probably unused. But this was where he had stored a lot of things [. . .] I hadn't thought about it until now, what happened? Mr Cadogan died or, I'm not sure. But certainly these things were there, and that room off the music room. Now [1994] that house is turned into flats, but I have crept into the garden and seen, there's still the circular window high up in that wall and there's still that small room off it, but I don't know what it is now. But that had quite an influence on my life, those brushes.[13]

It was at school in St Andrews that Barns-Graham says 'my art ambitions began':

> There was a marvellous teacher there called Miss Hebblethwaite, and she did wonderful chalk drawings on the blackboard. I remember her doing a daffodil and I think, 'I want to be an artist.' And the children had pictures put on the walls aged five, aged six, aged ten sort of thing, and, if only I could get one up. And one weekend I did a copy of the little figure on the marmalade jar [. . .] a little black figure, I think in a red jacket and blue trousers. Anyway I copied it

> but I reversed the – I made him have a blue jacket and red trousers, I reversed the colours you see. And to my amazement, that got on the wall, 'Willie Barns-Graham, aged eight years'. I've still got it. And that clinched it. I am going to be an artist. Then the other incident in my childhood was on a train when we were travelling from St Andrews to Glasgow, and my father was in the train [. . .] and my mother [. . .] And sitting beside me was a tall lady, and I was drawing with chalk into a book of triangles and squares, secret rooms really, I didn't want anyone to see them. And I was constantly doing this. And she asked me what I was doing, and I was livid with her, and my parents just shrugged their shoulders, said, 'Oh she's always doing that sort of thing.' And it was chalk – blue outlines and I coloured the interiors. But I wished now I had known who that was, because she took an interest in me, told us that she was on the staff at the Glasgow School of Art [. . .] I would only be about 12.[14]

When, despite her father's opposition, Barns-Graham finally started at art school in 1931, she felt that she was leaving the class consciousness of her childhood behind: 'artists still go into a melting-pot, you have to; we all come from different backgrounds but our aim is the same, trying to say something'.[15] Her student friends at Edinburgh included William Gear (1915–97), a miner's son from the Fife colliery town of East Wemyss. 'We had a scholarship for Paris,' Barns-Graham recalls, 'and we were over there, and I remember Bill Gear walking around a room, there was an exhibition of Van Gogh, and an American girl pointing to her mother said, "Mum, there he is!" Pointed at Bill Gear, who at that time he had red hair. It was a Van Gogh portrait, and I thought this was a huge joke.'[16]

This may have been during the five months Gear spent in Paris studying with Fernand Léger, before travelling through Italy to Greece, Istanbul and Albania. After army service during the war, Gear moved to Paris, exhibited with the CoBrA group in Amsterdam and in 1949 was one of the first young British abstract artists to show in New York. Gear was 'about ten' when his artistic induction took place:

> There was this occasion, I remember, when the teacher solemnly put a handbag on [. . .] a kind of table with a bit of paper behind it. And she announced that the one with the best drawing would get a shilling from my handbag, you see. So I won the prize [*laughs*] [. . .] You had to draw this, her handbag. This is it, this was still life, you drew the handbag. But the idea that in that handbag there was a shilling, that was incentive [*laughs*]. And a shilling to a kid of ten in those days was serious money. I remember going

> home and showing this my mother, 'Where did you get that?' But anyhow, that was my first inkling that I was good at art, so to speak.[17]

While Gear was at secondary school, the old art master died:

> and we got a youngish, a bright younger art master called Bob Morris, who had been at the College of Art in Edinburgh and actually was a friend of people like Gillies[18] and that group. I mean he had been to Paris even and so on, so he was aware of [what] you might call twentieth-century [art] and he, I suppose, he spotted me and encouraged me and gave me books, new books on Cézanne and modern art and so on to look at. And then I find myself being the top of the class and winning prizes, and deciding at the age of say 15 plus or 16 minus or whatever it was that I would like to go to the art school and being encouraged to do so by this art master and announcing to my parents that I wanted to go to the art school.[19]

He was surprised when his parents said, 'They didn't mind, this is great, that's fine.'

> But the other tradition, of course, in those families, especially mining families, most miners, most miners would say, 'My son's not going down the pit', you know, they would do everything to help. And, the lucky thing was, I didn't realise it at the time, but they encouraged me – but the lucky thing was that when applying for grants and through the Fife Education Authority, and they were very good and they did give grants to students going to university [. . .] And there was also the miners' welfare thing, and so one way and the other I got literally enough money to manage on as a student in Edinburgh, without being a problem – having to resort to my parents. And of course during the vacations I generally – well, certainly the summer vacation, I generally went berry picking in Perthshire with other students. So I wasn't a drag on my parents.[20]

What do I remember of the museums?: Paul Feiler and Josef Herman

Paul Feiler (1918–2013) grew up in Frankfurt-am-Main, where his father was director of the Carolinum Institute for Dentistry at Goethe University. Raised as a Lutheran, Feiler was unaware of his family's Jewish roots until the enactment of Nazi race laws in the early 1930s, when his father was dismissed from the university and Feiler was expelled from his school. In 1934 he was sent to England, where he studied at Regent Street Polytechnic and then the Slade, before being interned in 1940 as an enemy alien on the Isle of Man. Feiler later taught at the West of England College of Art in Bristol, while developing an increasingly abstract idiom in his painting. He bought a disused chapel near Newlyn in Cornwall, where he worked for part of the year. Photographs of the Cornish coast, or the patterns of field walls viewed from a distance, would become the starting point for apparently abstract images. Feiler locates his interest in photography, and in the figure of the photographer in the landscape, in both his own and his mother's early memories:

> I had a Brownie [camera] when I was a child, yes, and I took a lot of photographs. And I still have the photographs that I took with the Brownie. But, I don't think I was particularly good at anything, or rather, especially good at anything. I just did what everybody else did. My grandfather, my mother's father, was a great photographer and a pioneer in taking coloured photographs, coloured slides of flowers, that's all he did. And my mother remembers with agony having to carry his gear from place to place. But she was a dutiful daughter, so she did. But that's what she was. And I remember seeing those slides with an epidiascope and all, and they were very good, I mean they were exceptionally good.[21]
>
> [. . .] I used to go to the local museum and art gallery every Sunday after confirmation classes, not that I minded the confirmation classes but the museum was open in the afternoon, and I was able to walk across the bridge onto the other side of town, and I was very enamoured with a lot of the sculpture that was on display, as well as the paintings of course. And I had a very strong memory of a piece of sculpture by a German sculptor of the Renaissance called Riemenschneider,[22] a Madonna and Child carved in stone, and he was one of the major sculptors of Europe at that time. Incidentally I used to go to the art gallery of course and there I saw a famous Rembrandt and a famous Monet and a famous this and a famous Franz Marc, and I was very aware of having spent a lot of time looking at painting and sculpture. There was a fair amount in the house as well, at home, so it wasn't new to me, it was part of one's background, and I think part of one's education, if you were of a certain status so to speak, you had to be educated

> in matters of the fine arts, or the arts if you like. You had to sing apparently, and you had to play an instrument, neither of which I did. You had to enjoy art and music and poetry and all the rest of it.[23]
>
> [. . .] I found school a very narrow way, a very narrow form of enjoying life as a free person. I found being in with people who knew the answer to things when I didn't not easy. I think I have to say here that I was a loner. Although I had many friends, nevertheless I enjoyed being on my own. And I did start off painting when I was not only a child but almost prenatal. I was born with a paintbrush in my mouth. And I've painted ever since I can remember, non-stop until this very moment. [Like] you would say that you are born with a silver spoon in your mouth [. . .] And, since that is what I have always wanted to do, and it's never occurred to me that you can't do that, and since I was always encouraged to paint, and since I have records of myself being photographed aged two, three, four and five with a paintbrush in my hand, I think I'm justified to say that that is the case.[24]

Josef Herman's memories of his working-class Warsaw childhood date from roughly the same era. Whereas Feiler recalls always being familiar with art, both in museums and in the family home, Herman's first encounters with art took the form of shop signs and cinema posters. He recalls a Polish sign painter who happened to live in the same street, a certain Master Xavery Rex:

> I don't know whether you know continental signs for tailors, for cobblers – for cobblers it's usually a boot, a huge boot. For tailors it is sometimes a woman with a wedding dress. You know, these signs are absolutely fantastic [. . .] And men like Xavery Rex had no talent whatever, you know. But he painted all the huge posters for the local cinema, and you could see him actually do it, painting a letter, a letter O with the hands sticking out with a pistol, you know? Just a silly thing! This was the greatest art I knew [. . .] Oh, my God, I used to pop in. And every now and again I was privileged. He would ask me in, say, 'Boy!' He would have so many pennies. 'Go and buy powder *ultra*marine.' And I will never forget this word *ultra*marine. It starts with such fantastic magic, you know. And this was a great privilege to produce – to bring him the powder from which he will make a sky or something like it, you know. And to be able to see it. Because when I came back with ultramarine he never pushed me out. He let me stay in the workshop. Oh this was a greater experience than all the future museums,

> or all – I live in it with greater affection. You see, because whenever you were later taken to a museum, you were told, 'Shhh! Be *quiet!*' [. . .] But when you were in Rex's place [. . .] you were struck by a miracle coming out. A hand with a pistol [. . .] You must understand the sensitivity – the most wonderful thing about the sensitivity of great things in the child's life are really things which he will perceive and will remain with him. What do I remember of the museums? That I had to be quiet. This I remember most, you know? That I had to be quiet, and that I had not to move [. . .] And he [Rex] sometimes would chant, sing or whistle, and I would join in. And when he rested, yes, he had a mandolin. He would sit down and play the mandolin, and he will sing some Yiddish or Polish folk songs. It was lovely.[25]

My talent, whatever it was: Breon O'Casey and Patrick Heron

Breon O'Casey (1920–2011) was the eldest child of the Irish playwright Sean O'Casey, who had moved to London after falling out with the management of the Abbey Theatre in Dublin, where his early plays had been successfully if controversially staged. The family then relocated to Totnes in Devon, where George Bernard Shaw had advised O'Casey to send his children to the recently established school on the nearby Dartington Hall estate – an idealistic community founded by the American heiress Dorothy Elmhirst and her husband Leonard. Like Barns-Graham, O'Casey would spend most of his long career in west Cornwall, where he retained the Dartington ethos of equality between all creative activities, at various times producing jewellery, textiles, prints and sculpture, although he always considered himself primarily a painter.

> The war came when I was 12 [. . .] my mother sent for these swatches of tweed, because, you know, clothes were rationed here. And these little swatches of tweed came from Ireland, and they were so beautiful – ah, gosh, they were lovely. And I saw them, in a way, as little landscapes, little Irish landscapes [. . .] one was a sort of soft, misty brown, one was a pale blue, one was off-white, and it had little tiny flecks of vermilion in it, and little tiny flecks of emerald green, and other soft little colours. They were lovely, and they were hand-woven tweeds [. . .] To me it was the only visual thing that they [the Irish] were really good at. And I'll always remember those tweeds

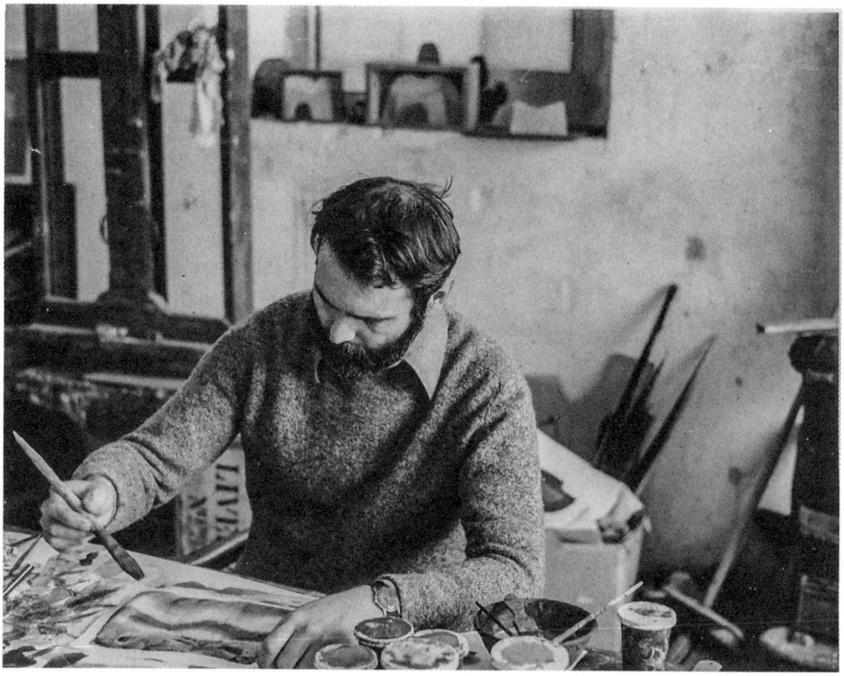

Breon O'Casey in Studio 3, Porthmeor Studios, St Ives, late 1960s. Photograph by Nicholas Elder.

[. . .] and I had three coats made from them. I had one coat that was this pale blue, and the other one was this lovely off-white with these little flecks of colour, and another was this soft, almost misty sort of brown. Beautiful. Beautiful. And another – it's funny – tweed is this, has played an important part in my life [. . .] I went to school in Dartington, and I had to cycle to school, and they – part of the [Dartington] estate was this factory which made tweed, and it was beside this little stream, and it was the mills – the mills were run by waterwheel. And along beside the factory was an old cider orchard, and it was terraced, because it was up a hill. And there were these old cider trees, and among the cider trees was this tenterhook frame[26] – these long tenterhook frames where they'd [. . .] wash the tweed to get it to hold together and hang it on these tenterhooks – so that's where the phrase comes from, 'on tenterhooks' – and – to stop it from shrinking. And so, when I would cycle to school, I'd sort of pass an exhibition, if you like, of tweeds, among these trees.[27]

> [. . .] My earliest memory of knowing I was an artist, in a sense – of knowing that I could see what – was when I was at nursery school [. . .] They had this woman come, and she was sort of genteel, but she painted – do you know that English sort of thing, where you are sort of an amateur, but an accomplished amateur? And she painted a sign for the school, like an inn sign [. . .] and underneath was a picture of these children playing. And we were all called in to see it when she'd finished it. And we said, oh, how lovely, and everything. But I knew in my heart that it wasn't any good, and I knew – I knew then, yes. Isn't that strange? Yes, I knew [. . .] But on the other hand, I wanted to – Walt Disney had brought out a book called *How to Draw*, and I wanted it, but my father wouldn't get it for me. But we were living in these flats in Battersea, and the boy downstairs had it. So I used to go down and learn how to draw these eyes with a – so that you had this little triangle going into the middle, so it looked like the eye had a light shining on it. I knew it was wrong, but I still wanted to do it [*laughs*]. So I was a fraud, as well as knowing.[28]

Patrick Heron (1920–99) spent his early years in Leeds, where his father was an entrepreneur and idealistic socialist. The family home, like the homes that Heron and his wife, Delia, would later make for themselves, exemplified an enlightened Arts and Crafts belief in the socially benign effects of well-chosen, thoughtfully arranged objects, patterns and colours. Heron was precociously gifted and largely self-taught as an artist, drawing initially on his admiration for the modern French masters Cézanne, Braque and Matisse. He would make his reputation in the 1950s as both a painter and a critic, helping to introduce European and then American abstract artists to the British public and raise the profile of his artist contemporaries abroad. As a boy, Heron's gifts were assiduously nurtured by his parents; in adult life, he would always regard his childhood drawings as equal to any other part of his oeuvre, as when he describes the marked change in subject matter that accompanied the family's move from Leeds to St Ives when Heron was five.

> Where all my drawing books in Leeds were filled with trams, traction engines, steamrollers, railway engines, cars and mill chimneys and great mills, all these were drawn with a linear pencil line in drawing books which my parents lovingly and protectively kept [. . .] their enthusiasm for my talent, whatever it was, was terribly total from the word go. And so they kept all these books, and even dated them. So I know exactly – I mean I can remember of course when I drew what, where. Anyway these north

country industrial scenes, which are the subject of the linear drawings in these drawing books, were suddenly switched to schooners and boats, and harbour walls and Cornish churches, and so on. And one of these books, dated 1925 by my mother, was completed at the house that we went [to], from Leeds.[29]

[. . .] Well, I've still got these books, and one of them – well, when we got down to Cornwall everything changed to ships and harbours, and one of them contained a drawing of a schooner, a three-masted schooner, in a rainstorm, with a bowsprit that went right out across the second page. I actually detached this from the second page, but I've still got the book showing where it came from, because I wanted to include it as item number one in the retrospective [exhibition] [. . .] with a beautiful catalogue, printed and designed by Lund Humphries with four-colour plates. Yes, you will find item number one, *Schooner in a Storm*. And that was framed, and used to stand, and still stands

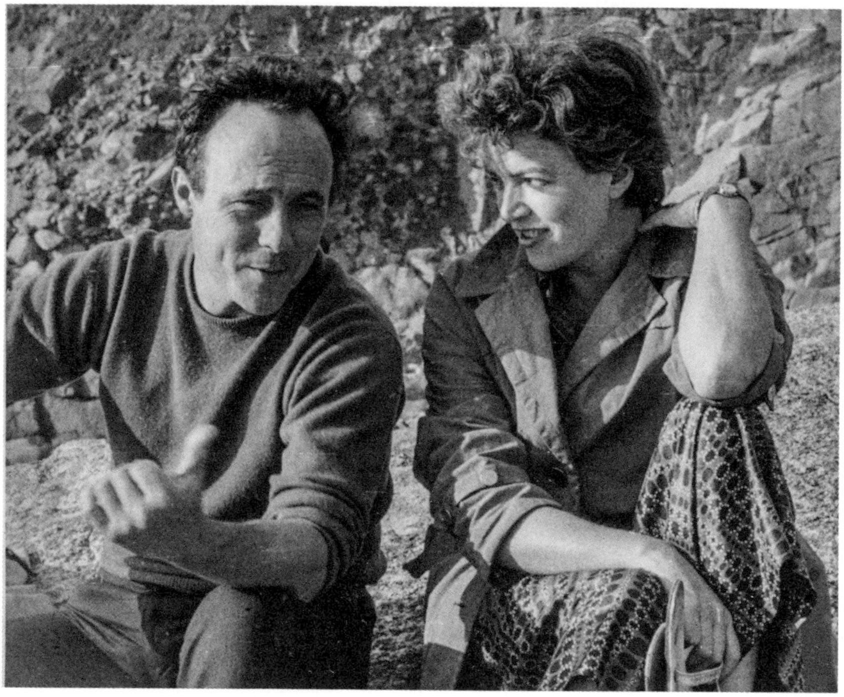

Patrick and Delia Heron at Cot Valley, Cornwall, *c.*1959.
Photograph by F.E. McWilliam.

> here, on this plan-chest top, here in the studio. It's been there for donkey's years. And Ben [Nicholson] was very intrigued by this drawing, and passing by one day he said, 'I still think that's –.' What did he say? 'I still think this is one of the best things you've ever done, you know.'[30]

One of Heron's schoolfriends was Peter Lanyon, son of a long-established local family who would later become both a close artistic associate and professional rival. 'We became very, very pronounced friends, very strong friends,' Heron recalls.

> We even exchanged works of art at one point. And curiously enough he thought he was – I'm now talking to you about, say, 1928, when I would be eight, and Peter was nearly ten, he might have just been ten, he was about 20 months older than me. And he thought he was going to be a sculptor, then, and I was always going to be a painter, and I remember exchanging a watercolour drawing of elm trees at night with him and on the back of it there's another drawing of St Anthony, which is a village just off the Helford River. Peter managed to tear this actually while it was in his keeping and so he stuck a label on the St Anthony drawing in order to preserve the elms at night [. . .] He apologised. And he lent me a plaster of Paris construction that he had made.[31]

One picks up all sorts of things: Bryan Kneale and Michael Sandle

'I think one picks up all sorts of things from the shape of toys, to cars, to aeroplanes,' observes the sculptor Bryan Kneale (b.1930), who grew up on the Isle of Man. Kneale originally trained as a painter, first at Douglas School of Art then at the Royal Academy Schools in London. He turned to sculpture in his late 20s, eventually becoming head of sculpture at the Royal College of Art.

> At that time [the late 1930s] there was a huge transformation, you know. For instance we used to have car racing over there [on the Isle of Man] and the toys themselves were reflecting the new forms. You know, I'm sure one picks up on a million things from just household articles.[32]
>
> [. . .] I can remember the lino, there was quite a lot of lino around the place [at home] and stair carpet, because that was very much Art Deco. I can remember that quite well [. . .] I think one of the problems of growing

up is coping with design, actually, because one does remember all these things.[33]

Kneale traces his theoretical as well as practical sculptural concerns back to childhood conversations with his brother. These seemed just as relevant, three decades later, in the context of the radical sculpture discussion sessions led by Anthony Caro at St Martin's School of Art (for Caro's account of these sessions, see Chapter 6).

> When I was a child I was very interested in what I thought was false and what was real. Anything that was plated, for instance, was false and upsetting. Anything made of plastic worried me. I had a great horror – I don't know why I was sort of afflicted with that [. . .] I was very conscious that things had to be real [. . .] I remember having a conversation with Tony Caro about it, because one of the sessions at St Martin's, they had a great discussion – which I heard about, I wasn't there – was whether a cube of steel a foot square was more real than a box made of steel, of half-inch plate welded together and ground off so you couldn't actually tell by looking at it which was real and which was false. And so they had a long discussion about how if you knew something was hollow it was therefore, it wasn't real. Anyway, I said, well that reminds me of an extraordinary thing. When I was a small child my brother came out with the same thing about Easter eggs, and he told me that the trouble with my Easter egg, which was very large, was [that it was] basically false, not real at all. So he got it off me and he blew an egg, real egg, melted down my egg and poured it into the eggshell. So I was then presented with this horrible little solid chocolate egg, which was real. So I told Tony about this and he was not amused in the least [*laughs*].[34]

Six years younger than Kneale, Michael Sandle also spent his formative years on the Isle of Man:

> I was always good at art, and I remember some of my drawings which I did received the disapproval of the schoolteacher because I remember doing burning tanks, which I can remember very clearly, a soldier being blown up, tank on fire, black cross on it, Nazi tank, or crashing aeroplanes. All the things I suppose that were very much in the air. I don't know why she didn't like it,

the schoolteacher, she told me I shouldn't be doing things like that. I remember that very clearly. And I remember the school doctor being very taken with an all-over pattern I did when most kids did sort of boring all-over patterns and I decided to do the complete royal family [*laughs*], you know, straight way up and upside-down, that was my all-over pattern. That was very original.[35]

[. . .] I used to go to Douglas public library and I got magazines like, there's a magazine called *The Artist*, and books on how to do it, and also books I remember on more sort of theory, and I got terribly into it. And I see it as a sort of escape from the sordid reality of that life between permanently quarrelling, often-violent parents – was a way out, so I became very, very intensely involved through these reproductions of – and I remember thinking at the time, and I was very, very young, how good Cotman[36] was. Then I got very much into, involved in the – you know, the Dutch still-life painters made a huge impression at that age. And then it just sort of took off from there. But it's interesting how one knows who is good and who isn't. For some reason or other I was ill, a bit later than 12, I suppose I must have been a teenager, probably 16. I remember having jaundice and my mother bringing me home some books from the library. She also bought me a book on American painting, believe it or not. I remember thinking at that age how good Albert Pinkham Ryder was, and he was Pollock's teacher.[37] And before that, how good, I knew instinctively that Velázquez was incredibly good. You know, no one said that – no one had said to me, Velázquez is *the* man. I just looked at it and I thought that I knew. Amazing [. . .] I can remember very clearly how I looked at them. I remember looking at the close-ups of the pigment, the way he put the pigment on and I was thinking 'Christ' to myself – though I didn't say 'Christ' 'cos I don't think one does when one's a child. But I remember thinking amazingly clear, that's what I want to do. I want that, this is it [. . .] It was a portrait of Philip of Spain, I remember. It was a close-up. It's full of wonderful pigment, the way he's got a lightness of touch [. . .] When I was a bit older, there was a hotel in a place called Santon, where the owner collected modern art, and I remember going there and seeing Matthew Smith, I remember, Christopher Wood, then that English surrealist – is his name Tanniel? Tannard?[38] And I met Bryan Kneale, who was a friend of a friend of somebody I knew. So I met him once or twice, and I thought he was the real thing, the real modern artist, and thought, I want to be like that. And he was quite wild in those days.[39]

A brightness in the wood: David Nash

'I've always felt,' says David Nash, 'that one is born with everything that you need, but it isn't in a viable form. Education is all about nurturing what is there rather than being treated as an empty vessel to stuff things in. And I had an education experience where the assumption was, I was an empty vessel to stuff things in. And there was just occasionally when, by chance, there was a right hit.'[40] He reflects on a series of formative early experiences, from taking part in a primary school play to the sight of timber being split by his father, and a moment of decision at boarding school: 'I can remember the spot that I was standing on.'

> There were plays, like nativity plays. I remember the tail of my rocking horse I used as a beard, I was a shepherd. And in one of those plays I can remember being introduced to the absurd or – I was a shepherd, Joseph and Mary came on to stage and asked me the way to Bethlehem, and I pointed in one direction and they went in the other direction, and it brought the house down.[41]
>
> [. . .] My brother got into reading war stories so I tried to read them [. . .] I used to read, when I was reading to myself in bed, you know, *The Famous Five*.[42] There was a lot of Enid Blyton stuff I can remember, because that was what I was given. It wasn't very inspired reading that I was offered [. . .] I can remember the kitten being rolled up in a jam roly-poly by the rats in the chimney and being very frightened about that, very upset about that. Peter Rabbit, Mr McGregor, was terrified of Mr McGregor[43] [. . .] Another Enid Blyton one called 'Mr Meddle', I had great sympathy for Mr Meddle and the sort of chaos which he would create. I guess he was my first meeting with an anarchist.[44]
>
> [. . .] My father had bought a little plot of land and he was the first one to build a house down this cul-de-sac, we were at the very end, where there was like a sort of turnaround there. But it was a rough road, it wasn't made up until after we left there. So we did a lot of what we would do in Wales in those plots of land, you know, digging trenches.[45] There was fantastic gang warfare against the neighbouring street, they had a gang of kids, so there was a lot of missiles toing and froing [. . .] And this outdoor activity was right there from the beginning again because of my father being a very practical man, because after the war, rationing, we had a lot of chickens, this was in Weybridge, my father was quite an entrepreneur too, and I can remember him cutting a tree down in our garden in Weybridge and splitting it into lengths to build a

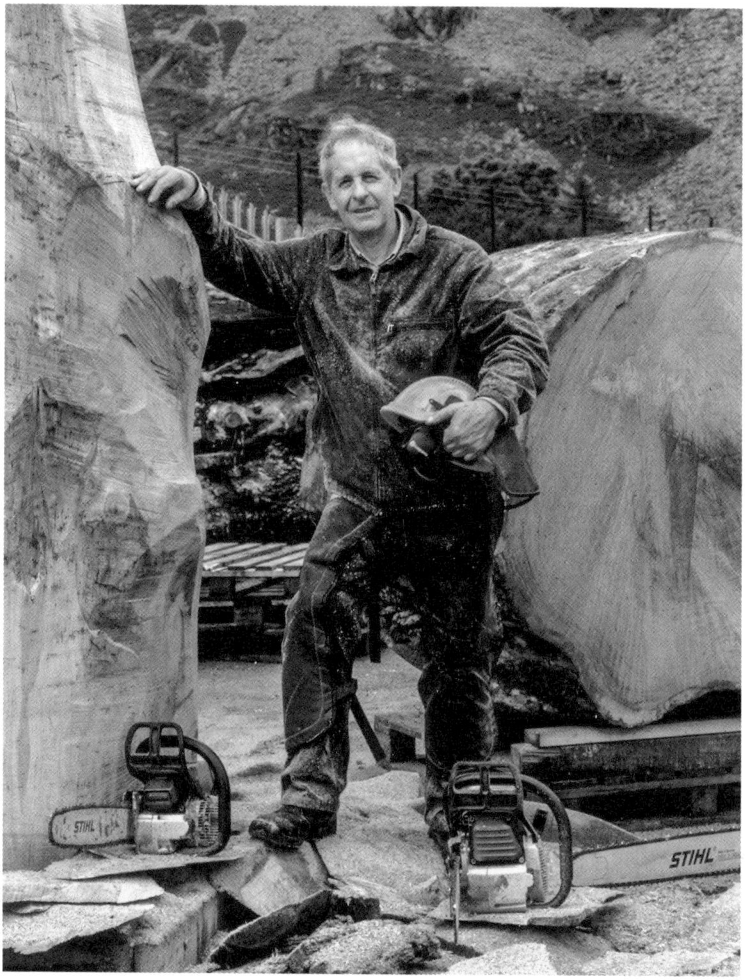

David Nash working on *Forms that Grow in the Night*, Llwyn Gell Workshops, Blaenau Ffestiniog, *c.*2007. Photograph by Ian Parker.

chicken house, and I can remember the gleam of light as it seems to be when you split wood open, fresh wood, there's a brightness in the wood there.[46]

[. . .] And there was a great deal of wood that came out of this part of the house which was demolished,[47] and there was a big scrap pile which was going to be used for firewood, and there was a big pile that my father kept which was useful wood. Because of the war and the rationing *et cetera,* we all got into the habit, everyone was still in the habit then of keeping whatever might be useful. So I used to make soapbox carts with this wood, and I built a fort, you know, with several storeys in it, I built a tower at aged ten, 11. So wood as a building-material-cum-play has sort of always been with me.[48]

[. . .] I was sent off to this boarding school where my brother had gone, and he had had a terrible time there, but my father was very determined that I should go there as well, and this school systematically set about demoralising me, and worked at destroying this confidence which I had managed to develop, and because I was – I got aware of myself probably a bit more than my peers were because of this stammering handicap, I could see what they were doing, and I was absolutely appalled. And I remember, I was probably in my second term there, being so angry, and I can remember the spot that I was standing on, and actually determining that I was not going to be moulded by these people, and I really declared war on them, and in a way I then declared war on my parents, because they were doing this to me, they were aiding and abetting what these people were doing, which were the staff, the whole ethos of the school, of what Brighton College was, what it represented, and this moulding one into these certain sort of attitudes.[49]

[. . .] In the middle of the fourth form I started doing art. And that's where I met Gordon Taylor, John Gordon Taylor, who is an exceptionally good art teacher. It was mainly drawing, drawing cubes, spheres, cylinders. He was a Bauhaus man,[50] in fact he apparently was continually being asked to teach in the design school in the Royal College, but his family were in Brighton and he just preferred his set-up. And he was very independent in his art room and he had an autonomy in there [. . .] He taught us life, taught us business. He taught in a way that, what real education is about, is that you teach into the young person for the future, that they can be able to use what is given them in life rather than for an exam.[51]

It's how you look: Phyllida Barlow

Phyllida Barlow recalls an occasion when she was 'maybe seven or something', visiting a girl of her own age whose father was an artist:

> We were painting, and I think we had both done the thing of painting the sky as a strip across the top. I remember him taking us to the window

> and saying, 'Where's the sky?' I remember it absolutely distinctly. And he said, 'Look, the sky is all round that house at the bottom of the garden' – it was like magic [. . .] So when we went back to our paintings, this thing of painting the sky all round, right down to the bottom of the painting where it met the rest of the composition was so exciting. It was thrilling – I suppose it was about translating what you actually saw compared with what you thought something was. I suppose when children do that strip of blue at the top of a painting it's actually what you might call a conceptual idea of something – it's how you look, isn't it, into the world compared with how it actually behaves visually?[52]

At the age of 14, by then thinking of applying to art school (see Chapter 4), Barlow attended a two-week summer school in Shoreham-by-the-Sea in West Sussex, run by a former Slade tutor and his son.

> It was just idyllic to be doing that every day, painting the immediate environment, the landscape – it was a kind of recognition that that was what I wanted to do [. . .] They taught in a very, very rigorous way. They taught you how to lay the colours out on the palette. I learnt so much from them, and some of the things still have a sort of incredible importance, like when painting outdoors and painting this surrounding Kent landscape, the space between the meadows and the trees. And I remember the older painter of the two just asking me where I thought the darkest place in the painting was and the lightest place – very, very simple things, and then saying, 'What colour is the darkest place?' And him adding, 'Because it's not black.' Sort of very simple things that when you're beginning to have your visual language expanded, you just devour it, the fact that the darkest colour isn't black, it's incredibly simple and incredibly obvious, but it's thrilling that it could be a very dark red or a very, incredibly dark yellow or dark blue – that you go way beyond the logic of dark to light to the reality of what is actually there [. . .] I remember this apple and his kind of question which also made me realise that maybe painting wasn't the only way for me – was kind of asking, what makes you know it's solid? Is it the apple itself? Or is it the space around the apple? And then going and looking at books of Cézanne and saying, what Cézanne did was make the tablecloth or the space around the objects really – I remember him using the words 'grip the object'. So you almost feel, if that surrounding colour and material – if that goes, the object would expand.

> These sort of wonderful descriptions which just made me have a completely new way of looking at the world around that wasn't just simplistic.[53]

The achievement of making: Lubaina Himid

Lubaina Himid (b.1954) was born in Zanzibar to a Tanzanian father and a British mother. After the sudden death of her father when she was just four months old, her mother returned with her to Britain, where they settled in north-west London. Himid studied theatre design at Wimbledon College of Art and worked in the theatre before becoming involved in the 1980s in organising exhibitions and other projects centred on the work of black women artists. Himid's work includes paintings on canvas and distinctive flat, painted figures, cut out of wood, like historic dummy-board figures from the eighteenth-century heyday of colonial wealth founded on the transatlantic slave trade. In 2001 Himid became professor of contemporary art at the University of Central Lancashire; in 2017 she won the Turner Prize.

> I didn't really start drawing at home a lot till I was about 11, something like that, I think. They were fantasy drawings really, I suppose they were glorified doodles really. Lots of drawing with black line, patterns that kind of grew out of other patterns, faces that grew out of patterns, patterns that grew out of faces, that sort of thing really. Psychedelic things I suppose you'd call them now, kind of hippy drawings. I think that was the beginning of how I – and the poetry I wrote was that sort of poetry as well [. . .] one line would [. . .] grow out of another line, which would grow out of another line. Sort of, a mixture of nonsense and fantasy, I suppose. And then, in a way, I think the drawings were the same sort of thing. Wasn't really very interested in drawing natural objects or real objects, and I don't think I painted all that much early on because of the mess it would make, but later on I did, you know. I was 15, 16, then I would paint in my bedroom, and I didn't seem to have made an awful lot of mess, but that was part of how you were in my house, you didn't make a mess, you know. Yes. I've always been quite interested in the Hogarth sort of cartoons, Cruikshank and Gillray, and they've kind of crept – that sort of inclination towards that exaggeration has always crept in and out. The drawings didn't really look like that, but that was what I was trying to do,

I think, make something that was slightly – I don't know, unsettling in a sort of way, but not realistic. So, but then gradually as I got older I would paint, again, almost fantasy paintings, maybe collage [. . .] I suppose teenage surrealist sort of things, cut up one person's body and draw a head, on that was somebody else's head and that sort of thing. Not really very interesting at all, but fun to do.

I had lots of scrapbooks too and I'd cut out, you know, just stuff I found interesting from newspapers and magazines. And then really never much looked back at those scrapbooks. It was the sticking them in, it was the doing them rather than the admiring them later or looking through them [. . .] I'm the sort of person that still really collects all sorts of bits and pieces, and then I don't really look at them again, but once I've collected them it's sort of stored. And I think that's – the cutting out of those things and the sticking them in the scrapbook was the storing them to memory for use later. I don't ever remember going through them and thinking, ah yes, that's a nice pink, I'll use that. But I don't do that now either. I look at a lot of things and then I'll drag it out later. And I know where it's come from, but I haven't actually gone back to the cutting in the file. But the act of making the decision about keeping them is what's important.

And I remember really quite an intense summer making work for my [art school] foundation year portfolio [. . .] I guess some of the other things that were around in those rooms of mine were things I'd made on Saturday morning [art classes], Camden Arts Centre, so I can remember a kind of twisty piece of metal, sculpture, tin sculpture sort of soldered together. I mean it was a terrible piece, I can see it now. But it took weeks and weeks to solder it together and learn how to solder and all that sort of thing. So I'd have things I made around the place, but not – I think I was making quite a lot of three-dimensional things as well, now I think about it. But I didn't really ever think they were particularly good, but looking at them I think I'd really understood the achievement of making them rather than how beautiful they were as objects. I think I understood that.[54]

3

The Sound of Bombs Falling

A Century of War

Few of the artists in this book treat war as an explicit subject, but most were born between around 1910 and 1945, which means that the two world wars were a formative part of their early experience. For those born in the first two or three decades of the twentieth century, fathers are often remembered as absent servicemen or returned war veterans. Kenneth Armitage, John Latham, Michael Kidner and others of this generation would later have their own first-hand experience war. Others, like Josef Herman, Willi Soukop and Paul Feiler, came to Britain as refugees from Nazi persecution. Artists born in the 1930s give us a child's-eye view of air-raid shelters and bomb sites, followed by a coming-of-age in the landscape of austerity, mandatory national service and the opening up of educational opportunities for young people from working-class families. Later still, the American war in Vietnam stirred a political consciousness that seemed to colour every other area of life and roused a desire for a different social order. In one way or another, the direct and indirect experience of war was common ground for almost everyone who grew up or settled in Britain in the early and mid-twentieth century, artists included. It shaped not only the physical environment of British cities, where bomb sites remained part of the urban landscape for many years after 1945, but also people's sense of what was possible and what most needed to be done.

He got through all that lot: the First World War

'I was aware of the First World War on a very strange occasion,' says Paul Feiler:

> I happened to go into the attic where I found locked up amongst a lot of things uniforms with medals on them, which were my father's, and he was – the only time I remember that he was angry, that he had been reminded of the fact that having been a patriotic soldier, to have lost the war, and that made him very angry. Nevertheless all my clothes were made from his uniforms subsequently of course [. . .] as a child you accept situations, and since we were a well-endowed family, all told, and all my cousins and relations were at peace with each other, and my home life was as agreeable as any home life could be, it somehow didn't occur to one that things that happened before, or things that happened at the time, could possibly be anything other than the way they were. And don't forget, I was born at a time when at the end of the war [in Germany] there was starvation, there was inflation, and there was occupation [. . .] I remember, and that's the only thing I remember about the whole of that part of my life, was the fact that one was forbidden to walk on the pavements during the occupation, when the French soldiers were walking up and down.[1]

Terry Frost was the only child of a brief marriage during the First World War. He was brought up by his grandparents in Leamington Spa, where his grandfather ran a small business hiring out bath chairs to the spa clientele.

> My mother had married again, having divorced my father immediately after the war when he came back [. . .] She lived in the same town, but it was a simple story, that she met my father during the wartime, and then, after the war she met her original sweetheart again when he came back from the war, and my father never had a chance, because he had only been a temporary wartime affair.[2]

After the divorce, though Frost barely remembered his father, he treasured mementos of his army life, as an artillery sergeant who had served in the Gallipoli campaign:

> Above the bed was a wonderful selection [of cards], which grieves me very much I haven't got them, or didn't get them, but they were all the wartime cards that my father must have sent home, but they were not ordinary cards, they were – what do you call it? It was – they were all done with silks [. . .] Beautiful, done with silks. There were two frames of those in the house, and

> they all went when my gran died, I was so upset about that. I don't know why I wasn't able to get there, perhaps I hadn't got the money. But things like that [. . .] were part of my life. And certain pieces of, I think there was a watch there, and a silver bugle, silver chain, which my father had got off some dead German officer in the wartime, loot, you know. Of course it wasn't called loot, it was victory.[3]

Ralph Brown (1928–2013) was born in Leeds, where his father worked as a school caretaker. His father 'wouldn't talk about the war [. . .] he would talk about things he'd done before the war when he was in South Africa and India and places, but he wouldn't talk about the war itself.'

> One of the curious things was that some years ago there was a marvellous series of programmes about the First World War[4] [. . .] And it was dreadful. And, I do remember one night in particular, it was showing a lot of these poor sods in trenches, and both I and my wife said, 'God! That's your dad.' And it was my father [. . .] standing against the side of a trench. And undoubtedly, there was no question about it, because I've got photographs of him. And that was terribly moving, I mean we just burst into tears, you know, oh God! Anyway he got through all that lot.[5]

Sheila Girling's father served in the original 1914 British Expeditionary Force to France. The story of his survival, and the empathetic tone in which Girling tells it ('I mean, he was only a young boy'), contrasts with the comic figure he cuts elsewhere in Girling's interview for Artists' Lives as the less hardy, less decisive partner to her charismatic mother:

> He was in the first batch to go out, you know, and he joined up, his brother joined at 18 and he joined at 17 because he wanted to get away from home I think and his mother. And it was a terrible time, I remember, the whole regiment was wiped out two or three times, and my father said they used to fight for dead bodies to put their feet on so they wouldn't get frostbite. But my father was very badly frostbitten, his feet. I mean, he was only a young boy. When I think of my grandson of that age, he's still a young kid. And he crawled, I remember, they had to crawl three miles, he couldn't walk, to get back behind the lines. You know, they told them to all get back and he couldn't walk. And he was in hospital [. . .] with his feet when he got back

> and they said well, we'll cut his feet off tomorrow, we'll have to cut his feet out tomorrow. And an old – well I don't know about an old nurse, but a motherly nurse – said, oh he's such a handsome young boy, leave them on for a day. And that night the blood came back, so he got his feet back. Must have been agony.[6]

Hungry days: the Nazi era

In the late 1930s, as anti-Semitic persecution in Warsaw increased, Josef Herman was repeatedly arrested. Between spells of up to ten weeks in prison, he stayed on the move, finding a bed for the night wherever he could:

> It means to me so much to understand the natural courtesy of the poor, the natural caring for each other, you know. For example [. . .] when I was already a youth and I was hiding from the police and I had to sleep one place to another, and I came once to a middle-class family whose son was a friend, you know. Now, there were about four rooms, and when I asked for a place to spend a few nights, he said, 'Of course, I'll ask my mother.' His mother came out and said, 'We have no extra bed' [*laughs*]. You know. Now this is a thing which would never happen with the poor. They will sleep on the floor, they will sleep on the table, they will sleep under the table, you know. There wouldn't be such a middle-class reply, you know. 'We have no extra bed!'[7]

After escaping from Poland via Belgium to France, Herman arrived in Bordeaux in June 1940, just as German forces were advancing on the city. Among the chaotic throng of refugees on the waterfront were Polish servicemen:

> The port was on fire, and there were sitting a group of about four or five Polish officers, being absolutely certain that nobody understands Polish. So they told themselves the great secrets, and one of the secrets was this, that in La Rochelle will be a ship which will take Polish soldiers to Canada [. . .] You know that you could hear already the canons of the Germans [. . .] And in La Rochelle the port was crowded with thousands of people, and there was only one ship, and in front of the ship French soldiers with machine guns. Nobody goes through. And there was one row of people who

> were meant to go up on this ship, and the rest, no. When I left Belgium I took with me a leather coat and a beret [. . .] I thought that a leather coat is better than an ordinary coat, for the simple reason that it can take more rain. And suddenly [. . .] two Polish military policemen catch me by the arm and ask me in a saucy voice, 'Where do you think *you* are going?' And I say, 'I want to get onto this ship, but I don't think that I have any chance. Look at this number of people.' You can't reason with Polish military policemen. They say, '*We* will see that you *get* onto this boat.' And they put me there in the row, *all* with leather coats and berets. And this was the uniform of the Polish airmen. And this is how I arrived here.[8]

In the event, Herman ended up in Liverpool, moving on to Glasgow, where he found a studio. In 1942 news reached him via the Red Cross that the Nazis had murdered everyone else in his family.

Willi Soukop (1907–95) grew up in a working-class Jewish family in Vienna; his father, like Herman's, was a shoemaker. After studying at the Academy of Fine Arts in Vienna, he was starting to establish himself as a sculptor when he received an invitation to work in England. He'd met a woman in Vienna, 'something like the secretary to the Elmhirsts[9] [. . .] I don't know how she knew my name, or somebody must have told her about it [and she said], 'I invite you to Dartington to work there as a sculptor, perhaps teach.'

> I was a little bit uneasy about it. First of all I didn't speak English, and then, it's an unknown place, you see, to go to England from Vienna you see. But anyway, I went [. . .] And what happened at that time, the Nazis came just into Germany, and a number of [artists], like the Jooss Ballet, they all escaped, and somehow Dartington offered them a place.[10]

Refugee artists were not only employed as teachers but were provided with studios in the many outbuildings and houses on the Dartington Estate:

> There were some American painters, Mark Tobey;[11] Hein Heckroth[12] was a German painter – he escaped from Germany you see. And so there was quite a colony of people who made their home at Dartington. There were all other countries, but the countries either threw them out or it was not liveable or whatever it is, or no income [. . .] I couldn't speak English yet, so it was quite a job [. . .] But talking wasn't that important. Working with

> people was important, you see. They gave me a little sort of room, and there in return for the room I taught sculpture to a few other people. There was never any money really, but a bit of woodcarving and so on, and that established me gradually at Dartington [. . .] And of course as there were so many German-speaking, we could talk you see. And there was the dance school, so of course that was interesting. I never saw dancing before.[13]

After having arrived in England at the age of 15 and been a pupil at boarding school, then an art student at the Slade, Paul Feiler was astonished to find himself rounded up and interned as an enemy alien at the beginning of the war, along with more recent Jewish refugees from his native Germany.

> There was a period when there was an exodus from Russia of Jews, opened the ghettos, who came and started invading Berlin, and I do know for a fact that a lot of well-established Jewish families [in Berlin] were very worried that this might cause some upset in their way of life, because they [the Russian Jews] were Orthodox, unruly, and gypsies so to speak, in the eyes of the Jews of Berlin, who had not only established themselves, but were part of the establishment. So, I can tell you now [. . .] when I was finally interned as an enemy alien, I met up with the most amazing range of people, amongst whom were at least two dozen Jews who were very, very, very Nazified, and who would have been only too pleased to be proper uniformed Nazis if it hadn't been for the fact that their name was Goldstein or whatever. And so, I have no illusions about any of that. I know it well from my existence, and I keep well away from aggro of any of this, because, it's to do with a human being and not their faith or their allegiance or their background or their race. People are people, and some people, as my grandmother would have said, and I can quote her now, and she said [. . .] 'Nice people when nasty things happen to them get nicer, and nasty people when nasty things happen to them get nastier.'[14]

Things in ruins: Second World War

Sheila Girling was 15, at home in Birmingham, when Prime Minister Neville Chamberlain broadcast to the nation that Britain had declared war on Germany. Just after 11 am on 3 September 1939,

> we all switched on the wireless and my mother screamed, 'It's war, it's war,' started rushing round and I got in a panic, and my father said, 'Look, calm down, calm down, calm down.' And we all – yes, it was a terrible moment. We thought we'd be bombed straight away. We put stuff all over our windows, so they wouldn't break. And I mean the bombing didn't start till later. We thought it would start that night, you know, we were all rushing round, putting mattresses under stairs and things. And next – we had a neighbour who had this son, we had a joint air-raid shelter, you know, it was dug into the ground with a bomb-proof roof, and when the sirens went we would all rush down. I remember being mortified because I still had curlers in and the boy next door would see me.[15]

Vivid recollections of nights spent in home-made bomb shelters, and of emerging in the morning to scenes of destruction, are a common thread in childhood memories of this time. City centres and industrial districts in the north and Midlands, and naval ports like Plymouth were subjected to particularly heavy and repeated bombing raids. Jack Smith was 12 at the time of the Sheffield Blitz on the nights of 12 and 15 December 1940. The morning after the second raid:

> I remember walking into Sheffield from where I lived, absolutely fascinated by what I saw. Skeletons of trams burnt out, just standing there like a skeleton. Visually totally absorbing, you know. One didn't feel, what a terrible thing has happened, which of course it was – people, many people had been killed. But already one was thinking, you know, what a fantastic object this is, and – then I remember seeing a paint factory going up in flames, extraordinary sight of that, late at night, during an air raid. And those kinds of things impressed me very much indeed.[16]

The Teesside iron and steel works were bombed by the Luftwaffe in summer 1940, when Basil Beattie (b.1935) was five:

> It was very vivid of course as a child. It was exciting, but you realised how dangerous it was. I remember, the typical evening would be to go to bed and suddenly to be woken up by your parents, saying, 'Get out of bed quickly,' the sirens had gone, you know. And make your way down to the air-raid shelter in the garden. I remember the air-raid shelter being delivered, and a pit dug for it, and then the soil put over the top, and we grew flowers on

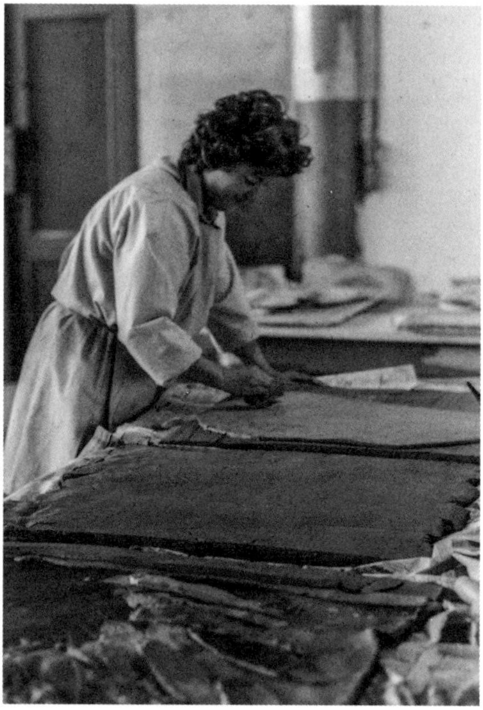

Sheila Girling at Margie Hughto's clay workshop in the art department at Syracuse University, NY, 1979. Photographer unknown.

it. So I remember it from the very beginning. But it wasn't a place that I enjoyed going to. It was very damp and full of spiders really, it would just be horrible. But I remember one evening [. . .] hearing the siren and realising my parents hadn't heard it, and calling them out of bed. And my mother and I just got down to the bottom of the stairs when the back door flew open, and there was a series of land mines that were being dropped. And this was unusual, this was very close to home, but we felt that the next one might be for us.[17]

In Haslemere in rural Surrey, Stuart Brisley (b.1933) turned seven during the Battle of Britain. 'When the air-raid sirens sounded,' he recalls, 'my position was under the piano':

> On this particular occasion it was an afternoon, and a very grey afternoon, and I decided that I didn't want to be under the piano so I looked out of the window. And there in the sky was this Messerschmitt [German aeroplane] in two pieces and a parachute and the whole thing just sort of – it was just amazing. And, if I had, you know, been a dutiful person I wouldn't have seen that. It was extraordinary.[18]

At school shortly after the war, Brisley and his fellow pupils were shown newsreel film of the liberation of the concentration camps. Many years later, happening to read a newspaper account of a similar school visit, he realised that, 'I had wiped it out of my memory':

> I suddenly realised that I had done that as well – that we had all gone off to – or they all come to the school, you know, I can't remember how it was. So, the war – I mean in 1944, of course, news about concentration camps was actually public. It was filtering out, and then when one heard about it on the news, and then there were pictures in the newspapers, and then we saw film. So that was an immensely affecting thing, no doubt about it. Because it came at the time when one was so impressionable.[19]

Michael Sandle was four when Plymouth was first bombed in July 1940. Between then and May 1944, the city and nearby naval dockyards suffered 59 air raids. War and the machinery of war would become a theme to which Sandle's sculpture often returned.

> During the Blitz on Plymouth, which as you know got bombed more than anywhere else, my mother decided she couldn't take any more and we left and moved to Bodmin on a farm, and I do remember very clearly that one day she got a letter and she burst up crying because the house had been bombed. I went back a year ago [1998], to see if I could remember anything about it. It's there, it's been rebuilt, but I could remember the lane where I used to play. Quite a steep hill, I used to go down on a wooden lorry, I remember that quite clearly. [During the bombing] we used to go to the shelters, and for me it was no fear or panic, my mother was in a bit of a state, but for me it was just a spectacle and an adventure. Yes, I remember the smell of the large underground shelters [. . .] We used to often go to the neighbour's backyard where he had one of those shelters made of corrugated

> iron and sandbags. I can remember that very clearly, I can remember the tinkling sound of falling masonry and the sound of bombs falling.[20]

In 1980 Sandle made a bronze sculpture titled *Untergang des Dritten Reichs* (*The End of the Third Reich*). A slab-like plinth – perhaps the base of an unbuilt or destroyed monument – supports a slew of broken or melted flesh, scattered with strangely intact objects, including an officer's hat and a couple of petrol cans. It represents 'Hitler and Eva Braun on their funeral pyre', says Sandle, and was,

> I would say, even though it's small, probably the best sculpture I've ever done [. . .] And a man came up to me and he said, 'I want to congratulate you,' he said. 'I was in Berlin at the end of the war.' He said, 'You've captured the atmosphere.' I thought that was good, I always like it when that happens.[21]

For those in their late teens or early 20s when war broke out, in place of whatever plans or ambitions they'd previously nurtured, there followed six years of military service or other war work – an enforced hiatus that would give a particular urgency to the late-starting careers of this artistic generation after the war. In 1939 the 24-year-old Terry Frost enlisted in the commandos:

> We had unarmed combat, and the commando knife, knuckle-duster affair [. . .] and I realised that infantry men are brilliantly trained in the sense of, it's parrot-fashion, everything is absolutely parrot-fashion, so that you don't have time to fear. You do what you are told [. . .] As soon as you come under real bullets, then that is when you need total and absolute discipline [. . .] people actually afraid that if they didn't do what they are told, rather than being afraid of the bullets.[22]

Posted to Crete in the spring of 1941, Frost was taken prisoner when German forces overran the island in May:

> We were completely surrounded and being dive-bombed at the same time. So in the end we had to send the CO [commanding officer], we had to give up [. . .] It is totally demoralising to be – because we had been doing very well really, we hadn't been beaten in a forward attack at all. You see when you've got aircraft, and you get fire coming from all round you, and there's

> nothing you can do about it, and you can see there's more and more of them coming, and more and more bombs being dropped on you, and you've got nowhere to go [. . .] There's the sea there you see. So, it was the only thing to do really, was to give up.[23]

During four years' imprisonment in a POW camp in Bavaria, Frost learned to be resourceful ('You might have had a Bible, but we smoked that, that was very good smoking paper for rolling you see, it's very thin') and to stay busy:

> I did a bit of drawing, because somebody else did drawing in the room, and a chap did caricatures, and I tried to do caricatures and couldn't do it, but I could get a likeness, and then of course everybody wanted one, and that's how I started to do it, which in turn led me to sit for the local art school. The local art school! There were half a dozen boys who had managed to get a hut out of the Germans, a broken-down hut, and they were using that on certain afternoons of the week to draw in, and paint in, and I went along to sit for them, and I saw what they were doing, and rightly or wrongly I thought to myself, well I could do better than that. So they let me go along then after I had sat for them, to paint. I did my first painting in there.[24]

Artists' materials had to be improvised.

> There was a young Scots chap could make the brushes. They used to cut the hair – when the sewage, the horses came in to do the sewage problems, the old cart horses with plenty of hairs down the bottom by their [fetlocks], and someone would get in while the chaps were busy and cut those hairs quick, you see. And then with the tin where they had coffee in or butter, they would make the ferrule for putting the hairs in, and they made my brushes like that you see. So that everybody had a sort of part in it. The canvas you got – you had a mattress which was stuffed with grass, and that was hessian, and so was the pillow hessian. So what I used to do was, I would do a portrait for a pillow; for a half, they would have to have that piece to do them [their portrait] on and give me the other piece for me to paint on. And then we used to size that with the barley soup, because it was very thin and it made a very good size. And of course any time we had sardines you kept the oil, because that made an oil to paint with.[25]

It was in the POW camp that Frost made his first painting of a life model – a burly soldier lying on a table in uniform. As a new recruit to the life room, he had last choice of the available paints.

> They gave me a tube of Prussian blue, and I think a yellow and a white [. . .] you have to use the colours you've got, which is quite an interesting lesson, because you can paint a green portrait if you want to, or a blue portrait or a red, anything [. . .] You can do it in anything if you get it right. And I didn't know about that at the time, but I was using just the colours that I had been given, because they were the colours they didn't want, and so, they weren't flesh colours, they're not flesh colour at all. So, that probably was a very good lesson for me, which I didn't know at the time. And from then on of course, because I could get a good likeness, I did about 200 portraits of different people.[26]

Born in Zambia, where his father was a colonial civil servant, John Latham (1921–2006) was about to take up a place at Oxford University when war broke out. After hearing Nazi speeches broadcast on the radio, he felt compelled to enlist in the navy.

> What came over was so absolutely intolerable that you'd have it on the radio, you'd hear the voice, the voice of this man shouting. And the things that he was said to be saying in the newspapers – it was reported of course in the newspapers – I don't think was exaggerated. I think we just said there was no way that we cannot in fact face it out, and we were brought up to do that. My father got his medal for being whatever it was that he did for his medal, he certainly didn't flinch at taking on some threat or other. And I think that's probably genetically transmitted. I don't like to be threatened or to be coerced in any way. I tend to make fun of it or to jump over it, pass it by. It's a sort of joke to me, I regard it as behaviour that's provocative, it's sort of ignorance, and respond in a way that would take it on. Rather than allow it to be going on, I would say, 'It won't do.'[27]

He chose to join the navy 'because I wanted to be at sea':

> I really was romantically interested in the sea. And I tried for the [Fleet] Air Arm. Seemed to be passing well to get flying, but the questioners on the panel found out that I was a painter. I'd had to acknowledge the fact that I

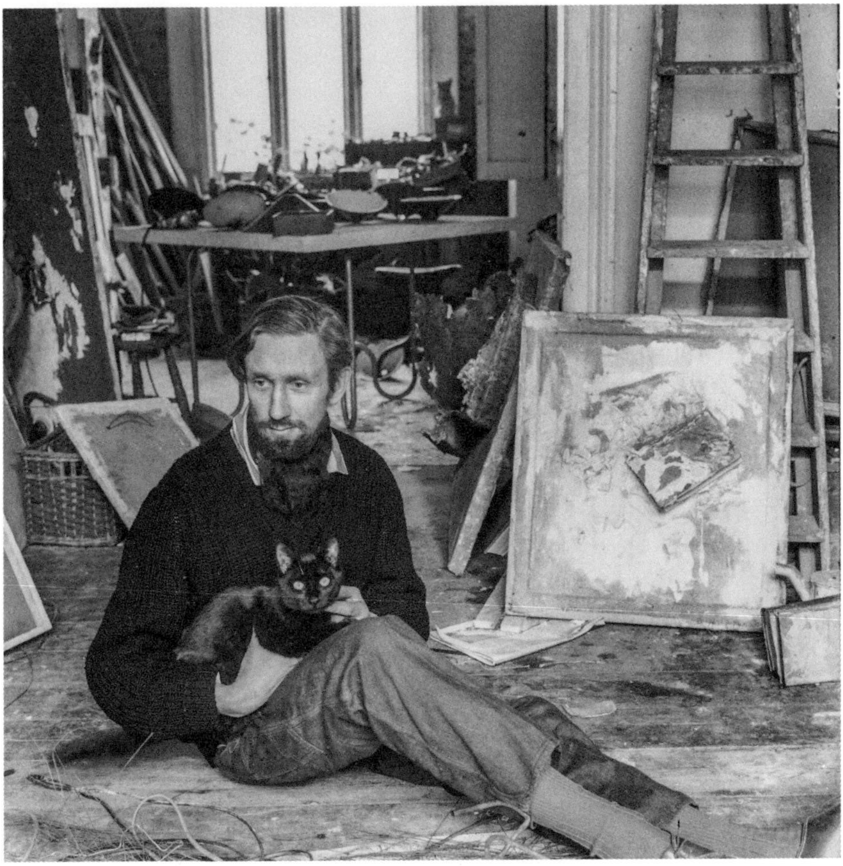

John Latham, 1963. Photograph by Ida Kar.

liked painting. Oh, they thought, well you must be an observing type, you'd better be trained as an observer. But I'd thought I'd prefer to drive, if I get into this thing, I want to drive my machine. No, they said, no, you would be an observer. But I didn't pass at the end because I had hay fever at the time, and they said that's a total bar, you'd never get away with flying if you have hay fever. Anyway, when that collapsed, I said I wanted to join up, go to Portsmouth and join up with the ordinary course of events and got into a squad which was dressed in bell-bottom trousers and a suit of navy blue [. . .] I didn't feel it a waste of time to be having to do it [. . .] I had an amazing time as a sailor in the navy.[28]

Michael Kidner (1917–2009) was born in Kettering, Northamptonshire. In 1940 he was studying landscape architecture at Ohio State University and staying with his sister in Canada. Since the threat of U-boats in the Atlantic made it too risky to return home, he joined up and served with the Canadian army for five years before preparations for the D-Day landings brought him back to England:

> We embarked in the Thames on a landing barge, and almost before we had left, a flying bomb hit a building right beside the ship. All their notepaper came fluttering down onto the deck, these kind of bills and receipts and things, it was semi-awe-inspiring. Anyway we went on, and all night long, these ships are like drums, and a bomb that falls in the water, or any noise in the water, is reverberated, even though it could be 60, 100 miles away. So all night long we had a kind of concert of bombs, if you like, and never knew quite, you know, we just went on. And then we had arrived off the Normandy coast, and the tide was wrong so we had to anchor, and there were air raids while we were anchored out there. And then when the tide was right we ran into the shore and disembarked the trucks. We had trucks, they all had to be specially sealed and they were driven off through fairly deep water and up onto the shore. And so the first thing we had to do was to get them off the beach where they were sitting targets, half a mile inland, in order to un-watertight them. So we did that, that was all in the afternoon. And then that night we set off to a campsite where we had been assigned, and on the way we were bombed, and one of the trucks in the convoy was knocked out, but the rest carried on, and camped in an apple orchard, quite near Caen. And what was absolutely crazy by army standards at the time was to camp in tents, you know. And so, the next thing we knew was that we were being bombed, and not only bombed but flares were dropped, so you felt like a sitting target, bright, as bright as day, just in your little circle. And so, this was in the middle of the night, and we had all gone to bed [. . .] And we woke up all in, noise breaking out, so we dashed over to our little slit trenches that we had made – that was the first thing we had to do, build slit trenches – and dived into these. And I discovered that in my undervest a mouse had crept in during the night, and I was busy in this trench keeping my head down trying to catch this mouse. Meanwhile there was all sorts of shrapnel shooting around. They were all anti-personnel bombs they were dropping. So, I mean it was a marvellous way to survive the attack, to be more concentrated on this mouse running around.[29]

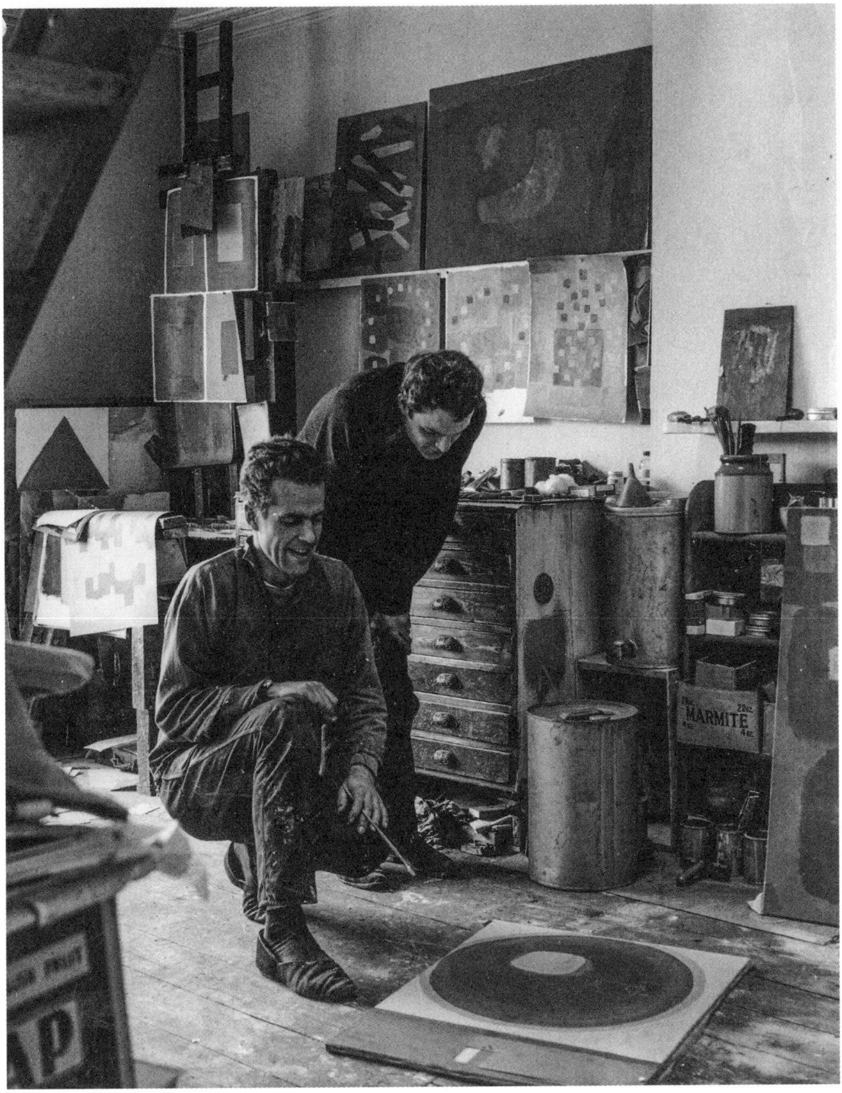

Michael Kidner (kneeling) in his studio in Belsize Park, London, 1960s.
Photographer unknown.

On being demobbed in 1945 at the age of 28, Kidner 'had no idea of what life was going to be like really. It was a blank. The new world was a very new world. I might have been born into it that day.'[30]

A totally different thing: the post-war era

By 1945 John Latham could no longer imagine returning to academic studies and his place at Oxford:

> I was so stunned by the experience of going [into the navy]. While in Italy I'd had a cousin, a female cousin [who] was in the women's branch of the special forces, working in Yugoslavia. She had a unit there and rang me up one day in the port in Bari. She said, 'I've got a Savoia-Marchetti plane,[31] and we're going to Rome in it and wouldn't you like to come with us, can you come with us? And we'll touch down in Bari for you [. . .] and we'll pick you up.' So in due course they picked me up and we flew with this Italian crew in their Italian aircraft, landed in Rome, got taken to see the Pope. We were all given an audience with the Pope who was, no great deal there because he'd been talking to Nazis. He was just chasing popularity, one might suppose. Anyway, after that, we went to Mussolini's palace. Mussolini's head office was the Palazzo Venezia in Rome, and in it there were stashed all the paintings which they'd managed to collect, a huge exhibition of old master paintings. Well, I went into one of these rooms, and without knowing what I was looking at I recognised that there were two pieces in there which weren't standard paintings, they were artworks by comparison. It was a totally different thing, absolutely electrifying to me, two small but vertical paintings. They were by El Greco. And I really got the message in there that there was something going on that I wanted to do, and it was an *affaire du coeur*.[32]

More prosaic, but equally idealistic in its way, was Basil Beattie's parents' determination, 'that I could do something that they had never been given the chance of, which was go to a college'.

> And I think, certainly the war did supply this kind of interruption. It's like a complete change of life. The world seemed to be very much different in many, many ways after those five, six years. And I think a lot of working-

class people found that their children could do things that they didn't do, there were more opportunities. But anyway, I enrolled at the local art school on a Saturday morning, that was while I was still at secondary school, and I used to go on a Saturday morning to the art school to make paintings.[33]

Conscription, which had been in force throughout the Second World War, was extended in peacetime in the form of national service for men over the age of 18 (later reduced to 17). Jack Smith had already spent two years at Sheffield College of Art when he was called up in 1946 for national service in the RAF:

> I knew I wanted to get to London where art took place, and where there were other artists. So when I was on leave in London one weekend I went to an art school called St Martin's, which was in the Charing Cross Road. I thought, what a marvellous place to be, in the middle of Charing Cross Road, all the bookshops and galleries. I could imagine nothing better. So I went inside and I said, 'I'd like – when I leave the Air Force in such-and-such a date, I'd like to come here, is it all right, is it possible?' So he said, 'Well next time you come on leave, bring your folder of work.' Which I did, I took a few things that I'd done. It was so easy in those days to get into college by comparison with now. He looked at the work and he said, 'OK. Come next term, September the so-and-so.' And so that's how it started. But, when September came, though I'd got my place at St Martin's, all demobilisation was stopped in the Air Force because of the Berlin airlift.[34] [. . .] I wrote home and I said that this had happened, that I'd got my place at St Martin's, and it started but I couldn't take it because of this taking place. Unbeknown to me, my father wrote to the MP, obviously a very strong letter. All I knew about it was, one day I was sitting in the billet with some friends, and an Air Force sergeant came in and said, 'You're wanted in the office immediately.' So I went to the office. They said, 'You're leaving here in 24 hours. Pack your bags, get your warrant, and go to Blackpool to be demobbed. But, before you go, the commanding officer wants to see you.' So I thought, well, all right. I went in to see the commanding officer, and he said, 'How the hell did you get a release? Who's your father? Is he somebody powerful and important?' I said, 'No, he's actually a senior clerk in an engineering works.' He said, 'Why are you going out?' I said, 'Because I've got this place at St Martin's School of Art.' 'Oh Christ!' he said, 'artists! We'll be bloody glad to get rid of people like you.' He said, 'Here I am, I've

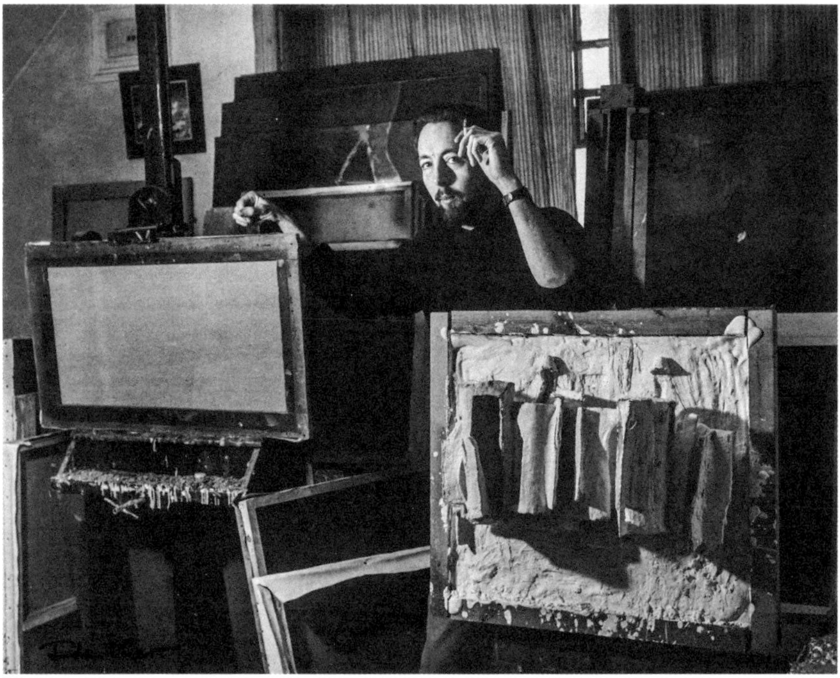

Jack Smith in his studio in London, 1959. Photograph by Ida Kar.

been in two world wars and getting ready for my third.' I thought, this man is insane, and not only insane, he's dangerous, because he's trying to provoke me. I didn't say anything at all. So he said, 'Go on, get out.' I mean if I'd said anything, if I'd really said what was in my mind, he would have kept me in. I'd have been in the clink [*laughs*]. Anyway, I got out.[35]

Born in Bartica, Guyana, in 1936, Frank Bowling immigrated to England at the age of 14 to stay with a relative and finish his schooling. On discovering that he would be required to do national service, he decided to volunteer for the RAF rather than wait to be called up.

It was an air-training station, and you had these young fellows who were either just out of public school or just down from the university [. . .] who were accustomed to batmen, waiters, you know, doing their every bidding. And this was all new to me. So after some vexed time I lost it, and refused to fetch this particular officer's pack. I think, it can't have been an isolated thing, I think he must have picked on me or something. Anyway, I just refused. You know, he stepped out of the aircraft and dropped his pack, as was their wont, and you were supposed to pick it up and fetch it back to the billet. And [. . .] I was immediately put on a charge, and, I was relieved of my bootlaces and buttons and all that, and put in the glasshouse[36] [. . .] I don't remember exactly the circumstances, but anyway, there was a marvellous flight sergeant there who, it seemed, was always about to rescue me, and this time he really did, claiming to the officer court thing that as an African and the son of a tribal leader, these menial jobs were done by other people. And you know, it wasn't expected that I should be [*laughs*] – I should be made a servant, right? And he got away with it. Because I was not an African. I don't think he knew where Guyana was, but you know, Guyana was good enough.[37]

They couldn't destroy the idea: Vietnam

In the 1960s, many artists and students in Europe as well as America were involved in protests against the Vietnam War, a proxy war fought by the USA in support of the South Vietnamese government against communist North Vietnam, supported by the Soviet Union. The anti-war movement gathered momentum after 1965, when the USA began large-scale bombing of North Vietnam. In New York for the opening of his exhibition at the Pace Gallery in 1967, Eduardo Paolozzi joined an anti-Vietnam march:

It had a lot of New York intellectuals in the group. And I remember walking past the Playboy Club in New York, and all the bunny girls on the balcony all shouting obscenities at us. And I think we were all embarrassed, because walking in the streets is quite harrowing, and you are quite naked. But also, when I did the exhibition at the Tate [in 1971] I seemed to be the only one that seemed to be involved in one's art in Vietnam, the war in Vietnam. I mean the cover of the catalogue was a boot, an American soldier's boot, and there was a group of bombs which had something to do with napalm, and I thought that that was the last of the great ready-mades, somehow, was a group of bombs. But it was very unpopular, I think the Tate didn't like at that time that kind of exhibition.[38]

In 1971 Roland Piché (b.1938) constructed *Bar-B-Q*, an enormous sculpture (15 ft high, with a 20-ft square footprint) consisting of a tent-like framework of steel tubes to which solid cocoons of fibreglass resin, suggesting body parts or organic growths, clung as if impaled. The piece arose, says Piché, from feelings of outrage about the Vietnam War, 'directly out of violation of the organic body and the beginning of fragmentation of the body into this collision between ideas of good intent':

> Like the White House would have a good rationale for why they went into Vietnam, and it seemed that there was a moral base there. But when it was put into action it resulted in the most outrageous atrocities to ordinary people, women and children, and that seemed to me to be so grotesque that it fed – because Samsone [Piché's second wife] was oriental, and my children are beautiful in their own right, and so this all became part of that emotional subconscious and unconscious dilemma. So, in a way, it's quite clear that the relationships I was in changed and charged my imagination [. . .] As it happened, I found myself very much on the side of Ho Chi Minh,[39] for the sheer power of the mind and the ideological position he took. With all the technology that America can muster, with all the power, they couldn't destroy the idea, and at the end of that conflict, that kind of wisdom came through and reinforced my own interests in different oriental philosophies, which I was much more attracted to in terms of trying to make sense of the world.[40]

In the early 1970s, Michael Sandle began work on a sculpture that became *A Twentieth Century Memorial* (1971–8), in which a gigantic machine gun is operated by the skeletal figure of Mickey Mouse. The sculpture 'took a long time to develop, but it was basically an idea about the war in Vietnam'. In Canada, where Sandle was working at the time, he'd met the American multimedia artist Alan Shepp, who was then teaching at the University of Victoria, British Columbia:

> I visited him there at the time of student riots [in May 1970], which is at the time when, I think it was Nixon [. . .] the Haiphong Delta and the war escalated, and there was a lot of student unrest, and I was in the middle of visiting this friend and we were walking up a road I think they call Telegraph [Bay] Road, which led to the university [. . .] and all hell broke loose. And I couldn't help but noticing, because it was happening in front of

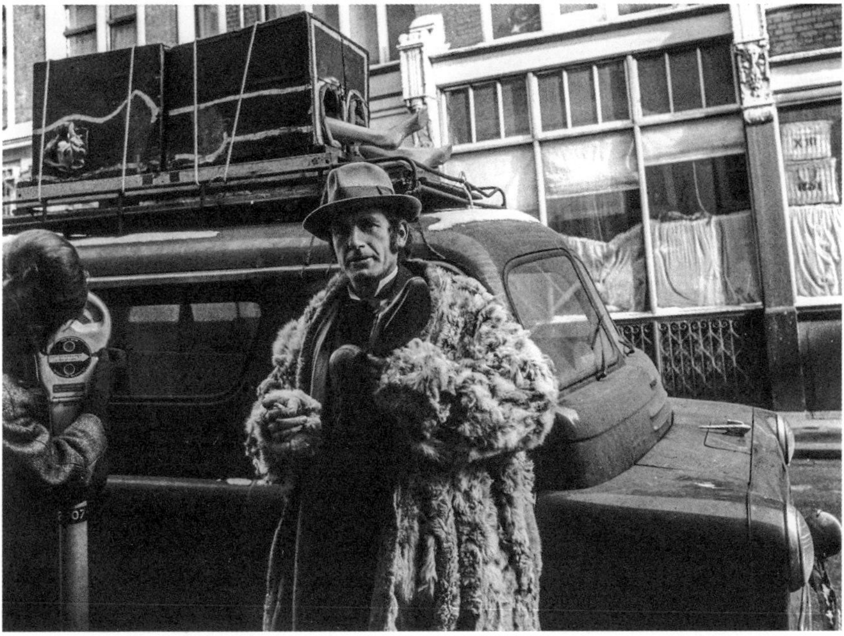

Bruce Lacey in Panton Street, London, 1963. Photograph by Lewis Morley.

> me – the state troopers put down this riot with ferocity. And it concentrated my mind that really one should do a sculpture about this, you know. It became an obsession with me that I had to do this sculpture.[41]

Bruce Lacey staged an anti-war protest in the basement of a London bookshop, Better Books, where the theatre director Charles Marowitz had just given a seminar on happenings (the term for performance-art events in which spectators were drawn into the performance, rather than passively watching it). 'And we all did a happening for all the punters – all about the time of the Vietnam War':

> So we were wanting [. . .] to drop ball bearings, or we were wanting to get bodies from mortuaries and drop dead bodies [. . .] But we can't afford a helicopter anyway, we were penniless. And also I'm a pacifist, so we can't hurt anybody with it. So, all the audience come down into this darkened basement, and – I'm upstairs first of all. Round the walls we've drilled holes, and I'm pouring red liquid down, so there was all blood running down the

walls. And then a whole trap door opens up with a chute, and all these dead bodies all covered in bandages, blood-soaked bandages, all slide down and crash amongst people. And I'm going round in a rubber suit with a helmet on, firing smoke everywhere like poison gas. And then at the end of the wall, which is like a brick wall, the whole wall collapses, because we've taken it all down and rebuilt it as a dry brick wall. And two surgeons arrive with nurses all draped in green surgical clothes wearing masks, surgical masks, and an operating table. And there's a pregnant lady in the crowd. They drag her out of the crowd, lay her on there, and they cut her open. Because she's really my second wife. Plastic bag all full of offal. And they're pulling out all this offal and stuff. And people are fainting in the crowd [. . .] So that was a real shock horror [. . .]

And later on [in July 1967], there was a thing at the Roundhouse in London about the Vietnam War called Angry Arts Week, and they asked me to make what would be called an installation, and I made something like a prison camp, all full of bamboo, growing bamboo, with all hands, all blood-soaked hands, all flying through the air, all trying to get beyond the cage. And the people who organised it were offended. They said, 'Look, there's more to war than death.'[42]

4

Self-propelled People

Going to Art School

Between Eileen Agar's student days at the Slade in the 1920s and Stuart Brisley's stint as a teacher at Hornsey College of Art in the late 1960s, British art school education was transformed. In the earliest era of art-school life recalled in the Artists' Lives recordings, two broad types of training were on offer. Firstly, there were metropolitan academies, like the Slade School of Fine Art and the Royal Academy Schools in London, at which students were prepared for life as an artist, preferably buoyed by private means. Many aspects of the teaching regime would not have seemed unfamiliar to Sir Joshua Reynolds two centuries earlier. Other art schools, especially in industrial cities like Sheffield and Leeds, provided training in technical skills intended to prepare students for employment either as teachers or in commercial applied arts such as textile design. Peter Blake, for example, lists 13 distinct disciplines taught at Gravesend School of Art in the 1950s. Each year, a few select students from provincial art schools would go on to pursue an academic–artistic vocation at the Royal College. It wasn't until around 1960 that educational reforms and radical new theories of art teaching began to change the landscape. Depending on their leadership and staff, art schools and departments responded in different ways, while artists would often work as visiting tutors in more than one school at a time. Frank Martin's innovations as head of sculpture at St Martin's School of Art opened the way for successive new waves of sculptural practice. Elsewhere, an academic curriculum based on observation from life continued, more or less under siege. Among the changes that resonate most profoundly in this chapter is the widening of opportunities and professional expectations for women.

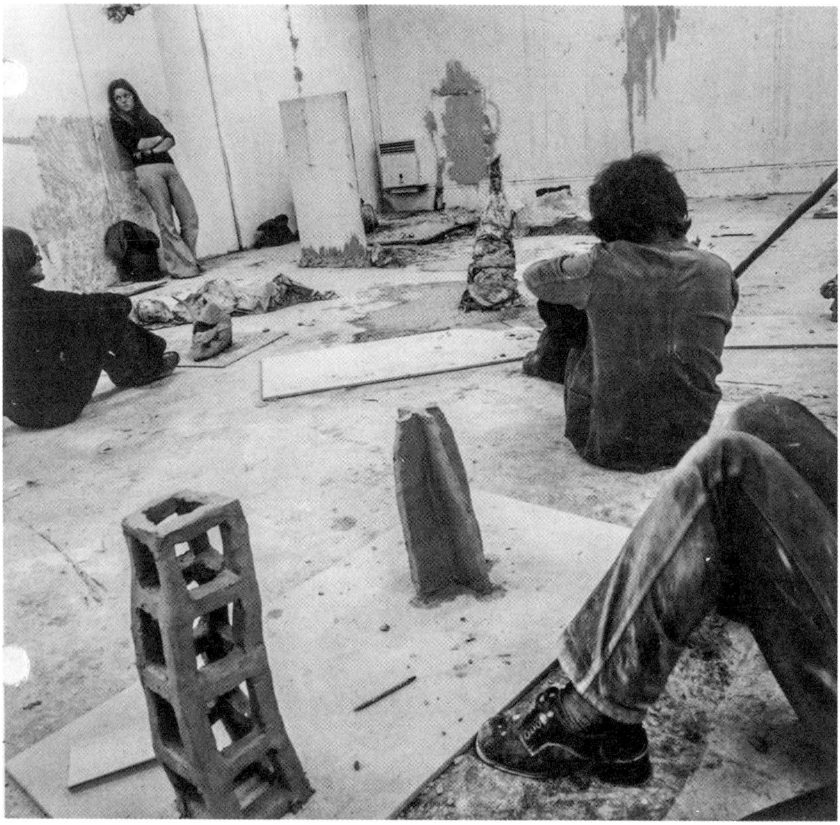

Sculpture teaching studio at St Martin's School of Art, 1960s. Photographer unknown.

Don't look at that French rubbish: Eileen Agar and Robert Medley

'I insisted that I wanted to be a painter, and my mother said, "Why don't you buy paintings if you're so keen on them".' At first, Eileen Agar 'couldn't explain to her that it wasn't the same thing'.

> It was a fight for my family, to even be a painter at the Slade, you see. Then a friend of my mother's said, 'Oh, do let her go. She has talent. You can see that by these little drawings she's done. Let her see what she gets done with other people's collaboration,' you know, 'with other people who are also there. She'll soon find her own level.' That's how it was cemented.[1]

The Slade, next door to University College in Gower Street, London, was at least a socially acceptable path for a young woman of Agar's background. At the time she started in 1925, some three-quarters of Slade students were daughters of upper- and middle-class families. The teaching was overseen by Professor Henry Tonks,[2] a former surgeon and war artist, whose exacting academicism and withering put-downs were a byword.

> Tonks used to say, 'Don't look at that French rubbish. It's all absolutely, it's wrong, and it's not English painting and they do also –' He was also thinking of the Impressionists, people like Seurat, whom I think is a marvellous painter, but at the time, Tonks wouldn't look at anything like that. He said, 'People aren't as thin as that,' or 'Trees aren't –' You know, he was absolutely for British painting, and trying to teach us how to paint, very academically.[3]
>
> [. . .] He said, 'The British, the Royal Academy, and the British, are the people who will lead art.' [But] we all swore that as soon as we were free of our parents, and our – everything else, and had the money, we'd go to France [. . .] I learnt how to stretch a canvas, and that sort of thing. How to keep your canvases rolled up, which side to roll them, and, but otherwise it was a very academic training at the Slade then, because of Tonks. And it was very finicky, you know, you couldn't draw in any impressionistic way, or anything like that [. . .] He would just have one model, a male or a female – and in those days, they were segregated, the women had a female model, and the males had a male model! Nowadays, it doesn't matter, but that's how it was. And Tonks would never – he didn't have any ideas, except just copying the things [. . .] and you couldn't compromise or experiment in any way.[4]

Male staff and students were overtly sceptical about the women's futures as artists: 'most men thought of women as muses, that is, they inspired the men to do great things, you see'.[5] The assumption was, 'Oh well, the women will get married and have children, and they'll forget about art.'[6]

Robert Medley (1905–94) was a contemporary of Agar's at the Slade, having previously studied briefly at the Royal Academy Schools. From the Slade, he went to Paris, where he met his future partner, the dancer Rupert Doone, with whom he would co-found the Group Theatre in 1932. As artistic director of the theatre, Medley was at the centre of avant-garde culture in inter-war Britain. He showed in the International Surrealist Exhibition in 1936 and in 1938 helped to set up the Artists' International Association, with its radical left-wing agenda (much watered-down after the war). Of his time at the Slade, Medley recalls,

> Tonks was a great character, but really not a very good teacher, let's face it. He was both rigorous and not rigorous enough. It was quite interesting. And the other teacher there who a lot of people got quite a lot from was Wilson Steer.[7] You either got a lot from Wilson Steer or you didn't. I didn't. And, he used to come round and say nothing really [. . .] but obviously he did drop the useful word to one or two students, but he never dropped a useful word into my eager little ear, as I struggled with an early life painting. And then I painted rather a good composition during the summer for the summer composition [prize]. I thought I was painting something like [Mark] Gertler and [Georges] Seurat, and it was a view of the back gardens of the houses opposite in Belsize Park Gardens, with a figure in it. There had to be a figure in it, you see, being in the Slade. And that caused for a moment quite a disturbance, because a lot of the students thought I ought to have had the prize, and of course I didn't, I didn't get anything at all. And so then I was of course ripe for rebellion all round, and this was in tune with the times. It was the times when 'significant form' was coming out, and Henry Moore, older than me, already leaving the Royal College [. . .] And there was a feeling all the way round of changing things.[8]

The phrase 'significant form' is a reference to the art criticism of Clive Bell, a leading figure in the Bloomsbury Group, into which Medley had been drawn through meeting the artists Duncan Grant and Vanessa Bell:

> You may think that Bloomsbury was a very provincial little group, but of course it was strongly Francophile, and people like Roger Fry and [John] Piper were enormously well travelled, everywhere, and though they were not the centre of an international movement they knew all about it, and when they went to Paris they were in it.[9]

It was the critic and artist Roger Fry who recommended that Medley should leave the Slade ('of course, Bloomsbury disliked the Slade very much [. . .] because they [Bloomsbury] backed Cézanne'[10]) to attend a teaching atelier in Paris, run by a trio of Cubists:

> The Académie Moderne [. . .] was run by Jean Marchand, [Fernand] Léger and [Amédée] Ozenfant. But I went there of course because Roger was a great friend of Marchand, who was a good bourgeois academic, post-Cézanne painter, a very nice man, but I found deadly boring, and I found the Académie Moderne also extremely boring. It was full of American girls trying to paint modern pictures under Ozenfant [. . .] So I split my time between going to the Académie Moderne [. . .] and painting life and things like that, and working in the Louvre. So every morning I went to the Louvre to copy.[11]
>
> [. . .] I learnt that art was a bit more than just being emotional about things – it brought one slap up against architecture and all kinds of things, how a picture was put together, for one thing, and also how extraordinarily everything is painted right through, in a thing like *Un Berger d'Arcadie*.[12] It's quite a free-ish Poussin really, and of course it's strongly poetic, which appealed to one. I don't think I could have painted a picture that hadn't got that. But I was just working in there every single day, and then when you get bored, throwing the brush down and going, wandering through a gallery, and then being brought up against a Chardin or something. Or going back and having another look, seeing how the Japanese [copyist] was getting along with Ingres' *Odalisque*. And then to have a look again at the Delacroixs and things like that. It's simply being – it accustomed one's eye to, well you may say I suppose just the old masters, but that didn't interfere with one's appreciation of one's contemporaries. Except that I never really came to terms as to what positively cubism was really about, and I doubt if anybody really knows that, even to this day.[13]

Evidently, there were still genres of 'French rubbish' that Slade alumni of the Tonks era struggled to embrace.

A certain kind of talent: Sandra Blow and Peter Blake

Sandra Blow (1925–2006) grew up in a prosperous Jewish family in London, where her father ran a fruit and vegetable business at Spitalfields Market. Art wasn't a feature of her upbringing, but an aunt noticed and encouraged her gift, and in 1941, at the age of 15 (not unusually young at that time) Blow started at St

Martin's School of Art. Blow's introduction to traditional art-school disciplines was a 'revelation':

> I just felt I was in paradise. I mean it was absolutely, absolute ecstasy to be in St Martin's, and to just draw. I mean it was so wonderful to me [. . .] Just drawing, the art, and the experience of painting and drawing was quite, it was ecstatic.[14]

Life drawing classes were accompanied by formal sessions in anatomy and perspective:

> I've got some of the old drawings still, tonal drawing from the model. Then we had various classes [. . .] There were anatomy, perspective, and there was this ghastly class of the – oh yes, anatomy I suppose. And we went to St Thomas's Hospital to look at – oh, kind of bits of corpses [. . .] the smell of the formaldehyde, it was in my nostrils, and when I became so neurotic about it, the smell of it stayed with me, and it was a horrendous

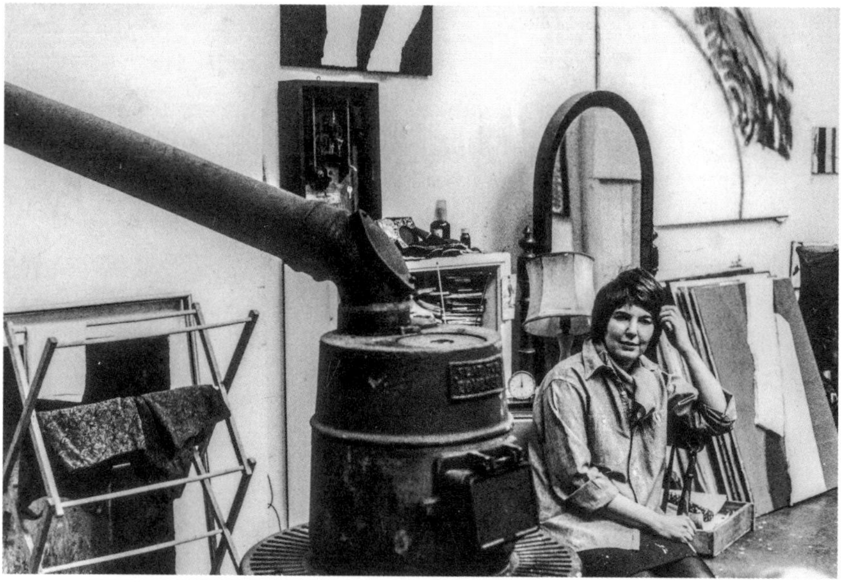

Sandra Blow in her studio at Sydney Close, Chelsea, 1966. Photograph by Roger Mayne.

experience. Anyway, and all my – the architecture, or the perspective, I'm not quite sure what, but I do remember drawing Greek temples, and I made all the columns look like milk bottles, it was so awful [*laughs*]. It was a total disaster.[15]

While the Slade relocated to Oxford for the duration of the war, St Martin's remained in its London home on Charing Cross Road:

And then the raids took place during – well, it was the [flying bombs] V-2s and V-1s occurred – and I can remember many occasions drawing the model, and then we would hear the bombs approaching. Of course I think, curiously enough the V-1 was the one that was called the doodlebug, and you heard it, then there was this great silence. I found that very unnerving. But the V-2s you couldn't hear and most people found that terrifying, thinking, any moment – but I adored the V-2s, I thought, thank God you don't have the noise [*laughs*]. I never logically really put two and two together, that you know – [*laughs*]. But I do remember being up there with a model, and the model saying, 'I'm not going to go down in the shelter with no clothes on.' So I would stay up there with the model, because she didn't want to go down into the shelter, or we went down to the basement or something. But she wouldn't go, so I often stayed up with all that glass [in the studio roof] waiting for the V-2s, or V-1s to appear [. . .] in many, many ways there was a very wonderful feeling in London at that time, it was – no, it may have been that everyone was generous and good-natured towards each other. I don't know [. . .] But it was a time when Myra Hess was giving concerts at the National Gallery,[16] so I would go down there with carrot sandwiches at lunchtime and listen to Myra Hess. And it was filled with divine young men, because all the free forces of Europe were there, and there were all these incredible Adonises wandering around. And of course it was in Soho, and the Gargoyle and the Mandrake [clubs] and Francis Bacon and Lucian [Freud], I was slightly friendly with Lucian, and John Craxton and various people.[17]

[. . .] You see what happened with me was, at St Martin's there was a structure, you went there every day and you had something to do, and there was a model and then all the anatomy, whatever. And what I did find was, when I left St Martin's, I really felt very lost, I didn't know how to organise my working day, and I didn't really quite know when I was on my own

> without the model stuck in front of me, what to do. And [. . .] I went on to the [Royal] Academy Schools, which I hated [. . .] they were cold and dark. And there was a teacher there, I think Dring, William Dring, who actually said to me, 'You nauseating female. You should be able to take one inch of your painting and go up to the model and not know the difference.'[18]

After art school, Blow's tutors expected her to become a portrait painter. In 1947–8, however, she spent a year travelling Italy, where the Italian abstract artist Alberto Burri became her mentor and lover. From this time onwards for the rest of her career, Blow remained committed to abstract painting, often on a very large scale (the Tate's *Green and White* [1969] is 10 ft square).

> In 1960 I was asked to teach at the Royal College, and so I had a salary [. . .] I used to do one day a week, and I usually had a group of painters who were mostly really interested in abstract painting but not always. I mean, it was a sort of exchange thing of which students would want me to teach them, or which I would want to, or whatever, but it had to be kind of mutually interesting. And [David] Hockney and [R.B.] Kitaj were there at the time, and I used to say to Hockney, 'I can't teach you anything, I just come in and enjoy what – every masterpiece I come and look at!' Because every time you went there, there was some wonderful painting that's now world famous, week by week [. . .] In one way I didn't like it because I felt that I would sort of start – I had been doing my own work, and then I would go there and then because [. . .] I became very involved with the pictures that I had looked at and talked about, I found it broke up whatever flow of ideas I had had about what I was doing. And so in one sense I was uneasy about teaching, but it was such a marvellous day there, because there would be those incredible students and their work.[19]

Peter Blake (b.1932) was born in Dartford, Kent, where his father was an electrician in a factory and his mother a nurse. At the age of 14 Blake enrolled in Gravesend Technical College and School of Art. Fascinated since childhood by the visual language of popular forms of art, entertainment and display – circuses, fairgrounds, corner shops – Blake began to introduce these motifs into his paintings while a student at the Royal College of Art (1953–6). He would always feel that the traditional, technical aspects of his training at Gravesend had provided him with skills that could be deployed in very different kinds of art. His first experience of life drawing involved the flamboyant gay male model and writer Quentin Crisp, who modelled in several art schools over a period of some 30 years and features repeatedly in Artists' Lives:

> So, if you can imagine, I was still in short trousers – so to be taken into a life class where – Quentin would have been in his 20s still, with this extraordinary figure with bright-blue hair, lipstick and blue fingernails. And I'd met one or two homosexuals by then, but I'd never seen anyone like Quentin.[20]
>
> [. . .] The profession of being a model was still very much a profession, so you would get families of Italian models, who'd do it as a family – they were professional Italian models [. . .] and they'd all arrive with the possibility of doing costume life, so they'd come with cases with their costume in, so you could choose whether it was costume life or life drawing.[21]

Blake explains how the introduction after the Second World War of student funding for further and higher education transformed British culture:

> I think that was the main reason for that kind of burst of a certain kind of talent in the 60s [. . .] that the kids of my age who, before the war, at that age, wouldn't have got to art school [. . .] were suddenly offered this chance of going [. . .] So there was a whole influx of talent from an area that wouldn't have been there before [. . .] There were the photographers like [Terence] Donovan and [David] Bailey and Don McCullin, and there were the actors like Terence Stamp, and artists like myself and Hockney, who wouldn't have gone to art school before the war [. . .] It was the Labour government, I think, and the grant system opened up the whole kind of floodgates.[22]
>
> [. . .] The year I did [the intermediate course] in 1950 was the last year of it in the form it had been in probably since 1850. So we would be taught silversmithing, metalwork, woodworking, carving, stone-carving, modelling – clay modelling – wood engraving, etching, life drawing, costume life drawing, architecture, anatomy, perspective – this incredible range of actual skills which could be taught, and which I've maintained since that these have stood me in good stead in the years. You had to choose a craft. My craft was Roman lettering, so I could do Roman lettering in spaces. So it was a very kind of disciplined education.[23]

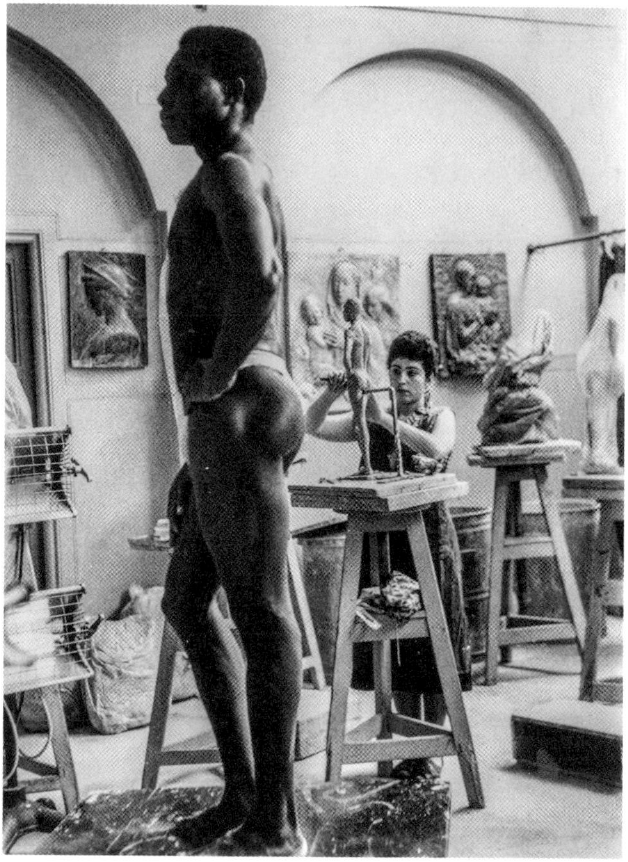

Sculpture student and model at Central School of Art and Design, 1957. Photograph by Roger Mayne.

[. . .] The art students of that generation invented wearing black and the roll-neck sweater, probably came out of Paris and existentialism, so kids at the art school were wearing black sweaters. One of my – the sculpture teacher – had been to the States and come back and brought a pair of jeans, and I was desperate to have a pair of jeans, and you couldn't – they simply didn't exist in England. So I bought a boiler suit and cut off the top part of it – your bib and tucker – it wasn't even denim, it was a kind of blue cottony material. So I made a pair of jeans [. . .] I can remember desperately wanting a corduroy jacket, and we couldn't afford one, and I remember my mum – one day, they must have saved some money – and she said, we'll go to London and get you one. And we went up to London, in the Charing Cross area, and bought a plum-coloured corduroy jacket, which I loved. And there was a second-hand bookshop with a book on Chagall, and it was old then, it couldn't have been very expensive, but again we couldn't afford it, but my mum got it. It's here, somewhere, it's one of these books here. So that was the first book, I suppose [. . .] as an art student that I'd ever got.[24]

Hiding behind my drawing board: Basil Beattie

One of the most widely shared memories of art school in the mid-twentieth century is the beginner's initiation into the life room. This was where generations of young men and women experienced their first sight of a naked adult of the opposite sex. The convention was for male models to wear a loincloth, while female models posed nude. Basil Beattie was 15 when he started at West Hartlepool College of Art in 1950:

I think the time when you're aware how extraordinary this occasion is, particularly when you're drawing from life a nude model, was the first week in art school, when you'd go in there, and suddenly you'd see all these clothed people surrounding, often a female without any clothes on. It was the most extraordinary event really. And I remember when I first went to art school hiding behind my drawing board and just peeping out, you know. It was a shock. But of course you soon got used to that. And the idea that you – I mean the model was often female, and without clothes on, was kind of ignored in a funny way. You know, you were talking about form, and – you weren't talking about sex.[25]

[. . .] And this was the first time I'd ever seen a nude woman, a naked woman. So, this was quite traumatic really. And, the extraordinary thing was that, the teaching always was, well, just keep your eye on the pose, and watch this rhythm here, and, see how the elbow joins to the arm, and so on. And the main thing of course, nobody was mentioning this highly sexually charged image, and a young lad just looking for the first time [. . .] And I'm sure the early drawings showed a certain shaking of the hand [*laughs*] [. . .] But of course you were soon weaned off any naughty thoughts, because everything was treated very formally, and it was very matter-of-

> fact. I suppose it had to be at that time. And it was like a discipline of pitting yourself against your perceptions – of shades and of tones, and of the rhythms in the figure. Often we were making figures and we weren't making images of people somehow. If you made images of people, that was done in the portrait class, when you just concentrate on the head [. . .] But, you know, Picasso did exist then. But there was no link between the artistic dimension of what I was later to associate with Matisse and with Picasso in these early days. You were simply, you know, your work was viewed in terms of how well you'd been able to see the proportion and the character of the pose. That's how it was judged.[26]

Completely in it: Barbara Steveni and John Latham

At around this time in the mid-1940s, Barbara Steveni (b.1928) won a scholarship to Chelsea School of Art. Born in Mashad, Iran, where her father was a diplomat, she'd arrived in London with her family after the war. The paintings in her Chelsea portfolio were 'mainly landscapes and trees':

> They weren't abstract at all [. . .] And, so, they were very well seen, hand-to-eye. I mean, my mother and father both hoped that I would do illustration, because I would go into the City and I would draw the Monument, and [...] that part of the Thames and everything, they would make them into Christmas cards and be immensely proud of me.[27]
>
> [. . .] The thing was that all the people that had been in the war were like 30 and 28, and we were all 17 or whatever it was [. . .] and I was absolutely dead scared of these older people [. . .] I was still immensely shy for some reason, and also very shy of men. And I would get quite a lot of interest from the men, and I wouldn't know how to handle it at all, and so I would slope off and do my dancing in the town hall sort of thing. And also, Chelsea School of Art at the time [. . .] you could go in one way and underneath the basement and come up at the other end, and I always used to do that to avoid all the men, who would stand at the top of the staircase, if you came up the stairs, and would point you out and comment on you as you would come out. So I thought, there must be another way I can get to the art school without having to run the gauntlet of these men. There was a special terrifying lot which was John [Latham], who was very gaunt with

blue eyes [. . .] And then there was the other guy, Vere Holden-White who, as you can hear from the name, was quite aristocratic also. And they would all stand at the top of the stairs, and that would be the terrifying – the ex-service people that one had to definitely get by.[28]

[. . .] One day I went into the still-life room, and instead of this faint painting of Vere's on the easel, there was a painting of a pot of flowers absolutely dripping with red paint, an absolutely marvellous painting, and it's like he [John Latham] had come through a catharsis, he was suddenly a painter. And I remember thinking at the time, he's an artist, you know [. . .] I remember feeling very strongly – oh, I felt that John, when I met him, I felt that he was an artist when I saw his things, he was also totally a committed artist, and completely in it and nothing else.[29]

[. . .] I remember this guy, who then became principal of Chelsea called [Frederick] Brill, and he was a man from Yorkshire, and he obviously had it in for me for being middle-class, one of the middle-class girls. So I remember him saying, 'Oh Miss Steveni – oh. Oh, you're very much better than I thought you could possibly be,' or something or other along those lines. And I also remember my father coming in at the time, with his rolled umbrella and his bowler hat [. . .] And then afterwards [H.S.] Williamson, who was the head of Chelsea School of Art, came out with a very amusing little grin on his face and said, 'I've had your father in here today, Barbara.' So I said, 'Oh yes?' jumping nervously, 'What did he say?' He said, 'Well he gave me a lecture on, when you were you going to earn some money and what sort of career was this?' And I said to him, 'What did you say?' He said, 'Well, I did my best to tell them that you were a very good student and that we hope that you would earn a living.'[30]

[. . .] When I was drawing, they always had to call my name out, because I was a scholarship person then, because I would have my materials free. And so they were calling out 'Barbara Steveni', and the model suddenly said from the dais, 'Oh, that's an unusual name, I have a great friend, Leo Steveni.' So, I rushed home and I said, 'Dad, I met a friend of yours today.' So he said, 'Oh yes?' I said, 'Yes, she's the model at Chelsea, very tanned and brown.' And, he said, 'Oh, oh Buki [Barbara], come into my room and we must have a little talk. Don't talk to Helen [Steveni's mother] about this.' So I sort of rushed in there. And it turned out that Dad was a nudist, you know, and went down to St Albans nudist camp, and everything. And so he tried to sort of, not win my silence exactly. So he whipped out all these

> photographs of these people in St Albans nudist camp, and he showed me this picture, and I shrieked with laughter, they were so sort of ugly [. . .] Because one is always having the nude figure, especially now, put to one, except in life drawings, as this glamorous, perfect figure, and here were all these people from the nudist place absolutely ordinary and falling all over the place. So I was sort of shrieking with laughter. 'Well what happens when you're playing tennis? Surely all your bits are jogging up and down.' And he was saying, 'Oh, well, no, no –', you know.[31]

Steveni and Latham married in 1951 and would later set up the Artist Placement Group (APG) together (see Chapter 7). In Latham's memory of his fellow ex-services students at Chelsea, they were notably 'self-propelled people who were enquiring and wanted to have the experience':

> I mean there were those that you could see going along with their easels and training themselves to be portrait painters or landscape artists or whatever it is for the market. But not my friends, they were genuinely concerned to be doing something which would show them what was interesting and what wasn't. Preparation for life of course, but you can't tie it only down to that, because one wants to be able to hold attention and not to hold attention when you don't want the attention. So to have to be in control of oneself, and all these exercises one does in an art school are very much in that direction.[32]

We'll do something with this: Frank Martin and Anthony Caro

When Frank Martin was at Portsmouth School of Art in the 1930s, the course consisted of a 'totally practical' routine of skills training, similar to Blake's later experience at Gravesend.

> It was straightforward craft-like work, and we did a little bit of ironwork, a little bit of pottery, a little bit of stained glass, and then painting, perspective, architecture, letter-cutting, and lithography was the other subject, besides drawing and painting and so on. It was apprenticeship-like, but nevertheless certainly had no history of art taught us ever.[33]
>
> [. . .] Rarely did we think of sculpture as being in it [the curriculum], believe it or not. That seemed much more like a craft activity. And I

> remember seeing and dwelling on [sculpture] quite a great deal with the memorials that were being set up, almost outside the college, the great memorials that were put up after the 1914–18 war, where the statues surrounding it, for instance the Portsmouth one [. . .] they were carved then by the Mancini brothers from Italy. They brought over carvers from Italy to do that, and I don't know of any sculptor around, at least at Portsmouth, that might have done [. . .] that sort of monument, it was beyond them.[34]

In 1952 Martin became head of sculpture at St Martin's, where one of his first appointments was Anthony Caro (1924–2013), a former engineering student who had then studied sculpture at the Royal Academy Schools, served in the Fleet Air Arm, and worked for two years as an assistant to Henry Moore. In 1959 Caro visited the USA, where he encountered the welded-steel abstract sculpture of David Smith. Martin recalls how, on Caro's return, the two of them immediately embarked on a radical overhaul of the sculpture department:

> Caro came back with this exhibition of Smith's [. . .] and showed me the exhibition catalogue and said, 'Keep that, we'll do something with this.' And so we seriously sat down and decided how we might approach this, and one of the things that we decided, we would throw out everything figurative within the studios. And we did this quite consciously, really cleared them, clinically clean – all the casts on the walls of the antique room days and any casts of any sort that one always found in art schools [. . .] We just pushed them into corners and other parts of the corridors and things like that. I mean Venus went very early on, and all those boy-and-goose and the gladiators and clapping fawn that every art school had from the British Museum castings [. . .] We cleared everything to do with that – the stands, the armatures that one had inside of figures, model figures, all the casts, and certainly in the end the model's throne. That was the last thing to go but the important thing, the symbolic thing to go, the model's throne.[35]

'When I first came back from America,' says Caro, 'I felt that I had changed, my work had changed.'

> I said [. . .] my work's changing but I can't teach you the new stuff, I've got to teach you the old stuff. Well that lasted for about four hours [*laughs*]! I couldn't go on teaching the old stuff, I had what I was discovering. That was

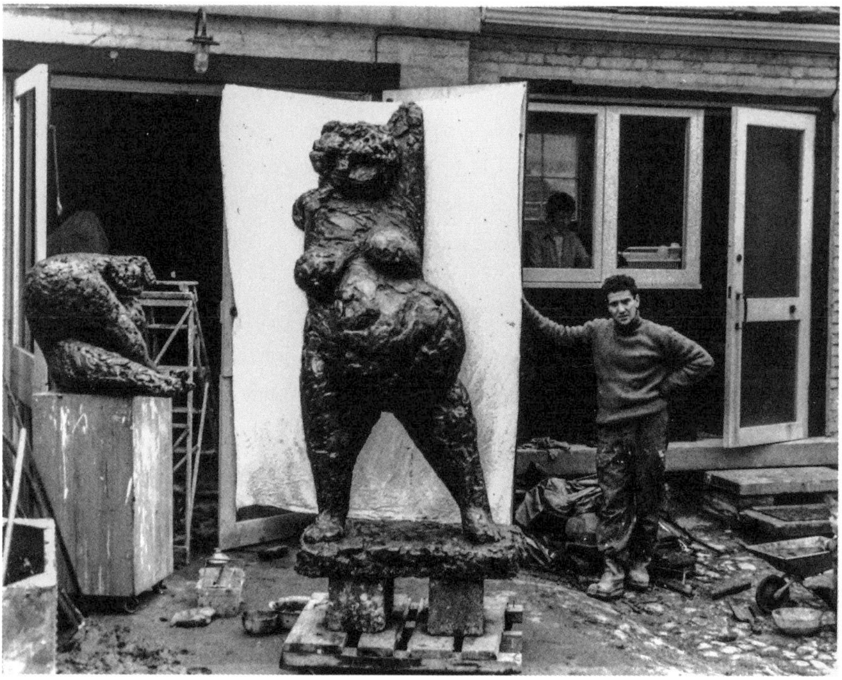

Anthony Caro with *Woman in Pregnancy*, Hampstead, *c.*1955. Photographer unknown.

why I was a good teacher, because I could teach what I was discovering, not what I knew. That's boring, you know. You do it this way because that's how you drive a car. Well that's all boring. Let's try and find out how to drive something we've never driven, and that was fun.[36]

[. . .] St Martin's became very much a sort of workshop situation, which I think was very good. There was a magazine we brought out two copies of called *First* at about that time, which was to do with everybody's thoughts and so on, but really as I developed after 1960, and as my teaching developed in parallel to my own work, the whole of St Martin's became a kind of workshop, so that there was no division between teachers, students, and very often – in fact Frank was very much blamed for it by the authorities and by the head of the school. People who had been students up until the previous year, or term, came straight back and taught, because they were right in there [. . .] And as a result it was very concentrated.[37]

[. . .] And we used to do evening classes, and very experimental in the evenings, which was great fun [. . .] from 4.30 to 6 we would have this rest, and then at 6 o'clock until 8.30 we would come back in and, well, I would set a subject at the beginning, and then later I got some of the students themselves to set subjects. Well there would be all sorts of things. Go into Soho and find any rubbish you can and come back and make a sculpture with it, or something, or – hundreds of things, I don't know. Make a sculpture of a scream, or a noise, or – I remember that one actually particularly, because Barry Flanagan[38] said, 'Make a sculpture for noise, of a sound.' And you know, people had made these things. And then, Barry said, 'Here's my sculpture,' and took a large piece of clay and threw it to the wall. Very interesting, and made one think, you know. It was much more of a sort of Duchampian statement in a way. Dozens of them, dozens of them. At Christmas time we would make masks and things like that, African-style stuff. In those days it was very strange to do these sorts of things in an art school [. . .] We must have kept those experimental classes going for five or ten years [. . .] there was something new every week.[39]

[. . .] And the feel of St Martin's was very special – and it was entirely devoted towards art and thinking about art, and thinking about the next, what was interesting us, and what was stimulating us. And I think that all the people involved in St Martin's – or I think why so many people, good or bad or indifferent, from St Martin's, have become successful sculptors. And I do say good, bad and indifferent because I think some of them are absolutely terrible, but [. . .] from their student days, they have had to put it first, you know. And – I wasn't interested in anybody who was going to commit artistic suicide by getting, you know, by not taking it seriously. They had got to address themselves to sculpture. And I think that that's why it has worked all right in a way for them.[40]

I just experimented: Kim Lim and Tess Jaray

At the age of 18, the Malaysian-born Kim Lim (1936–97) came to London, where she enrolled in the sculpture course at St Martin's. It struck her as 'kind of rambly and messy, and quite fun, and the teachers were a motley crew'.

There was Gore who was always – Frederick Gore – who did painting, who was always smoking a cigarette, and we would always wonder whether

> he'd burn his lip first or his eyelashes. And then there was a very nice Basque sculptor who was extremely helpful, I mean – I didn't spend all that long there, because I really didn't like the man who ran the whole [of] St Martin's, Frank, what's his name now? I can't remember. Martin. He was a bit pompous.[41]

Caro, whose earlier sculpture had developed during the time he spent as Henry Moore's assistant, was 'doing figurative things at the time, and not his abstract things, and when I tried to do abstract things, it was greatly disapproved of.'[42] The formal education Lim had experienced in Singapore left her feeling unprepared for the teaching approach at St Martin's. She found Caro 'very different from the kind of teachers I've had':

> very confrontational, which was meant to draw people out and be challenging, which is very good. But at the time I wasn't ready for that, because having come from a society where you listened and you never answered back or were asked to think, I found that quite frightening and difficult.[43]

One of Lim's other tutors was Elisabeth Frink, who had recently graduated from Chelsea and was one of very few professional female sculptors in the 1950s.

> She was very, very kind, and she said, 'Look, you're obviously not happy here, you know, why don't you go to the Slade?' And in those days there wasn't the terrible difficulty of getting into the Slade. I just applied, went for an interview, and they accepted me. As soon as I got to the Slade and had some freedom there to work [. . .] I started working in wood. But [my sculptures] became far more abstract. And of course, in my course of looking at things outside, I discovered Brancusi, and Giacometti and other things, and so I just experimented.[44]

The regime in the Slade life room, however, sounds anything but experimental:

> There was one [model] who was a very strange guy who didn't like wearing a loincloth, but [F.E.] McWilliam[45] objected, so on the day McWilliam was there he wore a loincloth, but the rest of the week he didn't. [McWilliam] thought it was immodest for the females I suppose. I mean it's a very kind of male thing isn't it? That looking at women naked is all right because of

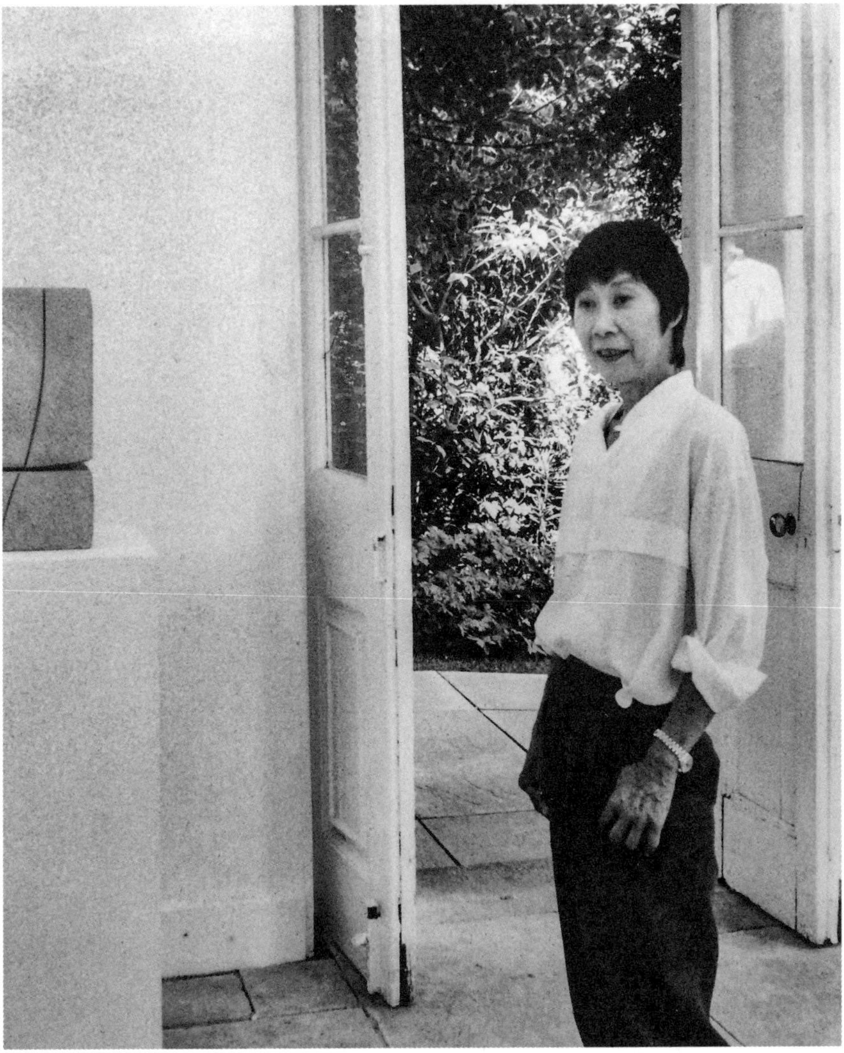

Kim Lim at Roche Court, near Salisbury, 1993. Photograph by Ferriel Waddington.

> all the tradition of, you know, nude paintings, but for women students who look at male parts is considered immodest or something.[46]

The sculpture staff, meanwhile, 'left you entirely on your own':

> They had this model standing there, year in, year out, in the same pose. I mean, different model but practically the same pose, and you had to do this life modelling. And the people in the sculpture department were very dour. They never spoke to each other, and they were so serious. They had this plumb-line mania, with calipers [. . .] these poor models would kind of shiver and cringe when they'd come with these calipers, and try and measure up, inch by inch. And in the beginning of term you'd see them put armatures up and the figures would be looking quite lively. At the end of the term, you know, they'd be all dying in clay.[47]
>
> [. . .] And I was very lucky. I was very kind of bold in those days, to go around looking for a studio, and I used to poke my nose – I lived in West Hampstead by then, I had a flat there – over people's gardens. And when I saw this shed with a glass roof, I knocked on the door and said, 'Is that an empty shed for letting?' And there was a strange couple who lived in this huge house, and her father was a chemist, and she said, 'Yes, as a matter of fact there's an old chemistry lab at the back which you can rent for £1 a week.' So, I couldn't afford £1 a week, but I found somebody else who would share it with me, so we paid 50p a week [. . .] And it was a leaky, marvellous leaky studio, cold with ice in winter, because there was this draught, but wonderful. It was my kind of hideaway, and I loved it.[48]

Tess Jaray was a student contemporary of Lim's in the painting department at St Martin's and then at the Slade. 'I wanted to go to art school as much to be in a more exciting environment as anything else. I don't think I really had a strong image of myself as an artist. I don't think I really knew what that meant.'

> There was a romantic idea in my mind that what I would have would be this studio, and in the studio would be one of those lovely old-fashioned easels that you wind up, and on the easel would be a painting that was absolutely perfect but not quite finished. So the door could always be open and people could always see it, and there would be this unfinished but still quite perfect image. Well, you know, that's a very, very long way from reality, because first of all, if one ever achieves something that is just about OK as a painter,

that sense of satisfaction probably only lasts a few seconds and then, you know, really what you want to do is wrap it up in brown paper and put it to face the wall. And if you haven't got to that point, you certainly don't want anybody else to see this unfinished thing which is going to look all wrong. So my idea was incredibly romanticised and idealised and not at all like life.[49]

[. . .] I think this is probably quite common for painters or for writers. It's not that they have anything to say; they want to learn about the language [. . .] They want to play around with the language of the medium and see what happens with that. You know, it's when people say, 'I want to be a writer,' it isn't necessarily that they have something to say. The something-to-say comes out of the manipulation of words and language [. . .] I don't think I did have any say at that time. I was rootling around, but I was obviously deeply interested in colour and space and surface and so on, without really knowing that that's what I was interested in.[50]

[. . .] We were taught how to lay out our colours on the palette. We had to make a palette to paint on [. . .] We had to physically make a palette. We would get it cut out of some kind of timber, treat it properly [. . .] with linseed oil, I think. I can't remember any more. But I did have it for years and years. And then we were taught how to lay out the cool colours together and then the warm colours together, and I suppose we must have been taught the difference between cool colours and warm colours and families of colours. And then a blob of white paint and then a blob of black paint. In other words, to organise your visual sense. It all sounds incredibly basic, but half the students I get now [at the Slade in the mid-1990s] don't know how to do that.[51]

[. . .] The very, very first thing he [Andrew Forge, her tutor at the Slade] said to me, we sat down, and he was an awkward man socially, he didn't find it easy to relate to other people. So there was a silence, classic Slade silence. And then he said, 'The problem with painting really is to know what to paint.' And you know, I have remembered that all these years, and there is a lot of truth in it [. . .] You don't have a thing to say necessarily that you then express in terms, in painterly terms. So that was rather reassuring that he said that to me, and obviously it must have struck a chord.[52]

British figurative painters in the 1950s tended to stick to a fairly restricted range of earth colours and muted tones. This was a legacy partly of post-war economic austerity (bright colours cost more) and partly of the kind of patient, unshowy realism practiced by William Coldstream, Slade Professor from 1949 to 1975. It didn't reflect Jaray's feelings about what she wanted to paint.

> I thought, why do I have to use this grim kind of colour? And I thought, I'll try something else. And I do remember setting up my easel in front of the model and using a completely different palette – pale yellows, oranges, reds, maybe a few pale greens. And I remember the painting, more or less I remember the painting I did. It was really bad. It was a terrible painting, but it got me out of using this other palette, and I think it made me understand that you can actually do whatever you want, and you can change. And you know, that sounds very simple and obvious, but it isn't. It's an incredibly difficult thing for any artist or student to try something different. It seems immensely courageous to do it at the time.[53]
>
> [. . .] A lot of teaching in art schools is not actually done by saying, you do it this way or that way, you know. It's done through a strange kind of osmosis of, you know, being in the presence of somebody who is an artist, and somehow learning indirectly.[54]

Jaray went on to teach at Hornsey College of Arts and Crafts, and then at the Slade. Whereas students in the 1960s 'were certainly expected to put in the hours', as she had at art school, the style of teaching was changing:

> Visiting artists and teachers became stars to some extent. That didn't really exist [before], although the teachers themselves did have glamour, you know. People like Derrick Greaves, Ed Middleditch, certainly Freddie Gore, they had glamour because they were older and established artists. But they didn't have that, quote, 'star quality' that came in in the 60s where it was certainly known for artists to come in and do – in fact I once timed somebody, who shall be nameless, I don't know why he should be nameless, doing seven-and-a-half minutes' teaching in a day. Now [in 1996], of course, those days have long gone.[55]

Out of interest, who was this teacher? 'It was actually John Hoyland. I mean, he was fairly well devoted to how many girls he could get in a day. I don't suppose any of this is going to be heard for a hundred years so I don't suppose it'll matter.'[56]

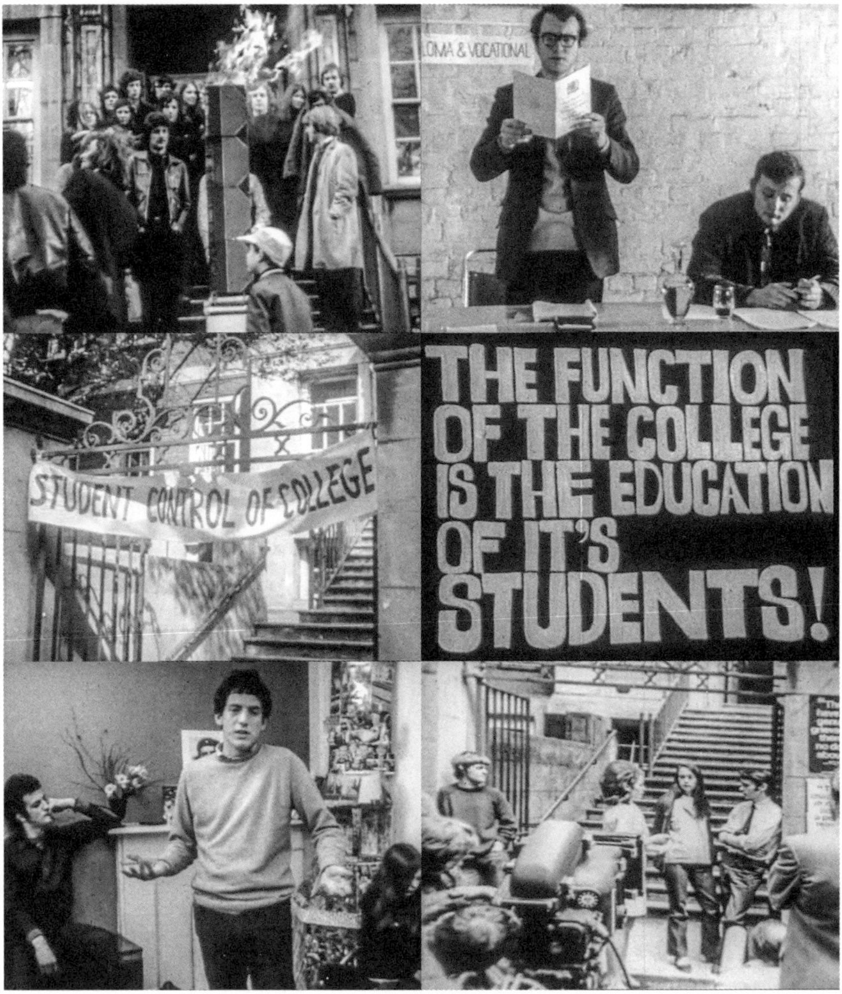

Film stills and photographs by Patricia Holland from *The Hornsey Film* (1970), a re-enactment of the student protest at Hornsey College of Arts and Crafts in 1968.

In 1968, after losing her job at Hornsey in the wake of the student protests, Jaray was offered work at the Slade. 'I met Willie Townsend[57] at a party and he said, "Oh why don't you come in and do a day's teaching?"'

> He was, as you know, this is not a secret, everybody knows he was fond of the bottle, he would be rather – this is not very discreet but I'm sure other people say it. He would go in in the morning extremely quiet and rather morose, and then he would disappear somewhere for a minute at half-past eleven, and he would come back rather more cheerful. So presumably it was the odd nip. So I think he was well tanked [. . .] Anyhow, he said come in next Tuesday or whatever, and do a visit, do a day's teaching. And when I woke up the next morning I thought, God! How wonderful, you know, to do some teaching at the Slade. And then I remembered that Coldstream had said that while he was alive, no woman – there would be no woman teacher employed, and that, what was his expression? 'No woman will step over the threshold as long as I am in charge.'[58]

What I liked about clay: Phyllida Barlow

When Phyllida Barlow initially applied to Chelsea School of Art in 1960, the recently appointed principal Lawrence Gowing was in the process of revitalising the school in preparation for its move to a purpose-designed building in Manresa Road, Chelsea. Gowing gradually removed long-serving traditionalists from the staff, replacing them with younger practising artists like Elisabeth Frink. On the day of Barlow's interview:

> I went with my mother and I was in my school uniform [. . .] I was 15 – and I went to the interview, and it was Lawrence Gowing and my mother, who was this very flirtatious, very vivid person. She really was the person who got into Chelsea art school, not this rather dreary schoolgirl in the corner [*laughs*]. But the one thing he liked were these two little clay figures that I'd taken along as an example of using clay. And when eventually I got to Chelsea and we had this first class with a reclining figure and it was with Robert Clatworthy, and he demonstrated how you could model – it was him and Elisabeth Frink running this class – model clay with hitting it with wood, cutting it with wood. They were talking about modelling where

you didn't use your hands and they were just saying, 'Find anything,' you know, 'go to the canteen and get a canteen knife, use a fork, use kitchen utensils.' It was just fantastic, but because I'd had this experience with clay I could respond to what they were saying absolutely instantly. And I knew that it has to be something that I would do. But painting was so dominant. Sculpture departments then in the 60s were places where there would be four to eight people in a year, as opposed to 60 or 80 in a year now. To move out of painting into sculpture was – not complicated, it was very straightforward but it was definitely a divorce. Because the areas – painting, sculpture – they were very distinctive and demarcated.[59]

[. . .] What I liked about clay was the fact that it was like paint. That you had this solid block and then you could attack the block almost as if it was a canvas that you were painting on. The great thing was that it wasn't a canvas, it was a block so that all the interruptions and interventions you made on that lump of clay were something that you had to do over and over again as you walked around it or as you spun the turntable of the modelling stand – these lovely modelling stands, where the wooden board that you were modelling on would rotate so that there was an automatic understanding that this was a 360-degree experience, unlike the easel that the painting goes on, which is a static one-dimensional, you could say, experience, that rotating stand just says it all. So this was like, in a way, painting in the round.[60]

Pressures and tensions: Stuart Brisley

Stuart Brisley applied to art school in 1949 on the prompting of his grandmother, who 'thought I should be a draughtsman because I did a lot of drawing'.

And my mother thought I should be an architect, because I was drawing, and so, she contacted the local art school – no a local architectural firm, and they suggested that I go to the local art school, which had an architectural qualification, that was Guildford School of Art [. . .] and I got in, with no interest in architecture whatsoever [. . .] And I remember being asked to design a bus station, a bus shelter, and then I remember having to do some drawings of drainpipes. And I was just so bored, quite honestly, and I had not an inkling of a sense of what a bus shelter should be. I mean, it was something that was completely uninteresting to me [. . .] So after a short

> time, I think it was two or three weeks, or a month, I transferred to the art thing.[61]

After art school, 'I really wanted to go on making work and I wanted to travel and I wanted to leave actually, leave, get out of here.'[62] Students who intended to earn a regular living from teaching he regarded with 'a sort of contempt'.

> I'm not saying I would think necessarily that now, but that was a way of thinking about it. These were people who were kind of giving up and going for soft options, and what the hell were they doing, you know? Because we were utterly committed, like a vocation [. . .] It's like Catholics and Protestants, if you're in Ireland, I guess, or Northern Ireland you could see it, you could tell. I can see them now, standing there. You know, go home for the weekend, blah-blah-blah-blah. They weren't committed to the – they didn't have a total – there were other people that did.[63]

All the same, Brisley would later have his own experience of teaching. On the staff of Hornsey, he took an active part in the student protest and occupation of the college's Crouch End Hill site in May 1968. The sit-in was triggered by a proposal to withdraw funding from the Student Union but quickly developed into an effective student takeover of the college, during which protesters and visiting sympathisers, including artists, drew up a thoroughgoing critique of the art education system.

> There was the sort of international event that was taking place in 1968, the Paris uprising and so on, the Prague Spring. There was all of that. So there seemed to be a climate in which there was a cry for more democracy in one way or another internationally. And I think, the Hornsey thing has to be seen in a broader context other than just the internal pressures and tensions that were within the college. And there were a lot in the college because of its sort of quick growth; because of the numbers of students and staff; because of the dynamism of some of the teaching practices; because of the interaction between people who had come, students who had come to the school with different sorts of aspirations, bumping into each other through this educational process. Because of the kind of lively atmosphere of London itself, both through student perspective and alternative street scene, alternative arts and all of that, allied to this sort of international trend towards greater democracy in certain areas. Seems to me that all this comes together in some way.

> And Hornsey is triggered by two events, one really internal, that is the withdrawal of funds from the Student Union, and two, by the international context, this sort of live event in Paris which was sort of like dramatic and powerful. So you have these two things, the much bigger one acting on the smaller one, and the smaller one having its own internal impetus for a protest to be made. And within, when the Student Union called the meeting on the 28th of May [. . .] the school was packed, the hall was packed with probably, I mean I don't think there would have been many students who were not there, and the staff, and within about an hour the demands had moved [. . .] to a demand for the educational process to be democratised and opened. And I can remember making – I think it was probably the first, or the second, staff speech in support of that, at the time. And I remember being invited to, being asked to stand as the staff – this is always my life – and I turned it down, I didn't want to lead it in any way. I just wanted to be part of it.[64]

The sit-in lasted six weeks and inspired similar protests at other art schools. It ended when students dispersed at the end of the summer term, and the college authorities moved back in. The same year, rather unexpectedly, William Coldstream offered Brisley a job at the Slade.

> I think Coldstream, who was rather a sharp guy, had decided that the Slade hadn't had any of this [student unrest] [. . .] So I was appointed as student adviser, which meant, basically the job was to invite people to the school to deal with alternative educational opportunities, which were not provided by the body of staff at the time.[65]

People have different views of Coldstream, he observes:

> but my view of him was of a sort of – as William Burroughs said, if you really want to be subversive, dress up in a suit. And I think mentally Coldstream must have taken that on, because he was so mischievous – as his mind was so mischievous, and he was so witty and sharp. And, I suppose that's how I remember him, as being someone that one would meet [. . .] and never be sure which way it was going to go, you know, whether one was – but always be sure that one was at a disadvantage intellectually, because he was so acute, really so sharp, and a very generous person. So he was both

ironic, you know, witty. But I learnt a lot from Coldstream, but the essential thing that I think I learnt from him was his notion of what the education was about. And he said, 'Undergraduate education in the Slade is to find out if you want to be an artist, and if you don't, well that's fine.' And he would be very sympathetic to people who were in doubt, who didn't know what to do. I mean he was, in that sense I think he was very enlightened as an educator [. . .] I said one day to Euan Uglow[66] [. . .] I could never understand why Coldstream employed me. He said, 'What do you mean? Of course, it's obvious.' And I said, 'Well what do you mean?' He said, 'Coldstream could never finish any work. It was always an unfinished process.' And he said, 'And here you are making performances,' he said, 'they're never finished. I mean, they're just things that take place and then, you know –' He said, 'It's so obvious what that connection is.' And I still don't understand it properly but that's what he thought.[67]

5

Strange Calm and Turbulence

On Painting

Painting is the most elusive artistic process to translate into written or spoken language. As Paul Feiler puts it, 'Painting is to do with seeing something that presents you with an inner experience for which you have no words that can be used as an explanation for your feeling.'[1] Sculptors can convey the physical sense of an object and the actions involved in making it; performance artists can describe and document what they did or where they were. But for painters, there is the unpredictable tightrope walk between intention and effect, the mysterious relationship between the liquid and solid substance of a painting and what that painting is and does. Some of the most thought-provoking, even moving, passages in Artists' Lives involve painters trying – not entirely successfully – to find the words to explain what it means to paint, circling around an activity and a compulsion that, even after a lifetime, can feel all but impossible to describe.

The big debate in twentieth-century British painting (in the post-war decades particularly) was between supporters and practitioners of abstraction and their figure-painting contemporaries. Both sides of the discussion are represented here, giving a sense of how British painters responded to a series of discoveries and stimuli – Robert Medley in the Louvre, Gillian Ayres with buckets of 'American' acrylic paint, Peter Blake enlisting office technology for his portraits. We eavesdrop on their inner worlds more than the outcome of their studio practice, perhaps coming as close as it is possible to get to a painters' subjective sense of what they are about. If one identifiable group is represented more fully than any other, it is probably women abstract painters. Wilhelmina Barns-Graham, Sandra Blow, Gillian Ayres and Tess Jaray are all very different artists and were never formally linked, but taken together their approaches to abstraction add up to one of the most distinctive strands in modern British art.

How ideas come: Robert Medley

'I don't know how ideas come to one,' says Robert Medley:

> I think I like pictures often which are painted out of people's heads, and not things that they see. I get tired of saying, 'Oh well a painting is all about seeing, or painting is all about looking.' You know, is it? Is it really all about looking? [. . .] It must be something else. You could hardly say that Michelangelo is all about looking, or Signorelli or anybody. It's about a lot of other things other than looking.[2]
>
> [. . .] I don't always work very well when I am in front of nature. I think one has to learn to look and to draw things properly. For instance, Daumier[3] hated painting from nature. In fact when he did portraits he used to pretend to paint the portrait when the sitter was there but used to paint it after they had gone [. . .] I think nature put him off as a whole when it came to painting. Even Degas was not entirely hooked with just looking, was he now? [. . .] I find that I do something and then I have to leave it for a year or two sometimes, and then I suddenly see what I really meant by the picture. Sometimes it means that I've got fucked up with all this looking business, which always with me leads to copying the damn thing. And once you start doing that, the whole of the creative thing goes out of the window, for me, totally.[4]
>
> [. . .] The other source of how I get my ideas, I get my ideas from looking at other pictures. The pictures I think – oh, I would like to – you know, this has something that I must do. And then I would try and – the picture builds up out of other pictures, and [. . .] I only get to understand what some pictures are actually about by reading other people, what they say about it. I suddenly realise that they have said something interesting about the picture, and then I think about that, and sometimes in the end I don't agree with it or I think of something much more interesting that comes out of it. Sometimes I will take a picture I have been thinking about – Goya – and I started to do some little groups of people in relationship to a kind of Goya-esque scale, and then I draw any little groups of figures, either nudes or [. . .]

> jugglers or what have you. Or it may be a group of people talking in the street or crossing the road. But it's [come] out of the scale and the looking at that picture, and trying to do it – perhaps doodling away, with people crossing the road, or people standing in a conversation. But then suddenly you realise, oh, that will make – you know, I can make a picture out of that.[5]

But there are limits to what pictures can be 'made out of'. Medley recounts how his friend Francis Bacon:

> wanted to paint a painting which would be as shocking as a real crime, and of course he got near it. But of course you can't in a painting do it, because a painting remains a painting – like a painting of a dog is never a dog, it's always a painting of a dog.[6]

A procedure of doing: William Gear and Paul Feiler

William Gear describes the situation for British painters in the austerity decade beween 1945 and the mid-1950s, when the scarcity and poor quality of materials affected their work:

> I worked a lot on paper for instance, I did lots of gouaches, and paper was accessible, but you couldn't just go round to the corner shop and buy a dozen canvases. One thing we did [. . .] it was quite possible to buy old paintings, I mean in a junk shop, and sometimes you could paint over them or use the stretchers. Or I had one or two army sheets, or when I went back to Scotland, I went to a local factory which made a kind of canvas, a linen canvas, and I got a few remnants. But it was a problem, and similarly paint. I mean, it was limited, and indeed you could get what you might call the basic, rough paints, but anything of quality was very difficult to obtain. It was very expensive too [. . .] The old-time French painters had no problem, I mean the Picassos and Matisses and Légers of this world. Well, they had no problem, they had their regular gallery merchants who could supply [them], but for the average artist it was really quite awkward.[7]

Discussing *Landscape Image No.1* (1961), a large, vertical, abstract painting now in Birmingham Museum and Art Gallery, Gear describes a working process in

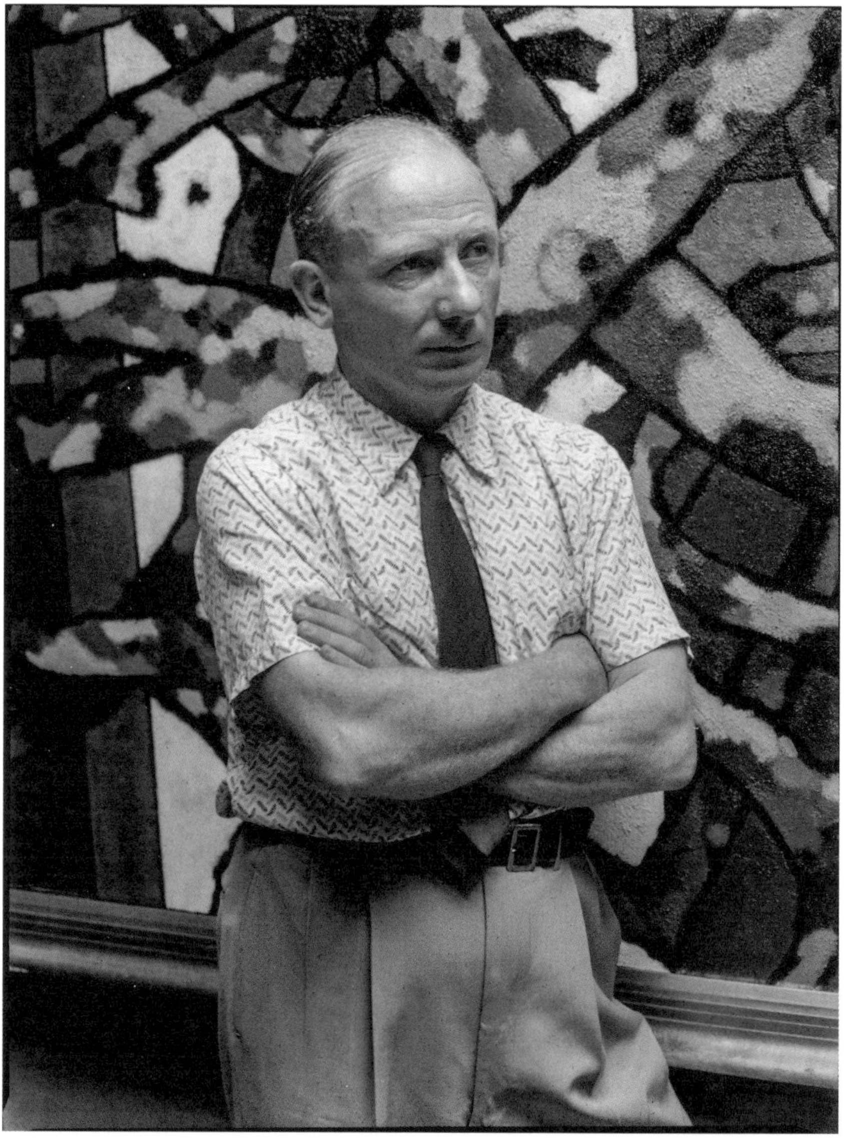

William Gear at his exhibition at the South London Art Gallery, Camberwell, July 1954. Photograph by Ida Kar.

which, though individual paintings relate to each other, each one is a new departure, making it impossible for an artist to retrace their steps or deliberately repeat a successful painting:

> I think the paintings like this, they depend so much on what one has been doing previously – one's mood at the time, what one has been seeing. You can't really explain how these things come about. It reaches a point where you are happiest doing this, working this way. Then you may feel on retrospect that you want to tighten it up or loosen it up or rearrange the colour, and so on [. . .] But this is how a painter works. It's not a question of 'knocking them off', so to speak. One has to adapt and investigate and allow for other suggestions or possibilities to come through.[8]

Landscape Image No.1 is built around a central thicket of upright black forms – jagged lines or poles that suggest tree trunks or, more distantly, human figures, though no one would call it a figurative painting. Gear doesn't talk of taking sides – abstraction or figuration – but of contrary though not conflicting gravitational fields. He tries to clarify by prompting the interviewer to look at the view through his window, where, he says, 'I can see my painting' – that building, that tree. It's all there:

> I was gravitating to abstraction and, of course, even in those early days, there was always a link with nature. I never denied nature, really. Even in those extreme abstract themes [. . .] there is an equivalence to observable form. I don't say nature in the naturalistic sense but of observable forms. They may be telegraph poles or stakes or trees or structures or – as I am looking out the window now – I mean, I can see my painting in two or three different ways. There is the severe architectural, modern structure over there, and at the same time trees and foliage and blossom and light through the tree. I mean, there is my painting, you see. This is where it comes from. I don't necessarily sit down and paint that, but I am aware of it, and I can see the equivalence to my painting. I don't say it's nature, but I don't deny nature. This is it. And I think it's impossible to deny nature really [. . .] There have been those severely abstract painters who might paint a circular disc and paint it red, and then they have a line across, and then they call it 'Red Disc' [. . .] But the human eye looking at this red disc is bound to associate it with the setting sun, or whatever. I mean, the physiological action of

> an eye looking at something is going to record and interpret in some way. So it's really rather pointless to say, 'My painting is purely concerned with proportion and structure and so on' [. . .] If you try to deny that the physiological aspect of an eye interpreting whatever you are looking at, then you are missing the point [. . .] Most of my paintings they have – well not necessarily, but sometimes they have a title. It might be *Summer Landscape* or *Spring Landscape* or *Garden Structure* or names like that. Again, looking at these paintings, you can see there is a basic dark structure which can be tree trunks, or stakes, or parts of buildings, or whatever, and then, additionally, the effect of foliage and blossom and light coming through the trees as you see it now. As I say, I don't depict it. I just paint the thing.[9]

'I paint every day,' says Paul Feiler. 'I paint for many hours every day. I get very tired, and I get very bored.'

> Because, to complete a painting, it takes not just days but weeks, and progress [. . .] is so slow and so unpredictable that it is just simply spending time doing it. And the actual procedure and the technicalities involved, and the practicalities involved, are so enormous that they take over as far as your image-making is concerned. So I do get very tired and very bored [. . .] There's a wonderful sense of silence, yes. And an enormous feeling of getting the ingredients together to make a meal just as good as the last one [. . .] in other words, you have to get into your kitchen and get your ingredients together, and there are a lot of practical problems involved which you have to deal with. And, you have to go through a procedure of doing, which requires a lot of energy, mental energy as well as physical energy [. . .] I do three or four hours in the morning, and then I do four or five hours in the afternoon, and I do that as a matter of routine, because it has to be done [. . .] So, a lot of what goes into it [painting] is sheer physical energy and mental concentration, all towards something that may or may not finally produce a wonderful sense of eureka, which does happen occasionally.[10]
>
> [. . .] It's like a kaleidoscope, just one tiny little turn and the whole scene completely changes. The whole combination of everything. Suddenly it's all red, from having been yellow. Suddenly there are little bits as opposed to big bits. And this is slow motion. And in painting it's such slow motion that you can't believe that it could ever speed up to a movement in the kaleidoscope. So that is when you think, phew! And you walk away and you think, good

Paul Feiler

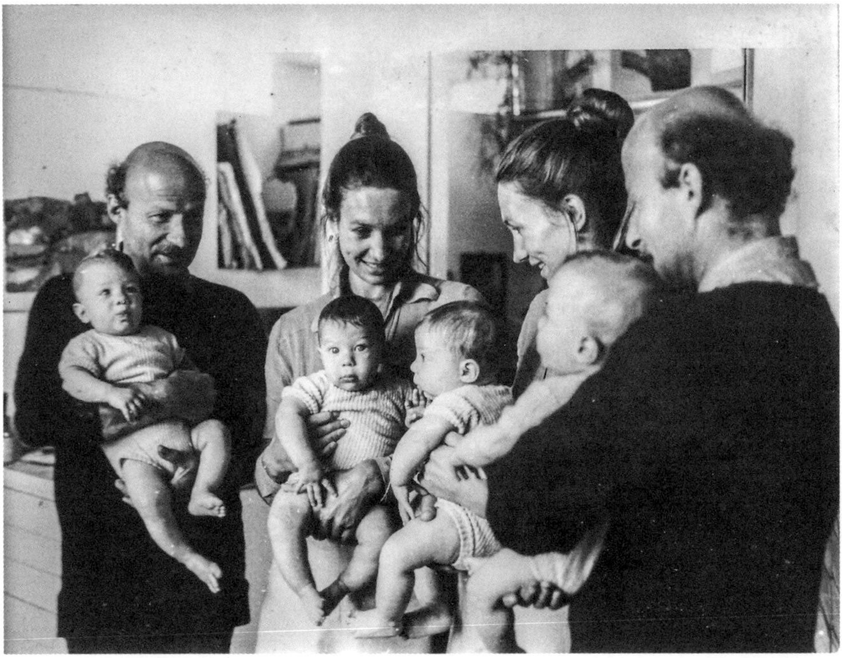

Paul and Catharine Feiler, with their twin sons Hugo and Adam, at home at Chapel Kerris, near Penzance, 1974. Photograph by Andrew Lanyon.

God! And you add something to it and the whole thing's gone. And you think, how can I get back to that, because that was it. But I've forgotten about [. . .] that, I must put it back, and as soon as I do, the whole thing is destroyed. That's what happens.[11]

[. . .] I feel that when you paint – when I paint – what I've taken with me from any experience is not only to do with place, but to do with my reaction to place, the sensation of the experience. And the sensation of the experience, as far as my own painting is concerned, is what I try to write down.[12]

[. . .] It's not the way it's [a painting's] done, because there are many who can do it just as well, but the way it's come about, and the way it has been a kind of mirror image whereby you recognise the strange calm and turbulence of one's existence. And it's just the way it is, in spite of the occasional smile.[13]

A physical shape and a thought shape: Wilhelmina Barns-Graham and Terry Frost

'I've noticed,' says Wilhelmina Barns-Graham, 'that when I'm under stress I sometimes do my best work.'

> I was under stress this time because I had a threat to my eyesight, and that's been overcome, but it made me concentrate particularly hard. Just a few hours' painting per day, and then thinking – a quick two hours – and I realised that thinking is as important a part as the actual work. And Barbara Hepworth once referred to that, the importance of thinking, keeping yourself quiet so that you have time to think. It's so important. And the funny thing is that, although I had to restrict my working time for only about two hours a day to begin with, and then I worked it up to a bit more by April, I did as much as I do when I work all day long and you scrape it out at the end of the day.[14]

Playing music in the studio was part of the discipline of 'keeping yourself quiet', arriving at what Barns-Graham calls 'a state of control'.

> I like Mozart and I like Bach, but I also like modern work, I like Stravinsky, Michael Tippett, I like – I also like real jazz, but that's more difficult to work [to]. It peps you up sometimes, but I like music that puts me into a state of contemplation or meditation, because I've done a lot of paintings that are meditations. When I was doing the 'Things of a Kind in Order and Disorder' [series of paintings], a lot of them were sort of prayers in my mind, and, I find it best to get a still mind, because I don't need to be pepped up with, or pepped down with tranquillisers or anything like that. I find that what one wants really is to get into a state of control. And there are many challenges down here [in St Ives] being a woman painter, and when I'm in stress, which I am from time to time, I find the best thing to do is to keep affirmative, come what may, and do another painting, in other words work, work, work. And I've even dedicated certain paintings to certain disturbances in my life. That's how I keep working.[15]

During the 1950s and early 1960s, Barns-Graham and Terry Frost worked in adjacent studios in Porthmeor Studios, St Ives. Frost's take on the relationship between life and painting – the kind of painting that isn't self-evidently *of* something – involves the artist in finding an equivalent for otherwise inexpressible experience. In his case, the experience is about a kind of body-memory of a particular place. Of his 1952 painting *Walking Along the Quay, Blue Movement,* he observes:

> This is a case of thinking about that walk [around St Ives harbour] which one did quite often, but standing here to think about it, so one sees the whole lot then – a sort of aerial view of it. But then you see, that's only a way of thinking as well as looking.[16]

Pointing to a reproduction of the painting in a book, he explains:

> You've got the golden section[17] running down there – and immediately I can see that without even bothering – and a square within a square basis, and then my rhythms will be – if you were to follow them through, you would find they connect up. And then, once I've got that structure in, I'm at liberty to do exactly what I want with my colours, if they make the painting work. So there is a freedom in it which is totally abstract. I'm not bound to do it – to try and do what I thought I saw. Instead I'm more inclined to do what I think I want to do about the situation. And it makes a blue evening, or whatever I want to make it [. . .] It's like – it's a capture, not just of a moment but many moments, because you walk by that [place], not once but many, many times over months. And so it's an experience which happens in a moment but quite frequently, and then one takes the sum total. It's like writing a poem about it, or a piece of music.[18]

Frost sounds ambivalent about the benefits of working at the heart of an artistic community, where other artists would regularly call in to see what he was up to:

> You always knew when you had done a good painting, because they didn't know what to say – because their envy, or jealousy made them talk about anything but the painting, and it always did the same to me. It's quite tricky when you see something which is really good and you haven't done it. I mean I'm talking about painters working at the same time and around you, that you want them to do a good painting of course, but you want to do one better yourself. This is I think quite natural.[19]

tly after arriving in St Ives in 1946, Frost had found work in Hepworth's eam of assistants who were tasked with the heavier carving of stone sculp- working to her directions and marks on the stone. He describes how his later habit of using collage in paintings 'relates back to sculpture'.

> When I worked for Barbara, that almost finished me for painting for about nine months, because I couldn't get used to the idea of a physical shape and a thought shape. I couldn't work the two out together. Because when you make a hole in a piece of stone, or when you carve a shape, you can't put it back on again, that is a fact. So you've got to make adjustments all the way round. And with a painting you can scrape off. And I was a bit disillusioned about the illusionistic side of painting, and I think that's what helped me to be stronger on the abstract side, and certainly helped me with the collage. Because if you use a collage you have to cut – well you don't have to, but I was cutting a positive shape, which gave me more satisfaction than having an expressionist brushstroke.[20]

Cut out the appearances: John Latham

When his wartime service on motor torpedo boats in the Royal Naval Volunteer Reserve came to an end, John Latham had enrolled at Regent Street Polytechnic and then at Chelsea College of Art. He was taught by Ceri Richards,[21] whose large painting for the 1951 Festival of Britain, *Trafalgar Square, London* (1950), with its Provençal blues and Picasso-esque pigeons, he may be describing here:

> [Richards'] approach to painting was technically far better developed than I would ever want to develop. I didn't feel that that was what I wanted to do, but I could understand where he got his forms from. An awful lot of them came from Picasso, a lot of them came from Matisse. He may have cast an eye across to Miró and others, but it was all forgotten. His best advice to me was, 'Well, you see, you know how to do that. That thing you've painted there – you've just – it's somebody else's. I know where you got it from.' Now that was good instruction, because I could see that I had borrowed somebody's forms. I'd borrowed a form from Cézanne, and of course I did a few. When painting with a brush it's very hard to lose allusions to other people's work, almost impossible.[22]

In 1951, shortly after his marriage to Barbara Steveni, Latham was introduced to a scientist couple, Clive and Anita Gregory:

> Clive Gregory [. . .] said would you do us a favour? We want you to do a mural for us for a Halloween night party, the night of the spirits is what we're interested in. And I was painting with a brush, just a very ordinary thing to do, but I didn't paint like other painters. I had got about four identifiable ways of making paint do something that it hadn't done before, so I was really keen on carrying that on, and I certainly didn't want to go and do a mural for some people that I didn't really have anything to do with. But it then struck me about a week after the invitation that what I had in my locker was an electrical gear for spraying paint, and it had been bought for the totally extraneous purposes of firing creosote at the outside of a bungalow that I was going to go and live in [. . .]
>
> Well, the invitation and the thought of this machine was the very thing which I should have seen before. It extended the idea of painting as the painting tradition, the painting trajectory had arrived at. It had arrived at a point where Jackson Pollock was very famous as having done drip paintings, which did nothing in the way of representing the world by appearances. That is very important. Cut out the appearances. Jackson Pollock took an awful long time getting rid of the appearances, or the drawing, the outlines of animals and things. Well, this idea of doing this painting suddenly electrified my idea, because a spray-gun mark made as painting had never been done before for a start, but it followed on to the drip marks, which were very famed, by Jackson Pollock. It followed on from the *tachisme* that was being done in Paris, and it followed on from the zero-action mark which was put forward by the minimalist approach to painting, which had left us with a proposition which said everything equals nothing. All of what's gone on to date is somehow dismissible [. . .] So we're into a very extraordinary state of affairs, which at this point I'd made the painting. Clive Gregory saw it, came in and saw it going on and said, 'Oh, very interesting. This is what we are going to be doing. It's giving us an idea of the spirit world.' I didn't want to know about the spirit world. What was interesting to me was that when marks go down on a piece of surface, something very much better than verbal explanation is happening.[23]

I had my own themes: Frank Bowling

After his release from national service, Frank Bowling's original ambition had been to become a writer. One of his part-time jobs was modelling at the Royal College of Art, where he became convinced that he had a clearer idea of what it took to be an artist than the students who were drawing or painting him. Bowling enrolled at Chelsea School of Art and from there, in 1959, won a scholarship to the Royal College: 'as luck would have it', the assessors noticed 'what I brought to my work, the things I wanted to paint about [. . .] I had my own themes'. It irritated Bowling that people consistently expected him to address Caribbean postcolonial subjects, 'because I certainly in doing my work never considered myself as painting out of any Caribbean intention. My own view of what I was doing was trying to paint, to make works that would stand up with the best works in the museums that I was familiar with.'[24] The settings of Bowling's early paintings, which got him into the Royal College of Art and gained him the silver medal to David Hockney's gold when they graduated in 1962, evoke the west London demi-monde of the post-war years. There was, says Bowling, 'this childbirth thing which I was obsessed by':

> because I saw this young woman giving birth in this incredibly derelict, broken-down basement flat in Notting Hill Gate [. . .] And this young girl, I'd seen her around, but this particular day, I think it was a Saturday, she was moaning and groaning, and, as a rule I wouldn't bother because I would think that, you know, she's carrying on her trade, because [. . .] to me a lot of these young women alone were whores, you know, I didn't ask. But – and they made a noise. But this was – this was a sound of somebody in pain, so I went to look. And this was happening, and so I called the ambulance, and by the time they got there the child had come out, with the cord round its neck. You know, I was just sort of – just a blur, like panic, you know, calling to the neighbour to help [. . .] Then the ambulance arrives and it was all taken care of. And for years I was obsessed with this business of how children come into the world [. . .] I was obsessed also with notions of existence. I was trying to read philosophy and – not trained, no one was guiding me, but I was stumbling around. I thought this was a very, very, very striking, important thing that you come into the world, in this agonising way, all the pain that goes with it, and all, just the mess that it makes, and the rest. So I was trying to paint those things [. . .] So people thought I was coming with fresh ideas.[25]

In 1960 Bowling married Paddy Kitchen, the Royal College registrar. In January 1962, waiting for the birth of his first child, Dan, Bowling began a series of white paintings. Years later, following Dan's sudden death in 2001, he returned to this theme. A friend had brought him some ready-stretched canvases, and though Bowling usually worked on unstretched canvas, 'it struck me that I should work on these canvases, because there were already existing canvases that I had made around the time he [Dan] was born':

> I made these [the earlier] landscape paintings in the snow, under the snow. They were directly related to him in the sense that, it was whilst I was waiting for him to be born, I was making these paintings of the backyard of [the] flat in which we lived.
>
> And then I had another bash at making these white paintings some years later when I was marooned in New York. So I thought that the thing for me to do to come to terms with this loss, with this very confusing business of – this man's life which seemed so full of promise [. . .] So I started working on these little white paintings. And I tried very hard not to make any prior decisions about what was going to go on these surfaces, right? I would just simply put down very thinly watered-down washes of pale colours and just watch – because the way I work a canvas, sitting on the table, and then I put the material on, and the container's usually something like this, or smaller, of the mixed paint. I would rest the container on the canvas [and] it had happened before I realised what I was doing. I just sat these containers in the pool of watery paint. And then a spread and bleed would take place, sometimes with the embryo of a sort of circle in the middle. And that's how I went at these works. I just worked at them in a way having emptied my head of any prior notions of what I was going to put down on these things [. . .] I had a session with the acupuncture people, and I collected the needles that was used to puncture me [. . .] On these surfaces, I laid them in the pool of pinkish or blueish liquid, and then leave it to dry [. . .] I thought that this was the thing, you know, the way to pathologise the hurt or the confusion anyway – the confusion that I found myself in with this man's death [. . .] I don't know how many I did in the end.[26]

Like nature but not like nature: Basil Beattie and Gillian Ayres

In the 1960s British painters began to adopt the relatively new, free-flowing, water-soluble acrylic paints that had made possible the abstract work of American colour-field painters like Helen Frankenthaler and Morris Louis. Unlike oil paints, acrylics could be splashed, dripped or brushed on in impulsive gestures. Broad areas of colour on huge canvases could be dry within minutes; and the colours were clean, bright and flat, leaving none (or much less) of the quasi-sculptural 'evidence of a hand' that viscous oil paint carries. Acrylic paints triggered a small revolution; British painting – especially abstract painting – almost instantly looked more expansive, more American, capable of more immediate and less laborious impact. Artists often had mixed feelings. Was this new medium too easy to handle, too facile? Basil Beattie explains that his choice of acrylic paint was 'primarily a philosophical one'.

> I've clearly shown in all the work that I've done, where the roots lie [in] the period at the Royal Academy Schools, where there was very much a drawing element, a very strong drawing element in the kind of – the work [of mine] that was influenced by de Kooning, there was a linear element. And then, later on, a complete rejection on my part of the evidence of the hand. Although there's a lot of control in the paintings, the work was less tactile, more vaporous in a way. There would be a link perhaps with Turner in a kind of almost unintentioned way, because the paint was drifted onto the surface. There was no evidence of a hand, and there was no particular incident. It was just an effect of light, it was an intensity of light that was evident. And in fact I was preoccupied with the absence of the hand, and [. . .] apart from being very conscious of someone like Morris Louis and Helen Frankenthaler, I was very interested in making something that was like nature but not like nature. Like nature in the manner of its operation, that it was formed through natural laws, like gravity [. . .] So it began to look like things that you could have seen in nature, certain aspects of nature. But that wasn't the intention. That was like a by-product of the process [. . .] I think that was something that I shared with quite a few artists at that time [. . .] I was particularly intrigued by that way of working, and it also [. . .] used the invention of acrylic paint. It was partly a product of the properties of acrylic paint that actually encouraged this particular approach. But I think the approach was

for me primarily a philosophical one. And I think it was a direct reaction to the hands being evident in the earlier work.[27]

For Gillian Ayres, the switch from oil paint to acrylic felt full of unexplored possibilities (you couldn't fill washing-up bowls with oil paint or splash it onto untreated canvas), though the chemical properties of acrylic paint (a form of plastic) could result in some less attractive effects.

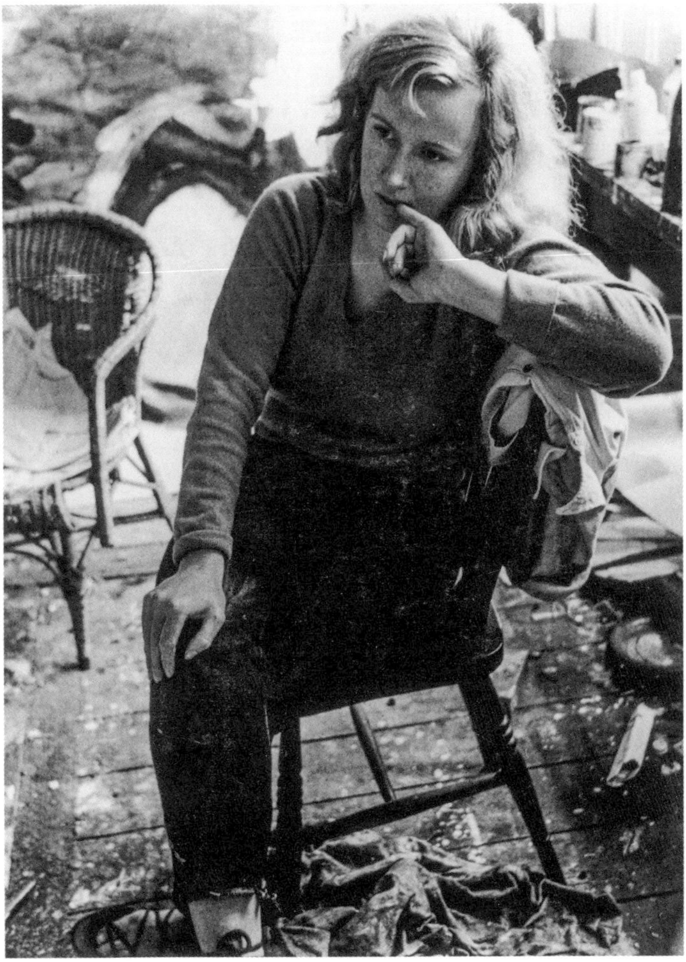

Gillian Ayres in her studio in London, 1960. Photograph by Roger Mayne.

> I'm critical, because I think now that the first way that acrylic was used, i.e. Frankenthaler or those early Americans, was where you could – if you don't prime canvas, it rots, oil paint rots canvas – and suddenly there was this new paint where you could paint straight onto white canvas or white cotton duck. And I think where they used it like great big, blown-up eighteenth-century English watercolours was tremendously exciting. I mean, I think when it came in it almost got used to the full [. . .] I don't like it [painted] thick, and I bounce back from it, I always think it looks like a plastic mackintosh. That's me, and that's my taste. I like it thin. Well I didn't, I used it sort of rather thin and rather flat. I'm fussy, I'm fussy about mediums [. . .] I went to a chemist and he made a note in his diary [. . .] 'Gillian Ayres knocked on the door and came and asked about the molecules of acrylic paint.' Yes, I did, I went into what you could do with it right at the beginning, and then I started to use it [. . .] and in the end one was mixing up great bowls and having great tubs of acrylic from factories, which kept the price down, from paint manufacturers. Beverley Road [Ayres' home] used to have great drums outside. God knows about health with this stuff. And then I used to buy pure pigment in sort of solvent, a mix-up. Great washing-up bowls of the stuff, yes [. . .] I mean, really, you know, to the day we drop dead we're learning, so one's always finding out things.[28]

Reviewing a lifetime of 'looking at painting, reading, thinking, and painting', Ayres reflects that she still can't fully explain why it is that she paints:

> I just sort of have to, and I always have, really for a very, very long time – maybe from ten, I think, I say 13. So, you still do whenever you can. There are times in life – I mean I have a mother that died of cancer, a father that had strokes for ten years. Sometimes life gets very problematic in many ways, so then, this happens to all of us. Perhaps we're ill sometimes or something. But, whenever I can and whenever I'm healthy and whenever I can find time, I will do exactly what I want to do. Nobody asks you to paint by the way, and – the world doesn't demand it.[29]

Balance of colour: Sheila Girling, Sandra Blow and Tess Jaray

When Anthony Caro travelled to New York in 1959, his wife, Sheila Girling, went with him. Like many British artists who crossed the Atlantic during the next decade, she found the contrast between New York and London 'terribly exciting':

> Everything was open, suddenly new materials were being used, new ways of using materials and the whole new concept of abstraction. It seemed, I mean the whole thing was just food really, and you hadn't seen anything like it [. . .] you believed in the people that were doing it, their sincerity.[30]

Helen Frankenthaler 'was revolutionising painting then by painting on unprimed canvas for the first time':

> She was pouring and using it [acrylic paint] like watercolour on – and that was again, I mean Morris Louis took from her and poured – I mean everything was happening, you know, people were using materials in a completely different way and the whole thing was open.[31]
>
> [. . .] Of course I'd learnt so much at art school about putting on the paint too, and I thought these people in a way hadn't learnt that and they were putting on paint in a different way than I would. But I mean it was wonderful, the fact that you could pour it or throw it, or Pollock was just throwing it. I mean all these things were wonderful, but for me it was [. . .] I would have been imitating and it wasn't me. So I think that was an era that had passed and I wanted to go back into the canvas, I didn't want the surface of the canvas to be, the whole thing, you know, not to break the surface of the canvas, I wanted to be able to get into a picture again.[32]
>
> [. . .] Well first of all I was just pulling the colour across the canvas so that the colours actually mixed on the canvas. And then, when I wanted to get more perhaps shaping and colour, and not leaving it so much to just [painting with] the arm, the way the painting was organised, I started to pour colour onto the canvas and then block it out with a ground colour, so that I would get something shining through [. . .] I poured the colour onto the canvas first and glazed it and then with this green I masked out the shape that I wanted. And at that point I'd just started to add a little collage. So it was all coming together [. . .] So I slowly sort of worked my way through [. . .]
>
> I think I have preconceived ideas, vaguely. They alter as you go, but I always mix my colours first. If I don't have the colours right the painting never succeeds. So I always get all my colours mixed to a certain extent, I

> know just what the colour is going to be on the painting. And then I have a, yes, the shaping I want is in my head so that I know, I can know where I want to start. Things alter, I mean the painting often takes over in a way you didn't expect it to and you think, oh gosh that's nice, or oh, that's a mess, I'll, you know, take that off. So it's a sort of dialogue, a painting, you know, with the way it's going and the way you thought it was going to go [. . .]
>
> The scale is usually the size of the canvas I put down [on the floor] [. . .] with a big painting, I know the sort of scale I want. But I often, you know, leave a border that I don't paint, so that I can turn it round, the canvas, the stretcher, and also sometimes you come in more than you intend, you know, you find that the image is – you need to constrict it more, so that really you're not painting on a square canvas where you're very conscious of the square, you're painting freely on a field of colour really. I don't like painting on a square, a preconceived stretched canvas, because you're always conscious of the edge really, and you're not conscious if you're painting on the floor, you're walking in it. You're sort of paddling in it almost. And then, when it comes to really the beastly jobs of sticking down the pieces [of collage] that you put on, I lift it on to a lifting table so that it doesn't wreck your back, which you can do if you're bending all the time. So really that's the way it goes.[33]
>
> [. . .] I think we ['painterly' painters] love the feel of paint, the application of paint, the colour, the sort of sensuality of the paint, just the – well not the smell for me even, but the feel, the touch and doing it through your hand and your senses. I don't think, you see, someone like Bridget Riley who's a very good painter, is a painterly painter because she can cut out the pieces of paper and somebody else paints them. I think if you hand over the actual – if you delegate the actual application of paint, it's a different ballgame really. It becomes something else, and I don't think that's where I would fit in at all. But I mean it's valid, but it's just not where I am, you know.[34]

Sandra Blow also sometimes preferred to work on paintings horizontally. Early photos show her mixing plaster, sand and other materials with her fingertips into paintings on boards laid on the floor. In 1988 she lowered an 8 ½ ft square canvas onto her studio floor, picked up a bucket of acrylic paint and splashed two explosive scarlet arcs across it. These were the opening actions for *Vivace* (1988), a case study in painterly alchemy in which resolute deliberation and insouciant openness to chance fuse in a single work:

> I put the work on the floor, because I thought if I had it up [on the wall] it [the paint] would just run down it, and then I think, I took my shoes off or something, I'm not quite sure, or did I put wellington boots on, one or the other? [. . .] I then mixed up a pail of the colour and then I walked over it, and I threw it where I wanted it. I directed it as far as I could, and followed it round the picture. I had to be very careful not to walk in the splashes and get footmarks on it. And I think the second gesture was probably done from outside the picture, but the first one I just walked across it. And then with, I think a broom or a mop, I pushed it where I thought it needed to sort of balance out. And then, there was one quick stage where I very quickly put [lifted] it up, and you can see in the picture where it's run a bit, and made a quick decision – what did it want? What did it want more? And quickly put it down again, and then added what I thought.[35]

Blow considered *Vivace* (now in the Tate) one of a handful of career-defining paintings. Here are her criteria for judging whether a painting (her own or anyone else's) has worked:

> For me there's a sort of – if I'm seeing it for the first time, I have a shock impact and a sense that it's right, and I feel very extended and I have a great sense of pleasure that – and excitement – if a picture does have that impact on me. And it's to do, I think, with the placing, the way the proportions of the picture connect, and the colour, the balance, and also perhaps – which I'm not quite sure whether it would come first or – is perhaps something very beautiful in a picture [. . .] I have described my work at times as architecture that doesn't have to function, that it's to do with proportion and space and balance, but it doesn't have to actually stand up and not fall down and you know, it doesn't have to have the architectural qualities that keep buildings up, but does have the elements of architecture [. . .] it's to do with that sense of it being an entity, that it has got the right balance of colour, of the areas, of the shape, everything working together and making a total. And I've sometimes thought that it's biological, that in order to walk we have to balance, we have to – our movements, we take them for granted but you know, if we lose our balance we fall over. I think in that way a picture has a kind of biological balance in it. I mean it's also to do with whatever colour means to us, and the balance of colour.[36]

Tess Jaray speaks in comparable terms of her own abstract painting: 'For me the paintbrush was a tool to put the painting on in a very quiet way, in a way that draws attention to nothing but the colour'.

> The more you draw attention to the surface of something, the more distracted you are from the purity of the colour, or the sense of the colour. That doesn't mean to say I didn't get huge enjoyment from putting paint on even, flat – I did, I mean brushing on – I've had times in my life when I haven't painted for a while, and I've really physically, desperately missed that action of actually painting, painting onto a surface. But because I've not done it, you know, like an abstract expressionist where I am relating to the thickness or viscosity of the paint, perhaps that's why it's been more important for me. You know, there is a graphic element to my work [. . .] it's not a word I like to use quite like that, because it's a word that's become a bit diminished, you know, it's usually preceded by the word 'only', 'only graphic'. But yes it is, it's a holding force, it's a rooting and a grounding, I think, a defining of something [. . .] it's building the foundations with a pencil.[37]
>
> [. . .] I don't think I understood for a long time how the whole thing just is a question of relationships, that's all it is, but then you could say that about practically anything in the world. But if you haven't got the relationship of one thing right to another in a painting, then there's nothing. And however much you understand it, unless you find a way of identifying completely with it in the painting, you won't be able to do it, otherwise great art historians would make great artists – I mean, we know they don't. So you can look at a painting and understand it, you know, fairly well, but that doesn't mean to say you can make one yourself. So that is simply through experience and ability and talent and luck, and when you were born and all those things.[38]
>
> [. . .] You put a colour down and what does it do to you? And that is utterly and completely personal, and it will only work, if it works, if it touches you at every level of your being but also communicates, you know? To be great, art has to be both personal and universal, and if it's imbalanced one way or the other it's just not good enough. So I don't think there is any answer to why, but [red and blue] have always been my colours basically. And there are certain colours I have never been able to handle. I don't think I have ever done a painting that I considered half-way successful which is

yellow, and yet it's Van Gogh's great colour and it's a marvellous colour, but it is a very, very difficult colour to use.[39]

[. . .] Whatever one talks about the reasons to make paintings, one of the most important things is that need to actually make an image that holds you, that grabs you. And this is something now that's gone out of the window a little bit. It's not really something that people talk about at all, creating an image [. . .] Suddenly now we are surrounded by so much imagery, it's so powerful – the media, the television, advertising. Advertising is so sophisticated, it's taken so much from painting. Painting in return now has taken so much from advertising. So many things have happened. But at that time, and probably for many years – and it will come back again, because I believe the power of the image is so strong, and the painted image is not like any other image. I don't think we can ever quite lose it.[40]

[. . .] In 1966 there was a painting that I called *Haven*, or there were a series of paintings around a simplified architectural theme where I was trying to evoke the colours of stone under a muted Italian light, that kind of feeling, perhaps in the evening [. . .] Greys, dull greys and greens. Now, what I did to arrive at that painting was to eliminate a lot of the shapes and to start to reduce it down [. . .] And whether it was something I wanted to draw out of the paintings, or whether the paintings themselves were dictating to me – because you know, that has to happen as well, you are not as an artist anything like as much in control as you think you are. Even the great artists have to rely on the paintings to speak to them. I don't believe that Rembrandt was entirely in control. But he was responding to something outside himself, and you were drawing everything from within [. . .] I mean, after all, there is nothing original under the sun. I don't think I was ever attempting to make original form. I was attempting to put together shapes and forms that are after all familiar, actually since the year dot. I was trying to create meaning or extrapolate meaning out of forms, abstract forms that had been used for different things for the last 30,000 years. And when I see marks on so-called primitive work, or maybe pre-Greek pots, a line of abstract marks that were made by whoever made those utensils, usually kitchen utensils, to me it's a kind of confirmation of the business of being alive and making a mark in the world.[41]

It's infinite: Peter Blake

Painting portraits is 'an intense business!' says Peter Blake. 'It's incredibly intimate painting a portrait from life. You're face to face with someone, and I just couldn't deal with it.'[42]

> The way I do a portrait, these days [early 2000s], is rather than have a sitter coming and sitting, as Coldstream would have done, or Frank Auerbach

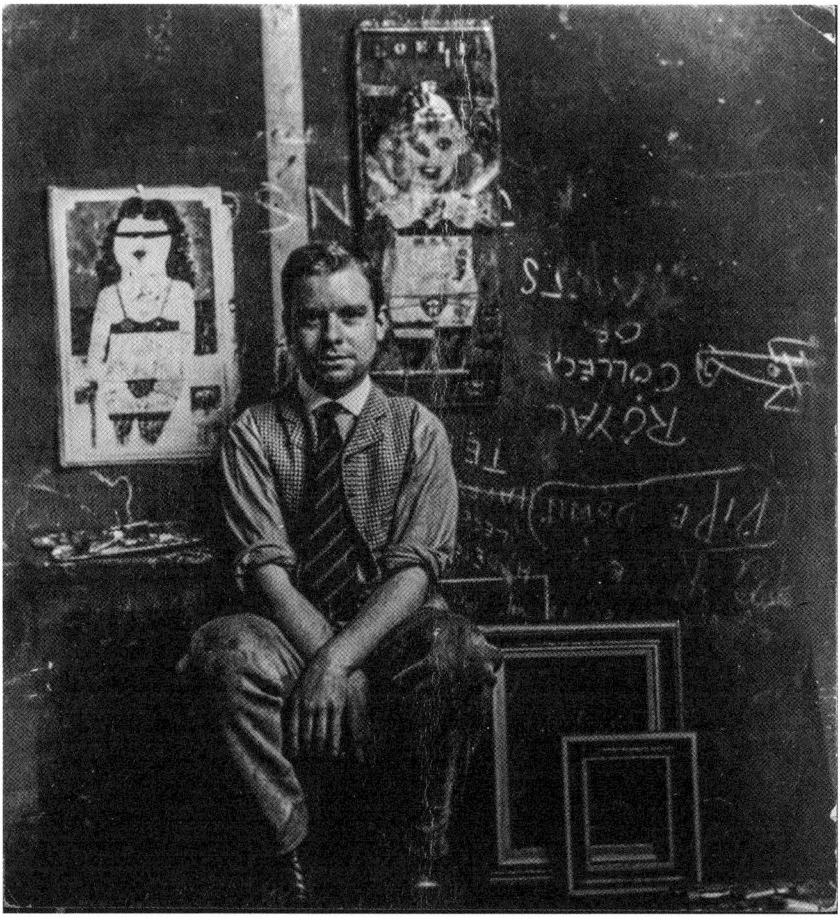

Peter Blake as a student at the Royal College of Art, 1955. Photograph by Robert Buhler.

> does, or Craigie Aitchison does, I assume that whoever I'm painting doesn't have time to do that, so they come and I take photographs, and then I work from the photographs. So the actual process [. . .] they're very casual photographs, I mean, I don't use a tripod. I don't pose people [. . .] And then I choose the one which I like most [. . .] What I would do now, same process [as photographic enlargement], but I would use a photocopy machine and photocopy it to the exact size I wanted [. . .] and then – photocopy paper is very thin, so I then would just put a sheet of transfer paper and draw on the photocopy. So that transfers a very exact image, so you're guaranteed a likeness, which is – as far as I'm concerned, that's the main thing in a portrait. It's got to look like somebody. Then I paint it as well and as beautifully as I can. What this short circuits is that other process of being an artist and having a sitter.[43]

With a sculpture, says Blake, there's a point when he knows that it's finished: 'I could add another piece of wood – but no, it's finished, it's polished, it's done.' With a painting, on the other hand, 'there's never a point like that':

> The way I try and work, I could always go on further, I mean [. . .] if I'm doing a portrait, you can start just by painting a pink circle, and it's a kind of portrait, and then you start to paint features, and you get a likeness, and then I paint the eyes, as detailed as I can. And then, to take it to the next stage, you paint the eyelashes, and then to the next stage, there might be a piece of dust on the eyelash. It's infinite, and so they're never really finished. Ever. So the moment of deciding when they're finished, normally, is just because it has to go. If it's something I'm painting for a show, the time for the show has arrived. But I don't think I've ever done a painting where I've been totally happy with and felt it's reached a conclusion. Well, it can never happen – there is no conclusion. Whereas with a sculpture there is.[44]

The placing of things: Lubaina Himid

At the start of her career, says Lubaina Himid, 'I wasn't interested in making paintings', but in cut-out figures, which were made from plywood and painted. Paintings, by contrast, 'weren't "in the room" enough.'

> I wanted to make things that were 'in the room', that weren't sort of special and distant, because I'd come from wanting to make theatre that was in the street, so the transition from theatre in the street to paintings in a gallery was enormous. So it took a long time to realise that paintings in a gallery were something that someone like me could make. You know, I understood that human beings had made them, but I still had that relation to them that they were otherworldly somehow, and I wasn't interested in that, in being that kind of artist. I was interested in being the sort of artist that you put a figure in a room – the room changes because there's another figure in the room that isn't real, but has a meaning. So it seemed at the time that perhaps works on the walls of domestic places were merely decorative. They were very pleasant but they didn't really make a difference to the room. But if you put a cut-out in a domestic place, domestic space, it changed how that space was. Doing theatre design made me very addicted to changing how space was. I knew that if you put an enormous table in a banqueting hall that was round, it was different than if you put a rectangular table. It just made the relationships and the actors different, so I understood that different furniture and the placing of things made a difference, and I wanted to make that difference in a domestic space, not on a set.[45]

Over time, Himid became more engaged in the technical and material process of painting the figures:

> I've always used the same paint and never used any other paint [. . .] it sounds nerdish somehow, but I've always used Liquitex acrylics ever since I, I don't know, I cannot remember a time when I didn't. And the great thing about them is the colour. The colour is incredibly pure. It's not chalky or you know, it has a fantastic quality, and what you put on is what you get, so it doesn't go darker or lighter and it mixes fantastically. So you can mix half a dozen different reds and get the real richness of red. As long as you don't use ultramarine ever, because it's always been sticky and it probably always will be. I don't know, they don't seem to get the mixture right. But there's something about those colours that I really love, and I use them in all sorts of different ways. You can use them as watercolours and you can use them like oils, so they come in sort of different consistencies and you can slap it on really thickly or you can thin it down to just almost nothing. And so I wasn't really particularly concentrating on, shall I say, the quality

of the painting, but I'm always, and always have been, most interested in the quality of the colour. So while I'm a person of many paintbrushes and many different ways of putting paint on, no one ever actually taught me how to paint [. . .] I'm a putter-on-er of colours [. . .] I very much mix paints on a palette, then I would mix it in jam-jar-fulls or vats full of colour [. . .] I've used it in all kinds of different ways actually. I've squeezed it straight from the tube and mixed it on the canvas. I have had whole periods of time where I paint it wet and then paint into the wet, where I've not primed the canvas, where I've painted straight on to wood so that it stains the wood rather than sits on the surface, or where I've primed the wood and it sits on the surface, you know. Whatever it is I'm working on I might do it a different way [. . .] I don't think I did any research at all, I think it was totally to do with 20-odd years of experimenting and seeing what works and what lasts, once I was into thinking, I hope this lasts a year and doesn't fall off the surface. No, I was never into looking at techniques or methods because I don't know, never thought about it. Never thought about pondering it in that way. Once I have an idea to do something, then I want to do it, so I try lots of things out.[46]

6

It Has Substance

On Sculpture

In this chapter, ten artists describe what it's like to work in a variety of sculptural media and idioms. Lynn Chadwick and Kenneth Armitage, who were born during the First World War and embarked on their careers just after the Second World War, are followed by a slightly younger generation, including Ralph Brown and Elisabeth Frink, who would also consistently base their work on the human figure, riding out the highs and lows of figure-sculpture's fortunes in the second half of the twentieth century. Their contemporaries Michael Kidner, Bryan Kneale, Kim Lim and Roland Piché, born between 1917 and 1938, are more concerned with structures and patterns, the properties and textures of materials, and the capacity of sculpture to embody or signify rather than represent. We've already encountered the moment, in Chapter 4, when a new phase of British sculpture was inaugurated – almost overnight, it seemed at the time – by Anthony Caro's first abstract metal constructions, and by Caro's radical rethinking of the way sculpture was conceptualised and taught. The reaction against object-based art of any kind that followed in the later 1960s and 1970s finds expression in Chapter 7. Born in the mid-1940s, David Nash and Phyllida Barlow (the youngest sculptors in the present chapter) both work with large, unwieldy components of the physical world beyond the studio – the way trees grow, the insistent otherness of *stuff* that confronts or obstructs us in street and home.

These curious figures: Lynn Chadwick and Kenneth Armitage

Lynn Chadwick (1914–2003) was born in Barnes, south-west London, into a conventional middle-class family. He struggled at school with undiagnosed

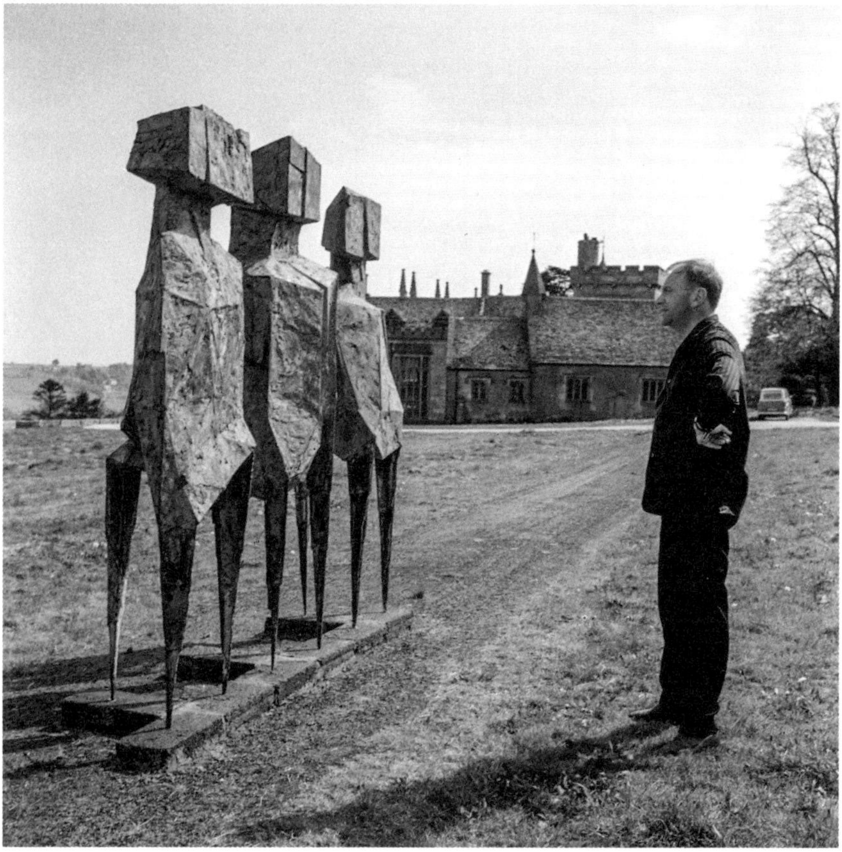

Lynn Chadwick with *The Watchers* outside his home at Lypiatt Park, near Stroud, early 1960s. Photograph by David Farrell.

dyslexia, became an architectural draughtsman and then underwent a few miserable wartime years piloting biplanes on Atlantic convoy duties. In 1944 he returned to his office desk, where post-war restrictions on building materials meant that he spent most of his time drawing parts for prefabricated housing and designing trade-fair stands. These he spritzed up with hanging mobiles. Chadwick always claimed to have been unaware of the mobiles that the American artist Alexander Calder had been making since the 1930s, but art collectors saw a connection and began to treat his work as art rather than design. By the summer of 1952, when Chadwick was selected with seven other youngish sculptors to represent Britain at the Venice Biennale, he was viewed as a leading figure of this new generation. At the 1956 Biennale, with a solo show this time, he won the International Sculpture Prize, for which the modernist master Alberto Giacometti had been widely tipped. It had all started, Chadwick recalls, when 'I was very lucky to be offered a small cottage in Gloucestershire, which cost almost nothing a week'.

> And I managed to survive there for ten years, on very, very little money. No, that was very good. It was a sort of formative period in my life, which allowed me to get on with doing something. I liked using my hands, making things. I was making mobiles to start with, and gradually I made things that were a bit more static, and gradually it came into sculpture, and I learned all kinds of things by myself. The only way I could learn is by having to do it. Sort of desert-island technique, really. You have to do it. If you have to do it, you do it.[1]

After taking a two-week crash course in welding, Chadwick evolved a personal method in which he used sheaves of narrow-gauge steel rods to construct a framework – sometimes resembling a human figure or animal – which he then filled and skimmed with very hard-setting concrete. He claims never to have known, when he picked up the oxyacetylene torch, what he was going to make.

> I used to weld something up, and I'd say, 'What does that resemble? What does that remind me of?' And if it's a bird, then I'd go on making it into a bird. If it's something else, an animal, I'd go on making it into some sort of animal, but not a specific animal. I couldn't do a portrait of an animal [. . .] Well, the actual welding technique that I use, tends to give more or less the form to my work, anyway. I'm very limited in that respect. I can't normally do rounded surfaces, not normally, anyway, certainly not volumes, rounded volumes. I can only do that by [. . .] doing my welding technique, and then adding something to it [. . .] I would love to [do rounded forms], yes. But you see, I mean, that my whole work would – would be no longer my work to other people. Whether that matters or not, I don't know, but anyway, I would no longer be recognised by my work. And I think that, somehow or other, we do like to be known for our work, the way we do things [and] it probably suits my attitude very well, the idea of the straight lines.[2]
>
> [. . .] Quite often the actual technique dictates what I'm going to do, but as I do it more or less instinctively, intuitively, I can't really explain why I

> do it. I don't know why I've got these lines here and there, in that particular place, it's the way they just come. And it's better – and it's better for me to let them just happen like that, rather than to be too intellectual about how they should be.[3]

In 1960 Chadwick produced a monumental group of three standing figures, titled *The Watchers*. Perhaps he'd have maintained that these massive sculptures too 'just happened'; yet, coaxed a little further, he hints at sculptural preoccupations that reach deeper and further than the strictly technical:

> They seem to be saying something [. . .] I haven't the slightest idea what they're saying, no. But, I mean, I can get the gist of it, the sense of it. I can usually get the sense of what people are thinking, but I couldn't say the words, but I know whether they're telling the truth or lying, that sort of simple difference like that [. . .] I used to watch, and I'd look at the Easter Island figure outside the British Museum, which has now been put somewhere else. But that always had a sort of message for me. I couldn't say what message it is, but a powerful feeling coming out of it.[4]
>
> [. . .] These curious figures, which I've made more abstract than the Easter Island ones, but they're just looking, apparently, into space, or – I don't know where. But that's the idea. And it's the – and the forms are merely to say it the way I want to say it. They're not, in any way, representative of anything. They're just shapes. Blobs on the horizon. You see, the Easter Island things, for me, have this great intensity of – of message, as it were, and I wanted to do the same thing.[5]

Another of the sculptors at the 1952 Biennale – the 'geometry of fear'[6] line-up – was Kenneth Armitage. He and Chadwick had first met at the annual boat-race party held by the artists Julian Trevelyan and Mary Fedden in their Hammersmith home. The two sculptors' careers would run parallel, until a bitter falling-out in the early 1970s, followed by reconciliation in the last years of their lives. Armitage's account of their meeting, recorded in 1991 while he and Chadwick were still estranged, reminds us that there are always at least two sides to any life story:

> People crowded into this [house], because they had a front-seat view of the whole thing going past the window [. . .] And there I met Lynn, and so we became almost instantly friends. And this friendship developed over a few

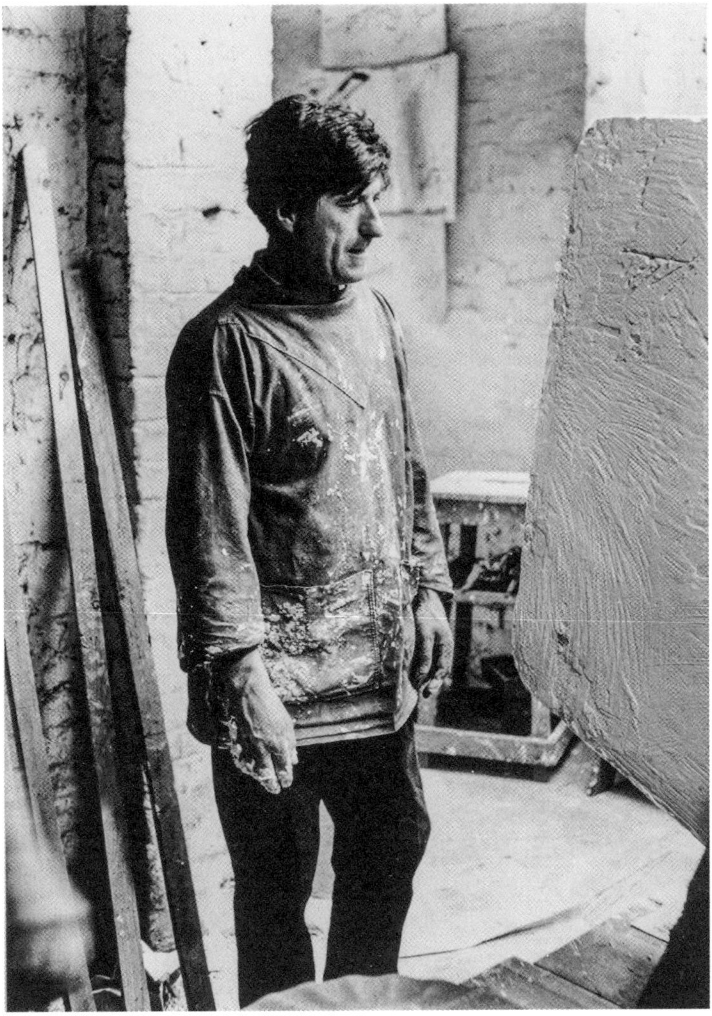

Kenneth Armitage in his studio in Notting Hill Gate, London, 1957. Photograph by Roger Mayne.

years. We made journeys abroad and so on. I was attracted really by his – he was very funny, and was great fun to go abroad with, that kind of thing. He was then working in metal, he was making mobiles *à la* Calder.[7] He went to try and find Calder. He went to America, but Calder wouldn't see him. He said, 'I don't meet imitators', which is a clue to the problems I had with Chadwick later. I liked Chadwick, but he had – he was totally different from

> myself and from Reg [Butler] in his attitude. He believed that you could help yourself to anything that anyone did. He said, 'We all do it.' Well we don't all do it. We do get influenced, but we didn't know that we're being influenced. But he ruthlessly picked what he wanted. For example, Reg Butler called the little figures in his maquette for the Unknown Political Prisoner [Competition],[8] *The Watchers*. Lynn liked that title, and he called almost everything *The Watchers* for three or four years. It went on and on and on. He liked the idea that Liz Frink had done polished areas, and he used polished areas[9] [. . .] He also got the idea of having an armature, filling it with filler, and then rubbing the armature down so that it was exposed, leaving little lines. He said he got that idea from me, but I don't want – this is only a technical device, I didn't attach any importance to it [. . .] Sometimes people said, 'We can't tell the difference between your work and Chadwick's.' And it also confused me. I found that sometimes when I was working, I would be thinking of him, you know, and it was just no good. Now, one thing I have not been short of is ideas to follow up, [whereas] Chadwick has remained with the work that he formed at that time. Now, I am not really running Lynn down, I'm just saying there was a difference.[10]

'He is a very good sculptor,' observes Chadwick of Armitage:

> The forms are very good and all that. But that's not quite the point. I like, like him. Yes, it is that. It's because the actual sculptural quality is right. He – he doesn't want to hear that, apparently. He wants to think that people can appreciate his expression, what he's saying, the violence to be coming through. And he likes that – that's what he wants to hear. And I don't want to know about the violence of his work.[11]

It was Chadwick, in fact, whose series of howling 'Beasts' and angular, visor-faced figures were often associated with anxiety, if not outright violence. Armitage's description of *People in the Wind* (1950), one of the sculptures that launched his international reputation at the 1952 Biennale, strikes a more humane note. This small bronze consists of a kind of clump of arrowhead- or wing-like torsos supported on stick legs. Tiny heads sprout on extended necks, while rudimentary arms and hands stretch out, as if in greeting. The fused figures are canted forwards, like people pushing against a stiff wind.

I got fascinated with Le Corbusier.[12] Now this affected my work, and so, instead of carving I started making little models, first of all maquettes, of things with an armature, which was standard, the way he – steel rods, iron rods, inside. I gave up clay modelling and modelled direct with plaster over wire netting, the usual kind of thing, with scrim on top [. . .] But first of all I made these little [clay] models. Now, I started – going back to the joins in the terracotta, I started joining figures together compulsively, I had to. And more and more, until they were one mass. Two or three figures would be unified into one mass, and then I could arrange the arms and legs as I wanted. Because if you look at a crowd, you don't count the arms and legs, you just see the odd arms swinging and the odd leg moving. You don't say there are six legs there and six arms and so on. And so I could use the arms as I wanted in the design of the maquette, which was a completely free thing to do. And then, one day in London [. . .] looking out the window on a very windy day, I saw a woman walking, holding two children, all three leaning against the wind. And I thought, oh, this is an idea. And I started making tiny maquettes with I think three figures, long necks, and they had a little bunch of arms in the front, extended forward with hands. And also, surrounding them were clothes flapping out in the wind, rather like washing on a line. Now, there were two or three things involved in this piece. First, seeing the actual people in London; second, the studio door had a little plant outside it, which I often – I saw every day, and it had half a dozen stalks coming up from a small area, absolutely upright and straight, and opening out at the top. And this impressed me; and also seeing washing on the line.[13]

'I had been very lucky in the 1950s,' reflects Armitage some 40 years later:

I had sales and exhibitions all over the place [. . .] But due to the British Council exhibitions abroad, I was better known abroad, and was better received abroad than I was here. About this time [1960s] the English habit was to follow American ideas on art, and perhaps still does. But the idea began to crystallise with people that I was wrong on two counts. I was wrong for being figurative, that is there was a figure basis to my work. This was a phase of abstract art in England.[14] There were various kinds, minimal art, there was all kinds of art, but it was not figurative art, and people had read that it was now something else. And so they thought, oh right, I'm stuck in the mud with something that had been done in the Renaissance and much earlier, for millions of years [. . .] which is of course nonsense, because figurative art goes on [. . .] Now the other thing that people attacked me for was using bronze casting. This I think they felt was a very ancient technique. It is, what, 4,500 years old? And we had the Bronze Age of course before the Iron Age. And this irritated people. It's very strange that in painting people accept that the technique is much the same. Oil painting is still used, and of course acrylic. But whereas oil painting has no corporeal reality, it's just marks on a surface, sculpture has a three-dimensional reality, it has substance.[15]

The individual image: Ralph Brown and Elisabeth Frink

'I remember being impressed, very impressed [. . .] by Armitage's sculpture of these figures in the wind,' recalls Ralph Brown. While at Leeds College of Art between 1948 and 1951, he'd been introduced to the work of contemporary European figurative sculptors Marino Marini and Giacomo Manzú:

I thought, well this is modern sculpture, but this is figurative, it's not like Moore and Hepworth [. . .] Because, at that particular time, in most art schools, particularly at the Royal College, the students were doing sub-Moore, sub-Frank Dobson, sub-Barbara Hepworth sculptures, this was the avant-garde. And so, many of us then, and there was a group of us in Leeds who had a strong reaction against this, and wanted to go back to figuration.[16]

Brown went on to study at the Royal College; in 1954 he was offered the chance to work in the Paris studio of the Russian-born sculptor Ossip Zadkine, whose colossal bronze figure *The Destroyed City* (1947–53) had recently been installed in Rotterdam. 'I used to say that he's not so much a sculptor as a good pastry-maker actually, but, not in front of him,' says Brown. 'I didn't particularly like his work. I quite liked the bloke [. . .] But it was useful being there.'[17]

When I came back from Paris, I didn't think of myself as a student. I felt completely different to them. I felt as if – I was thinking of myself as an artist, because I'd been living in a city which was full of artists who were

> working as artists [. . .] And, coming back, my motivation was much tougher than it had been before I went even. I'd done a lot of drawings when I was in Paris, of *clochards*, beggars, and I think perhaps because of Berger's influence,[18] maybe, I was very concerned about making, if you like, socially motivated sculpture [. . .] I wanted to make a great life-size sculpture with a great wall, and it would have been almost theatrical, really, with a whole group of figures sitting on benches and walking and sleeping.[19]

In 1955 the critic John Berger identified Brown as one of a number of young British artists, including the sculptor George Fullard and the painter Derrick Greaves, whose work he championed for its honest engagement – as he saw it – with social and political injustice. 'I don't think it's the right thing to do, to be socially motivated about one's work, in that sense, now,' Brown reflected in the late 1990s. Even in those early years, his sense of a sculpture's 'identity' sounds more physical than ethical:

> I started making complete figures which had their own image, as it were, and I began to become more preoccupied with the individual image, the individual identity of the objects that I made, so that they had – I wanted to make things that would live in a space, like a creature would live in a space, actually, in a house. And I had this feeling that I wanted to make something that was memorable in the sense that, if you walked into a sitting room and found a cow standing there, that would be memorable. And I wanted my sculpture to be memorable like that, if you see what I mean. You know, like – 'I remember that room because there was this cow, sculpture, whatever, standing in the middle.' Something which had an identity.[20]

In 1960 Brown was commissioned to make a public sculpture for Harlow, one of the new towns constructed after the war in response to the devastation and overcrowding in central London.

> They asked me whether I would be interested in submitting a maquette, a sketch model, for the Market Square. And in fact I didn't much like the Market Square. I didn't find all the contemporary architecture very endearing actually. It was all sort of very – it seemed to me to be rather sterile, and rigid and, not terribly sympathetic. I suppose, Harlow was only just starting as a town, and it was rather a bleak and empty and open space.

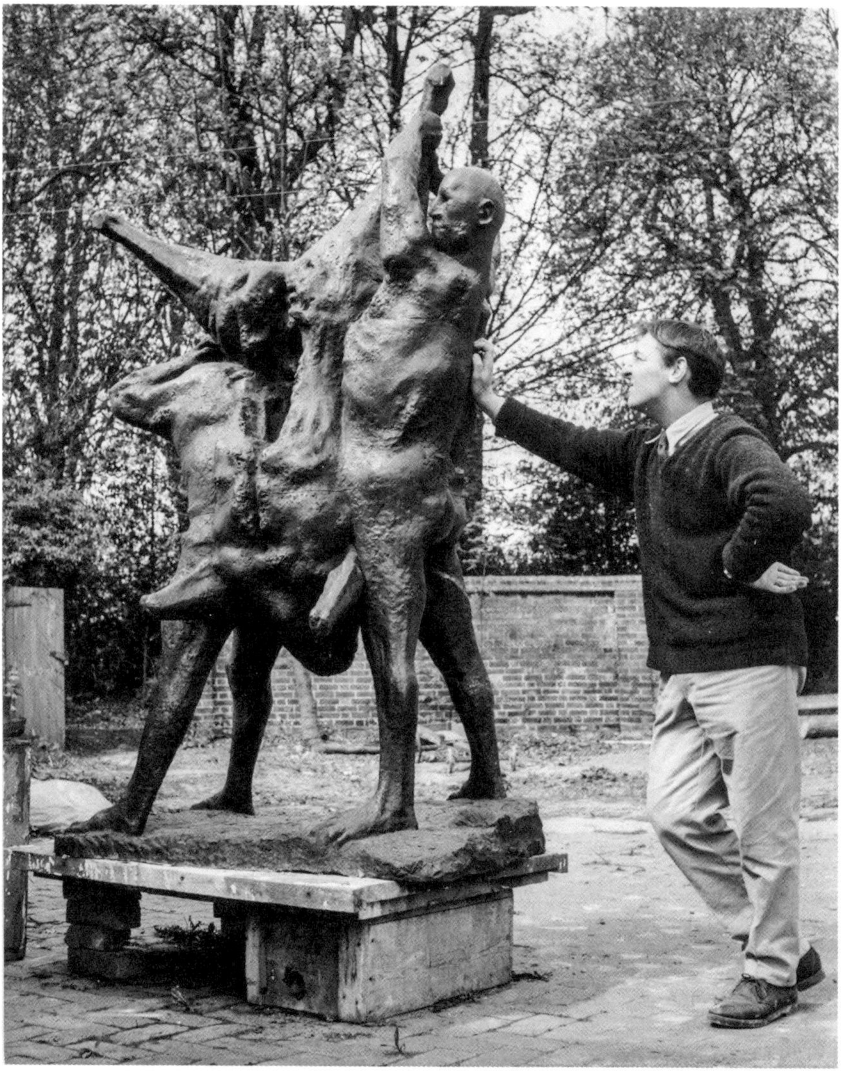

Ralph Brown with *The Meat Porters* outside his studio at Digswell, Hertfordshire, 1959. Photograph by D.J. Williams.

> And I thought, the best thing to do is, drop a few bombs in the middle of it actually. And so my sculpture [*The Meat Porters*] was really rather like a sculptural bomb actually, it went off in all directions. And it was dirty, and it was about blood and men working hard and sweating and all this sort of thing. It was, I suppose – it wasn't a social-realist sculpture, but it was what I tend to dislike about sculpture [. . .] it tended to be rather rhetorical. But it made the right shape in the space. It was an organic shape. But I put an enormous amount into that sculpture of myself, I think. There were a lot of natural forms in it. I went down to Smithfield[21] and did quite a lot of drawings of the bummarees, the porters at Smithfield, and carcasses and things. I was also very impressed as well by a picture that I'd seen in the *Voices of Silence*, in Malraux's book,[22] of Rembrandt's *Flayed Ox*, and it combined all sorts of things. The textures in the sculpture had to do with rocky surfaces, the sorts of surfaces which I enjoyed and liked as a rock climber and a potholer, all that sort of thing, which I still used to do at that time, going up to Yorkshire and Skye and Wales and things, rock climbing.[23]

Late in life, perhaps feeling that, by the 1990s, his commitment to a sculptural idiom he'd first developed 40 years earlier looked anachronistic, Brown states his case:

> Sculpture is making things, sculpture is nothing – if it's not the art of making things, then I don't know what it is actually. I mean, I suppose really it comes down to that. So far as my own work is concerned, I'm a reactionary old bastard actually, if you like, and, I've found that I can look back now and get more pleasure out of looking at Egyptian sculpture, or looking at sculpture of the eighteenth century. Even marble carvers like Bernini and Canova – I'll look at this with a fresh eye.[24]

Elisabeth Frink (1930–93) was born in Thurlow, Suffolk, and studied at Guildford School of Art, where she was taught by Willi Soukop, then at Chelsea School of Art, where she started to sculpt in plaster on armatures, a method she would use throughout her career. The first of these works to be cast in bronze, *Bird* (1952), was acquired by the Tate when Frink was just 21. She describes her early sculptures as, 'Men and birds, and horses' heads, very strange, sort of gothic, rather apocryphal figures, very gloomy.'[25] There followed a series of falling figures and winged men, including a 1964 public commission for Manchester Airport.

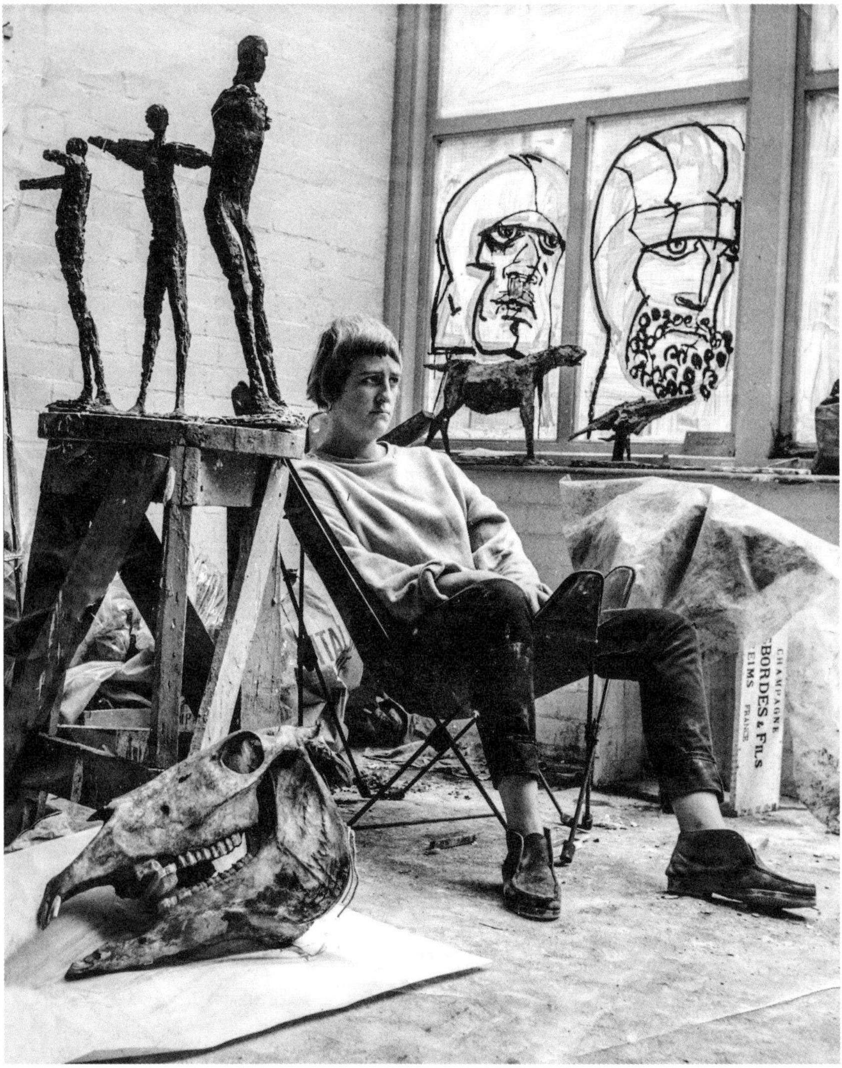

Elisabeth Frink in her studio at Fleming Close, London, *c.*1959.
Photographer unknown.

Frink's later life-size and larger male figures and horses have a muscled, athletic solidity, reminiscent of classical sculpture (she admired the ancient Riace bronzes).

At Chelsea between 1949 and 1953, Frink recalls:

> We were all immensely cheerful, and busy getting on with what we wanted to do, busy enjoying ourselves, because after the war, it was fairly austere, because I was still on rationing when I went to Chelsea Art School. The clothes were terrible! [. . .] Well, I mean, we had to take our jerseys in, or paint them, or cut down our jeans, or do something mad. And we all used to go off to the jazz club [. . .] I don't think any of us were particularly aware of what was going on in America. Probably the older people were, I wasn't. I mean, we were very insulated [. . .] And we still couldn't go abroad much. None of us had any money. I mean, petrol was still very short, and my next trip abroad was when I was 20, when four of us, or five of us, went to Paris, and that was wonderful [. . .] Oh, I discovered Giacometti, Brancusi, the Museum of Modern Art, the Musée Rodin. Fantastic! [. . .] And I saw Giacometti, you know, sitting in a cafe. Well, once we knew he went there, we used to [go] and sit quietly in a corner, like little mice, and look at this wonderful face. You know, it was fantastic. And we lived on bread and tomatoes and cheese. We had no money. It was great.[26]
>
> [. . .] I suppose my earlier role model was Rodin, probably. And, after that I discovered Giacometti and the way he built up in plaster. And I moved much more in that direction, and I worked in plaster of Paris then, and I still do, direct.[27]
>
> [. . . Using] scrim and chicken wire, yes, and then, finally, solid plaster, and, very much the technique that I'm using now [. . .] I used to work it down with an axe [. . .] and then eventually chisels and files, any old thing, really [. . .] I can get something up very quickly, which is the wonderful thing about plaster.[28]
>
> [. . . In 1964] I did the Manchester Airport, big aluminium flying figure. A memorial to Alcock and Brown.[29] It's a big, 14-foot long, horizontal winged figure, and it was nude [. . .] It had a helmet on. And when he was installed in the airport, I mean, there were people shouting 'Disgusting!' before they had the wrap taken off. And then the mother, the great-granddaughter of Alcock, or Albrown, or whatever the hell they were [. . .] She came up and said – she had a fleet of children behind her and said, 'It's disgraceful!' she said. 'Disgraceful!' she said, 'Why does it have to be nude?'

And I said, 'Well, I want it to be a symbolic figure, and I didn't want to do just another old flying man.' And she turned on her heels and walked away, with all these kids following her! [*laughs*] [. . .] I was in a tail end, when I did that birdman, it was the tail end of my birdmen period, anyway. I thought it was entirely suitable, that's really why I did it. I knew it would be controversial. Still, it's still there somewhere, stuck up round the airport![30]

[. . .] At the end of my stay in France [in the late 1960s], I started doing horses again. I mean, really, for the first time in sculpture. Because, apart from the horse's head previously – very, very early – I didn't involve horses at all. And this is mainly because I bought a horse, to teach my son to ride, and also to ride again, myself, down there. And also I got to know the Camargue horses, which are wonderfully wild, primitive animals. And I was fascinated by how they moved and looked. So all the next series of sculptures of horses and things, are all based on that. The horse in its primitive sense [. . .] I'm much more interested in the relationship between the man and the horse, and not particularly the shape of either, if you see what I mean. But the nice thing was that this horse used to be in the stable under the studio, and he used to sleep, lie down, and never minded when I pottered in there to have a look at him. It started me off on a whole series of lying-down horses [. . .] They have a very close relationship, for millions of years, man and horse, that's what interests me. You know, the horse has done so much for man – works for him, carries him to battle, and yet has retained its independence in a strange way, that it can, in a flash, transform everything by chucking him off. And I like that idea [. . .] But also the horse is very put-upon, of course, because man has this capacity of loving the animals who live with him but also being very cruel.[31]

[. . .] I mainly think of sculpture for the outdoors, if I'm doing a big piece, yes. Although I do like to see my big pieces inside, confined in a gallery, because it gives them a marvellous sense of busting out, which I quite like, for a change.[32]

Behind the scenes: Michael Kidner and Bryan Kneale

Michael Kidner (1917–2009) was born in Kettering, Northamptonshire; after academic studies (history and anthropology at Cambridge) and wartime service in the Canadian army, he briefly attended an art and design course at

Goldsmiths' College. In the early 1950s he studied in Paris with the Cubist painter André Lhote. By the 1960s Kidner was exploring colour and form as pure optical sensation, showing alongside Bridget Riley in the exhibition 'The Responsive Eye' at the Museum of Modern Art, New York, in 1965. In 1969, wanting to see what happened when the illusory three-dimensionality of Op art painting became actual, Kidner began experimenting with sculpture.

> I got rather suspicious of painting at a certain stage. I felt it was too easy to hide what you didn't want to show in a painting, you know, just to present the Garden of Eden and not anything else. And I felt that once you went into three dimensions it was like looking behind the scenes. And so, more and more, in the 80s I was making three-dimensional objects.[33]
>
> [. . .] I had seen a column in an exhibition in Washington at the Henry Gallery,[34] which had rather impressed me. And it was to do with colour, and it was a column where there were little gold flecks sunk into the surface, so that the surface seemed to be deep, rather like looking into water. You could sort of look into the surface. And I thought I would like to try and achieve a surface like that, but I didn't – I started by picking up a stick out of the garden and painting it, and thinking every day I'll paint another coat and another coat. And this would go on for at least a year, building up a surface. And then I thought, well this is silly. If I'm going to paint this stick and it's going to take me a year, I might as well paint something more interesting. And so I began to play with – actually it was with some of Og's[35] building bricks, I just began to see what sort of shape I could get interested in. And then I built this column which has two profiles, one with a single curve in it and one with a double curve, and that seemed interesting. And so then I – another thing which has bothered me in my career is always confronting new techniques and never being a real master at any. But in order to make this column I got into fibreglass and making – there was a teacher, one of the technicians at Corsham[36] was a specialist in fibreglass, so I was able to get his directions and advice. And I must have spent months making this wretched column, first out of these wooden blocks and then skinning the wooden blocks with P38,[37] stuff you mend cars with, and then polishing it and separating it and then casting the mould in order to cast the column, and so on. But anyway, I eventually got this column. And then the column began to interest me as a – the fact that a wave changes according to your angle. And so then I began to wonder how I could in fact paint a

> three-dimensional line, is what it amounted to, and so I started rotating the column and recording the rotations, and evolving a pattern. And that occupied me from '69 till '72 virtually.[38]

Possibly referring to his fibreglass and elastic constructions of the mid-1990s (when Kidner recorded his interview for Artists' Lives), he observes that, 'sculptors don't regard it [my work] as sculpture'.

> It's three-dimensional [but] it doesn't seem to have a category [. . .] I know Phillip King[39] said that I'm not a sculptor. I don't know what he would call it [. . .] I certainly see it as three-dimensional, and if I take [Naum] Gabo's kind of description of sculpture then, yes I do.[40] It's sculpture of volume. You see, whereas I think painters are mainly concerned with space, sculptors are mainly concerned with volume. Yes, and it's a bit of a sort of hybrid between those, because – I don't know how I categorise myself.[41]
>
> [. . .] If your mind does wander when you're making something quite systematic, where can you let it wander to? Because you can't stop the job in hand, or it'll go wrong [. . .] Half the things I think about never get realised, they sort of pass by. It would be nice to do this while I'm bored doing what I'm doing. It would be interesting if I did this instead of that. And sometimes I make a little note on a piece of paper, but I very rarely pursue them. And I must say, when I go up [to the studio] with no idea I don't often think of these ideas that I've, as it were, shed. They don't seem to have much substance, but they are prolific, sort of prolific unrealised. If I stopped to think how I would do it, I might not do it. But when I'm bored but occupied, they come of their own accord, you know. If I'm not occupied and I'm waiting for them, they don't come.[42]

Like Kidner, Bryan Kneale started out as a painter, studying at the Royal Academy Schools between 1948 and 1952 and then making a reputation as a portraitist. By his late 20s, he recalls, 'I was going round in a circle, nothing was progressing and I wasn't happy at all.'

> I went back to the Isle of Man, and we had a little cottage up in the hills and I decided to start all over again as if I'd never painted a picture in my life. And I went out and drew hedges and things, and eventually I ended up working in a cave, and I did a lot of drawings and watercolours and things –

well, ink drawings – of the inside of a cave and the outside of a cave. And I realised that I was doing a head, I was getting inside the head. And that was a breakthrough, because I thought, well, I'm going to actually make a head, I'm gonna go through it, and I've painted the outside and inside. And I did several paintings, quite a few paintings on that idea [. . .] And it's, around that time – I had always resisted the idea of making three-dimensional objects because I'd seen myself as being a painter. And I didn't want to know any sculptors. I knew Frink very well actually, but I wasn't connected with the idea of making sculptures. Anyway, my brother-in-law, who actually was a farmer, and he did a tremendous amount of metalwork – welding and so on and so forth – and I'd resisted the idea of having a go, and one day I said, well, would he show me how you weld metal together? And the instant I laid my hands on this, I realised that this is what I should have been doing.[43]

[. . .] When I first started making sculpture, the thing that really amazed me, there were so few people making sculpture, certainly in an adventurous sort of way, there were hardly any people doing it. The great era of the early 50s, when you had the people like Robert Adams and Meadows and Chadwick and Butler, was long over. And the second explosion took place in the early 60s. I mean there'd been the other side of things, there'd been Liz Frink, there'd been Ralph Brown, Bob Clatworthy and various other people who were continuing to work in the figurative tradition. And there'd been George Fullard and Hubert Dalwood,[44] who later became totally abstract. But there really were very few people making sculpture in the early 60s. Anyway, by the end of the 60s there was a vast army, all Caro's students of course, apart from anything else. There was Phillip King and [William] Tucker and [Tim] Scott and all that lot. Anyway, what we thought was people would positively rejoice to see all our wonderful stuff. Far from it. We met with rage and hostility beyond belief. Beyond belief. In fact it was quite shocking some of it. I remember Garth Evans showed in Cardiff an enormous steel piece, and it took him about three years to get over the reception. In fact the next time he showed a piece in the Holland Park show,[45] it consisted of a dustbin with a tape recording of the vile comments from the local rags in it.[46]

In 1962 London County Council commissioned Kneale to produce a sculpture for Fenwick Place housing estate in Lambeth (it has since disappeared), for which he decided to work in slate.

> I was very used to the idea of using slate, because it was the farmers' material from the Isle of Man for making gates, hedges and things like that [. . .] There were very few trees in the early days so they used slate instead. And you saw the iron emerging from the slate gateposts and of course going back, these great slates were carved into the old Norse crosses.[47] So I was very familiar with it as a medium, and I still often think about the way it was handled. Anyway, I went up to north Wales and in the quarries in Blaenau Ffestiniog, which was then still just about operative as a working quarry. I rootled around and we went down into the bowel of the quarry. We went down almost a mile. It was extraordinary, because it was like a cathedral of slate, and the men used to blast and then they'd go down there and they'd chain themselves to the walls of the quarry and prise the huge lumps of slate off, and sometimes they came down with the slate of course. And I remember saying to them, 'What happens?' And they said, 'Ah well, we'll show you the accident book when we get up to the top.' So sure enough, there'd been a lot of broken limbs and dead bodies [. . .]
>
> There was a place called the Oakeley Quarry,[48] and it was like a huge extinct volcano with a hole in the bottom, which was actually just like the descent into hell. There was this terrible hole, and with the loose slate held back by massive conglomerations of chains, and then a vertical ramp going right down. You got on a trolley, and you could see far in the distance two tiny specks of light, and they were the lights and the lamps of the miners' hats, and you'd go down there to the very end, and then you'd go down another level and another level until you were well under a mile – it was very hot down there by the bottom there – and it was a terrible place.[49]

How the surface is arrived at: Kim Lim and Roland Piché

Travelling between London and her native Singapore, Kim Lim would stop over in India, Greece and South East Asia to visit ancient sites. She loved the gentle geometries of Cycaldic stone-carvings and the graceful lines of Chinese Han Dynasty bronzes. Lim carved her early sculptures from wood; from about 1980, however, she worked increasingly in pale stone, often shaped into horizontal or vertical blocks and incised with delicately curving, quasi-geometric lines and fissures.

I really want the lines [carved in the stone] to actually in the end look like something that flows together and that you're not conscious of each line, you know, you just look at it and it's there. And then, of course, when you start analysing, you realise it's a line that stops there, and then another one that stops further along. But the first impact I'm always trying to get at, is to see the whole thing as a kind of finished piece, a kind of melody that's there with a tune, if it doesn't sound daft [. . .] I have a piece like this that's been going on since 1989 [for six years] and I still haven't finished it. It's a piece in granite, and it's just very difficult, and I've changed my mind at least 50 times [. . .] I keep on chopping, and it's getting smaller [. . .] It was quite a big block, so at least it's lost 6 inches all over, you know, and I just keep cutting it. And it just doesn't work for me, so I just leave it and go back at it [. . .] It's a vertical block with grooves running up and down vertically. But I had – I think the problem was that I had too many ideas for that, and sometimes that is a mistake. You can't put too many things in one piece, it just can't carry it – for me anyway. I mean some people can work in a very complex way and get away with it, but not for me. I need to have a simple structure that holds. At least it doesn't work for me for the moment, still, and I'll keep at it [. . .] And then sometimes when I'm working on another piece, my eye keeps shifting to it, and then inevitably I move – I mean that's a very bad thing, I should cover it up, because it distracts me from what I'm doing. But, it's one of the ones that's really challenging me, and I think, one of these days I'll get you! [*laughs*][50]

[. . .] I was very aware of water, because everywhere I lived, you know, I was very close to the sea, spent a lot of time seeing things floating, and very aware of rain, there was always torrential rain, and so the rhythms of water running was one of the elements that's very close to one's being [. . .] I love it when I'm inside and I hear rain at night. It really is, really heavy stuff, you know, I really love it. [The quality of light in Singapore] would be very dramatic, either it would be very thundery and the whole sky would go very grey, or sometimes there would be shafts of sunlight and – I mean never the very soft, all over non-light, like winter here [in Britain], which is what depresses me intensely. I feel as if I'm living under water, because it's murky and I don't like that. I like it to be really kind of clear and bright, and the light there is never murky.[51]

[. . .] I've always liked repetition, and things that create a vibration by just having more of it than just one. I don't know where that's come from, but it's certainly a very strong key to my work [. . .] I think sometimes I like to kind of build up a sense of repetition so that you can continue it yourself without actually doing it. I think if I can infer something in a work, I would like that very much [. . .] I just think that you could go over the top, repeating too much, but if you just set up a pattern, you know, it creates an image which the person looking at it would respond to and continue. I think in the end that's what one tries to do really – a metaphor to trigger off a response in a person, because obviously the observer would come with a totally different set of references from your own, so you can't always impose what you want to infer on the person. I mean there's a great hope that they will get what you're trying to do, and if they do it's a great bonus. I mean sometimes when people have seen exhibitions of mine and have written to me, and I've never known them at all, and say how they feel about it, I mean it's the greatest pleasure for me to find that, ha! You know, they have actually got it – that I'm not mad.[52]

[. . .] I suppose when I'm making them [sculptures], it doesn't actually occur to me at all, wanting to communicate, I mean, I just have the desire to make this thing [. . .] and I suppose if you look back in the early things [in museums], that repetition appears a lot in the decoration and embellishment of things that people made [. . .] I mean decoration in the best sense of the word, of trying to [. . .] add something and enrich your experience, and not just elaborate for the hell of it. Because I think decoration has got a very bad [. . .] meaning these days, because it's kind of slight and things, considered, you know, not important. But when you look back in the early, early parts. We went to Turkey in September and it was a wonderful experience, because we went to this [archaeological] dig, which is the earliest human urban habitation found to date, called Çatalhöyük,[53] and you would think that people who made pots and things there would just have crude vessels for functional use. But no, they have the most beautiful kind of decorations on them, paintings, and very abstract designs. A great sense of balance, or else a kind of geometric repetition, you know – very, very thoughtfully and sensitively done, in very basic colours. But my goodness they were beautiful. So it was in a way very reassuring to see these things done 6,300 years ago, where the need is there.[54]

Roland Piché (b.1938) was born in London and studied at Hornsey College of Art, followed by the Royal College of Art and a year assisting Henry Moore in 1963–4. By his late twenties he was already having considerable success, with sculpture selected for the landmark 1965 'New Generation' exhibition at the Whitechapel Gallery and a solo show at Marlborough Gallery in 1967. Piché's work has always eluded classification: in the 1960s and 1970s he constructed geometric space frames, around and within which stretchy-looking organic shapes swing, hang or stick; by the 1990s he was carving or casting hieratic figure sculptures.

> Before I went to Hornsey College of Art, I was aware of Reg Butler, Henry Moore, and I used to make sculptures in the garden, and I would go to bombed churches, because there was a lot of bombed buildings in those days, and get metal and bring it back. And I'd wire it together to make structures, and I'd need cement to seal it, and I'd get stone and wheel it back from Tottenham, I remember, to make stone sculptures, and carve and set the stone inside these metal constructions. And I was also interested in using coloured glass to find an equivalent to experiences that I might be thinking of. And I made about five to eight sculptures which didn't look like any one sculpture, but they originated from Reg Butler's working in space.[55]
>
> [. . .] When I was at Hornsey, Oliffe Richmond,[56] a New Zealander who'd worked as an assistant to Moore, came to teach at Hornsey, and he took us down to meet Moore, to see the studios in Much Hadham. And Moore for me was a giant. Everywhere I looked at contemporary sculpture, Moore blocked the path. Yes, there was America, there were other ways of going, but he was someone that one had to face and come to terms with. So when we went to see the studios down there and we were lined up on this nice sunny day to meet him, we were introduced. And I was at the end of the line, I was in my black T-shirt, being very physical and he said, 'And what do you do?' And I said, 'Well, I'm a sculpture student.' And he said, 'Well I knew you were,' he said, 'because in my day you'd either go to the boxing rings in the fairgrounds to make money or you'd go into sculpture.' That's romantic enough that isn't it? But he was such a disappointing man. He's just a little guy, very apologetic and very nice, I couldn't acquaint this giant I'd formed in a line that makes these huge wonderful sculptures.[57]
>
> [. . .] A first principle of sculpture [. . .] is how light hits surface, i.e. its surface tension, which is the most difficult, the most sophisticated principle of all in sculpture in particular – how the surface is arrived at, between what's inside and what's outside and the way light hits it, which has been a

traditional concern within sculpture from Rodin [. . .] and into the kind of sculptors I was interested in.[58]

[. . .] I put this huge 25 foot x 25 foot sculpture [*Crucifix in 4 Parts*, 1972] up in Holland Park, London, which was as a result of, well what do you do with a big sculpture like that? [. . .] And I remember the site they'd given me was by the peacock garden, and it was on a great sloping part of the park, so I had to build up these six different platforms, and then erect it with cranes and everything into position. And then there were these 25 foot steels going up. And having done all that, I then had to go up on ladders and paint it, and it was windy on the day that I was going up there, and 20 foot off the ground on a ladder that you've tied so it won't fall, on sloping terrain with trees moving around in the wind, and you're painting it with a reddy-pink colour. And I remember the path came round where the people would go, and I remember this person saying, 'I hope you're not going to leave that here.' So I'm holding on for dear life, like on a boat, painting, and he said, 'I have this walk every day and I really object to you putting this here.' And I thought, well, I'm doing it for you, out of the kindness of my bank manager, and I'm putting myself at risk – however, that's my problem [. . .] Well, the moral of the story is that people instinctively don't like what they don't understand. I didn't like maths at school because I didn't understand maths. I didn't like Latin, because I didn't understand it. Just because you don't understand the language, doesn't make the language have nothing to say.[59]

Object and process: David Nash and Phyllida Barlow

David Nash talks about the different ways in which he has shaped and worked with trees, from his first experiments with a felled ash and an axe to *Wooden Boulder* and *Wooden Waterway*, both of which he started in 1978. *Wooden Boulder* was a huge, roughly carved ball left on a hillside in North Wales, from where it travelled – slipping, rolling, river-borne and sometimes pushed along, until, after a long disappearance, it reappeared in 2009 in the Dwyryd Estuary. Nash constructed *Wooden Waterway* during a residency at Grizedale in the Lake District.

The local council decided to make some playing fields [in Blaenau Ffestiniog] and they cut some trees down, one of which was an ash, and

I bought it for £1 this trunk, which was about 16 inches in diameter and about 10 foot long. And they dropped it over in the road for me and I rolled it across the road into my front yard, and just using an axe I just cut just a very simple round form. And I was then consciously trying to address this problem that I am still having with anxiety and about the process of working, how to work, and sort of realising that I wanted to make a real wood object, and how would I make that? And I would use an axe, a very, very simple, you know, age-old tool, and just to cut the very simplest form. And when that roundish form came off the main trunk of the tree, that would be it, and then, I found that object so interesting and the process so satisfying I just went and made another one and another one and another one, and I actually changed the sides of the axe as the tree got smaller, so that the mark of the axe on the wood would remain consistent with the scale, though the pieces were getting smaller. And I just had nine of them. And it was just like an exercise I had given myself as an experiment in a process, so that the object was a pure result of the most simple process of working with wood.[60]

[. . .] I gradually worked more and more into the reality of what wood is. So at first I thought I was working with wood, and at first it was unrecognisable – they were planks and old bits of demolition wood, beams, that had been squared up. And then working with fresh wood, and the fact of it cracking and bending and warping – there was a behaviour. And then, when meeting the anthroposophy of Rudolf Steiner, there was quite a comprehension of the elements and of the temperaments. And realising that of course wood is a weave of earth and light. If you look at an acorn, the whole tree is in there, the whole potential, but it needs a whole activity and environment and a drawing-in of these elements for it to actually fulfil the potential which is in that contracted seed. An acorn is a contracted oak tree. And it became quite obvious that really what I was working with isn't really wood, or tree, it's the elements [. . .] emphasising the various elements. The *Wooden Waterway* in Grizedale and the *Wooden Boulder* emphasise water, the presence of water. The *Wooden Waterway* in Grizedale, to go back to Grizedale for a moment – Blaenau Ffestiniog has 120 in of rain per annum, and one of the things that we were really looking forward to, going to Grizedale, getting out of Blaenau, was to getting out of this rain. And then we discovered Grizedale is the second wettest place in Britain, and all through February it rained, and then to March, six weeks it was raining. And then, it continued to

> rain but the ground was drying out, but I realised it was all going up the trees. As the spring began to unfold the trees demanded the water, and although it was still raining it was drying underfoot. And I was aware then, physically aware, of the incredible tonnage of water which is involved in the process of trees growing [. . .] and I wanted to make something which said something about water and wood, and about the flow of water in wood. And I found two trees which had fallen down and were lying downhill, and they were near a stream, and I was able to divert [the stream] through troughs. And I imagined it would only last a few weeks, it was purely an experimental piece. But it was astonishing, now we are 17 years on from there, and it's still running, and people have looked after it [. . .] and people walking by and people who actually spot it, and they go and they understand what was meant, you know, there are bits fallen off, or the trough isn't aligned right and they will straighten it up or take stones out of it, leaves out of it. So water and wood, *Wooden Boulder*, *Wooden Waterway*.[61]

Phyllida Barlow talks about what it was like, in the early 1990s, making sculpture at home but receiving little external encouragement and few, if any, offers to exhibit her work.

> I took work onto the streets. Those works up there are the few out of about 30 that survived. They survived on the streets for about six months, actually, and then I decided to bring them back into the house again. One was down – just on a very nice, old-fashioned rubbish bin [in] Kings Cross. Another one was stuffed – there were two lamp posts, and I rammed one in between it. And then, yes, various other ones – but I never took photographs. I *have* taken photographs of things I've left on the street [. . .] I think, looking back on it, it was the most liberating time, because, sort of releasing the objects into the world, and not knowing whether they would survive or not, in a way meant they truly had a life without me. And I remember taking some of the smaller ones and very late at night, on Waterloo Bridge, just throwing them into the Thames. And that was fantastic. And then a passer-by got very annoyed with me, because they saw it as extremely dangerous, and it was about two in the morning. And they were right, you know. They were saying, what happens if a boat goes . . . ? And I, in my fervour to do this gesture of finding a place for these works – because that's really what it was – was hell-bent on chucking them in the Thames, regardless of who was

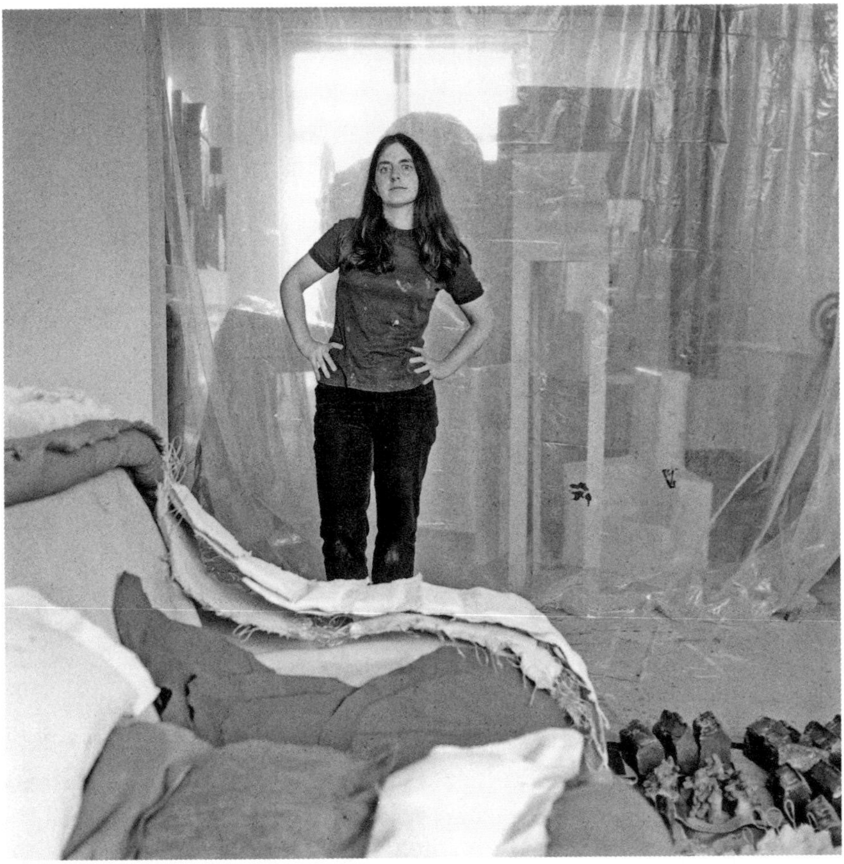

Phyllida Barlow in her studio in Finsbury Park, London, 1971. Photograph by John Malcolm Couzins.

underneath! [*laughs*] Which was very selfish in some ways. But yes, it was very liberating. But there was a haunting fear that the work was worthless – I don't mean in terms of money, but in terms of its creative worth. It had no worth, it had no – the only point it had was my desire to make it. And that, I suppose, taught me that that's actually quite an important experience to have – where going it alone is something where you are open to all sorts of experiences about making, because there is no responsibility to do anything else [. . .] [In 1995] I had a small show at the Henry Moore [Institute], in the library, and that was an absolutely, a fantastic experience.[62]

Ten years later, Barlow was exhibiting large-scale sculptures and installations internationally. Her *untitled: upturnedhouse, 2* (2012), now in the Tate, stands about 16 foot high and resembles an improvised cabin, clad in a patchwork of painted wood panels. Tilting to one side, as if about to topple, it feels both four-square and unstable, simultaneously a refuge and a hazard. Barlow recounts the story, heard by chance while listening to the radio, which sparked off her series of three 'upturnedhouse' constructions.

> There was a big documentary on Radio 4, which I'm sort of addicted to when I'm alone in the studio [. . .] And the reporter had gone to New Orleans quite soon after Katrina[63] had happened and was interviewing some of the people who had been stuck on the top of the stadium building [including a man who, when the floodwaters subsided] decided to go and find his house [. . .] and he set out on the journey, and he described his journey of leaving the centre of New Orleans [. . .] and how, as he walked, the mud, which was becoming solid, got thicker and thicker until he was wading through it, up to his knees, and he was trying the whole time to get his bearings, but the entire landscape, the urban landscape, had changed beyond recognition, and then way in the distance he recognised this tree, that was stripped of everything [. . .] and then far away, beyond the tree, was this, this strange image that was, that had this colour, this very pale-blue colour, which was the colour of his house, and yet it didn't look like his house in any way at all. So he walked towards it, and by then it was really treacherous, he didn't actually know what he was walking on, but he had to get to this pale-blue structure, and it *was* his house, but it was turned completely upside down [. . .] His shock, and his description of how he confronted this upturned house, when he finally realised it was his own home, was so sculptural, and so vivid, it was to me as though he was describing a piece of sculpture [. . .] and it was just an incredibly moving, vivid, very, very special account of a structure, you know, I don't think he mentioned the word 'house' [. . .] it was all, that very poetic thing of being able to actually describe something without naming it, you know, that I thought was so compelling. And that's where, for me, these three 'upturnedhouses' have come from.[64]

7

The Strength of an Idea

Conceptual and Performance Art

We've already met John Latham as a former painting student, picking up a spray gun as a way of 'making paint do something that it hadn't done before'.[1] By the 1960s, Latham was pushing his work even further towards performance and conceptual practice. 'The whole business about conceptual work,' he explains, concerns 'the strength of an idea'. It seemed to him 'that an idea was as strong and as lasting, if it was a good idea, as a work, as an object.'[2] The belief that an artist's primary medium is thought rather than paint and canvas, chisel and stone, wasn't exactly new; earlier in the twentieth century it had been forcefully articulated by Marcel Duchamp and Naum Gabo, among others. But the second half of the 1960s were a tipping point, when media such as photographic installation, video and performance art moved from the margins into mainstream exhibition spaces and the public consciousness. Artists in Europe, America and Asia explicitly rejected art's 'collectible, tradeable, valuable objectness',[3] often – as in Latham's or Paul Neagu's work – creating objects that were then destroyed or consumed in the course of a performance. Artists also sought direct engagement in the social and political arena, in a way that felt very alien to the British art world's habitual manner of going about its business. 'One of the main functions of art that people of my generation [. . .] wanted to do,' says Michael Craig-Martin, 'was to demystify art, to make it more accessible, to make it so that it was used.'[4]

The emphasis on idea rather than object made common cause between artists in Britain and abroad. The expatriate Romanian sculptor and performance artist Paul Neagu describes his concept of 'palpable art'; Latham's wife and collaborator, Barbara Steveni, describes their regular contacts with artists of the Fluxus movement, including the Japanese performance artist Yoko Ono. Around the same time, radical innovations in the art-school curriculum by tutors such as Richard Hamilton at Newcastle University and Roy Ascott at Ipswich Civic College introduced a new generation of British students to conceptual practice, giving it equal status, even precedence, to traditional fine-art disciplines.

Frank Martin and John Latham separately revisit the moment in 1966, while Latham was teaching part-time in the painting department at St Martin's School of Art, when Martin decided that the time was right to focus on conceptual art as part of the degree programme. This is only six years, you have to remember, since Martin and Caro together revolutionised the sculpture programme. The next student generation would define its aims in contrast to all forms of 'object making', including the constructed abstract sculpture that had recently seemed so radical. In the process of seeing-through these successive reinventions of his department, 'I lost all my sculpture,' says Martin:

> I was a very skilled sculptor in the old sense, carving wood. Abstract sculpture didn't suit my style, and I didn't want to work in it [. . .] It was the skill of making, the skill of carving, the skill of modelling in clay that was something that involved me anyway. But then, I was somehow doing another thing in education [. . .] the concept around it all was very much what I was involved with, and we did then – do understand – it moved from even abstract sculpture on to conceptual sculpture of a variety of people, as you know. Richard Long, [Richard] Deacon, all those sort of people, George and Gilbert, all came out of the conceptual ideas that started to be used within the group. And we had two areas of study going on then, called A and B, and within those areas certain attitudes of sculpture were developed that were the mainstay of what happened beyond ordinary abstract sculpture [. . .] people like Deacon and [Bill] Woodrow, all well-known now of course, were all within that field. Yes, a completely different principle around it.[5]

In Latham's account, the new approaches to sculpture had less to do with formal 'areas of study' than with discussions in the pub, where he met up with a postgraduate sculpture student, Barry Flanagan. Latham by this time was already experimenting with alternative materials, having made the first of many assemblages using books, *Burial of Count Orgaz* (1958, titled after a painting by El Greco), a few years earlier. He had no time for the view in the sculpture department that very little could be learned from a painter:

> Frank Martin when I saw him said, 'No I'm sorry, there's nothing doing.' And I said, 'What you mean, there's nothing doing, I'm here, paid.' [*laughs*] [. . .] And that was really all that I saw of him. But I was able to talk to one of the new, younger students there, Barry Flanagan, who was post-Phillip King, post-Tony Caro and the new English art scene, the sculptors – Bill Tucker and that lot. And Barry and I used to be able to meet in the lunch hour in the pub. We couldn't talk in school because it was non-U[6] for the painting department to have anything to do with sculptors. Or rather this was a sculptural principle that, who are these other people around the place? Are they supposed to be artists? What do they do? Well anyway, Barry and I had quite a lot of convergences of view, and we decided jointly to hold a show. I was offered a show in Bangor in North Wales and we had a show there.[7] And we had this 'still and chew' party, which ended up in the New York museum [. . .] and it's one of those pieces of, one of the slices of fortune which showed me really that I couldn't be communicating in England, but I appeared to be able to communicate overseas without difficulty.[8]

This is a reference to a notorious episode in August 1966 that resulted in Latham being sacked from his post at St Martin's. He hosted a session at his home at which a group of students 'chewed over' pages ripped from a library copy of *Art and Culture* by the American critic Clement Greenberg. Since Greenberg had been an early, highly influential advocate of Caro's abstract sculpture, and was a revered figure at St Martin's, Latham's action was a political statement rather than an impulsive prank. The masticated pages were then mixed with yeast and chemicals and allowed to ferment. Instead of returning Greenberg's book to the library at St Martin's, Latham delivered a phial containing the fermented 'essence' of Greenberg. After his dismissal, he retained the phial and the overdue notice from the library. Combined in a leather case with other documents and residues of the 'still and chew' project, these eventually constituted a work in their own right, *Art and Culture 1966–69*, which the Museum of Modern Art, New York, acquired in 1970.

Who were the women artists?: Barbara Steveni

In September 1966 Yoko Ono arrived in London for the Destruction in Art Symposium, a gathering of artists, poets and scientists from across the

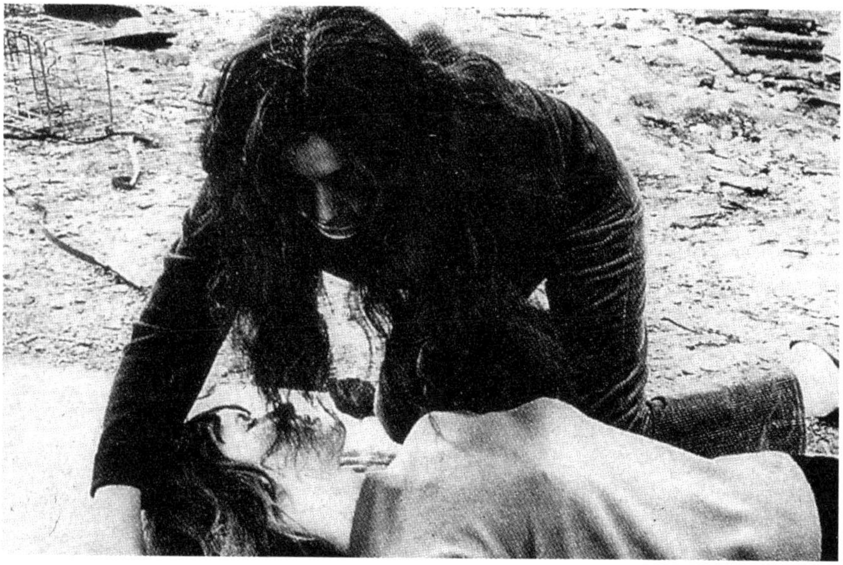

Barbara Steveni (lying down) and Yoko Ono performing Ono's *Shadow Piece* as part of the Destruction of Art Symposium, Notting Hill Gate, London, 1965. Photographer unknown.

international alternative and counter-cultural spectrum. She stayed with Latham and Steveni, as Steveni recalls:

> She arrived with her stash of works that she was going to do. And [. . .] the fact that she was a well-off lady meant that she arrived – she could buy great big lofts in America, in New York or whatever it was, where they would all do their events and stuff. She had the money to do that [. . .] But she was a strong artist, she knew what she wanted to do [. . .] But, it did make a difference, I think, at that time. I think I'm looking at, who were the women artists at the time? And I didn't see myself as a woman artist at the time. Although I had been at art school and I had done these things, I didn't actually see myself as a woman artist, that came much later, because I was in a culture, and living with a quite a bit older male artist, and all men, and all artists were men at the time. So I was very much participating in – as was Stuart Brisley's wife [. . .] in *Studio International*[9] at the time there was Deborah Brisley with her guts being pulled out, you know, meant to be being pulled out by Stuart Brisley

and being cut up and everything, on one page of *Studio International*, and on the other side there was me being, you know, burnt in a gallery in Aachen, all wrapped up in books, and just my eyes showing.[10] So we were very much participating in our men's events without thinking that we – without thinking how much we were giving or doing or initiating or anything. So it took me quite a long time to pull out of that and claim what I was doing and notice myself, because I was in that culture at the time where the man was *it*.[11]

[. . .] Yoko and I got on very well together, and she was about the first woman artist besides Carlyle Reedy,[12] who I met a bit later [. . .] And so we got on very well together, and she told me about her piece, *Cut Piece* (1964), which she had done before in America, which consisted of her sitting on a stage and inviting the audience to come up and cut off her clothes, and I arranged to go and get, for publicity purposes, from Biba's, some clothes that would get cut off, so we had all these different costumes for her to have cut off from Biba's. And, this was done in [. . .] the Africa Centre, which still exists in Covent Garden. And, she sat on this platform, and had her clothes cut off, her Biba garments cut off, one by one. And again that was interesting [. . .] in Yoko Ono's show at the beginning of this year [1998], how very different it was, the way the people cut the clothes off now and what they cut off Yoko at the time. And it was also interesting that, it was the men that came up to cut all the clothes off, whereas in the present day a lot of the women came to cut the clothes off, and so that was another interesting factor. And, but I remember when, when they had all been cut off, Yoko then had her long hair down to, came right down to her shoulders and she just sat cross-legged on the platform, and she looked very ancient, because she wasn't very ancient then, she looked like a Buddha, because she had this slightly olive skin and her hair like that. And, well to me she looked like a Buddha, and it was a nice thing that I've always remembered about her.[13]

This whole other area: Barbara Steveni, John Latham and the Artist Placement Group

In 1966, following the Destruction in Art Symposium, Steveni and Latham initiated the Artist Placement Group (APG). They proposed to release artists from their isolation within the art world by setting up placements in industry. In this way, not only would artists be able to realise their potential for contributing to society, but their contribution, whether in terms of work produced or new ideas, could be quantified, putting a measurable rather than notional value on art.[14] Steveni explains how the idea for the APG grew out of a search for junk props for a Fluxus performance:

> Daniel Spoerri[15] and Robert Filliou[16] were going to put on a show in Gallery One,[17] a sort of Fluxus show [. . .] they came over, and they stayed with me while John was in America, and, they wanted – this was where my idea for APG, which was the Artist Placement Group, as it was to become, became born – because they wanted a whole lot of material for scrap. And I took them to an industrial site, just outside London and collected some scrap for them to make their show, sort of stuff for their show. And a bit later than that, which must have been '65, '66 [. . .] and, I got lost on the Outer Circular Road. This was when I was on my own without the Fluxus group people coming with me, and I got lost on this industrial estate. And it was at night-time, or at least it was dark, it was about sort of 10 o'clock, and there was this huge, enormous industrial complex, humming away, and there was a Mars factory and a clock factory, a Timex factory. And I thought to myself, well, instead of just picking up buckets of plastic and material, why aren't we actually associated with this world that we don't seem to be touching? And, I came back with this idea in my head that we needed to be, you know, artists needed to be in this whole other area, and that was the beginning of my idea which grew into the Artist Placement Group.[18]

Steveni describes, step by step, how a mildly disquieting accidental experience developed into a semi-institutional programme, after Latham took her initial idea to Frank Martin, who in turn opened his address book of influential contacts. In its way, her account presents a model example of the kinds of routes by which, in the latter half of the 1960s, offbeat ideas were finding their way from the fringes to the centre. It began with her conviction 'that there was a whole part of society that was humming away about which we [i.e. artists] had nothing to do':

> and it consisted of people, actions, it consisted of the manufacture base of the country upon which apparently we ran [. . .] Yes, when we say political, that's a tiny, weeny 'p' and it's not left–right political, but it's very much going towards a whole structure where art is part of a whole structure and not a bit that is on the outside and that we are allowed to, you know, this is where you make your contribution to society.[19]

> [. . .] And when John came back [from America], I told him about it, and he thought that that was a very interesting idea and he liked the idea. And he had just been given one or two teaching days at St Martin's School of Art, and he told Frank Martin, who was head of the sculpture school at the time, and the sculpture school had all sorts of people, like Gilbert and George and Tim Scott. And I went into Frank Martin's office one day, and he said, 'Oh Barbara, why don't you get in touch with –?' Because I had said industries and everything, you know. He said, 'Why don't you get in touch with this guy?' And he was reading the pink *Financial Times*, and he was called Sir Robert Adeane, who was I think connected with the Queen [. . .] And he said – because he's chairman of all these companies, like Shell, this that and the other, he had got about sort of ten chairmanships, as they all do. So I sent my paper to Sir Robert Adeane,[20] and he said – I rang him up and said, 'What did you think?' He said, 'Well, come round and have a drink, my dear.' So, I went round, and he was standing inside his Cheyne Walk house, he was standing in front of the fireplace, needless to say, astride of a tiger rug with its great big head [. . .] And, he said, 'Well, very good idea, my dear. I'll be on your committee.' So, I thought, 'Oh my God! I'd better have a committee to put this man on, this is obviously very good.' So, I rushed round and got a committee of the sort of people you would have on a committee, which would be [William] Coldstream, you know, Frank Martin, Julie Lawson joined it. She was then, she was secretary to Roland Penrose,[21] and we got Michael Compton,[22] who was at the Tate, and we formed a trust called Artist Placement Group.[23]

Latham's parallel account of APG takes us into the technical workings of the scheme. Arcane and complex as he makes this sound, the essential issue is that the artist's contribution should be assessed not in terms of material value but as intellectual (i.e. conceptual) property. Tate curator Michael Compton seems to have been unconvinced: how, he asked Latham, could you measure the conceptual contribution of great scientists and philosophers? Not a problem, according to Latham: APG would make Freud and Einstein rich, though it might be a different story for Karl Marx.

> What is taken from an artist and used when in placement should be assessed for its worth, what value is it, on five different levels, the lowest of which is national benefits, the highest of which is conceptual, the top level is

> conceptual paradigm shifts. And when that idea was brought out, I should say, I showed it to Michael Compton at the Tate and [. . .] he was going to argue against it, and one of his arguments [. . .] was well, how do you account for the damage that artists do? And the other one was, how would you account, for instance, for the work of – and then he named five of the beacons in history, such as Newton, Einstein, Freud, Marx and Hegel. Now those are the five. And I thought well, let's have them all placed in different [government] departments, and we'll write a fictional account of how what happened with each of them to illustrate what would happen if nothing happened at all and what should happen if one got one very big answer [. . .] And the big answer that I got for the strong end was energy as reported by Einstein and energy as thought of by Freud. And so the story was, Einstein had been asked to get it together, or Freud had been asked to get it together in a different department, and they'd got together because they had this problem of what is human energy and how do we account for that kind of energy? [. . .] Well, the proposition was, they arrived at the Freud–Einstein equations, and that entitled the IP, the Incidental Person [i.e. the placement artist], to endless drawing rights on the international scale, United Nations fund, wherever that could be put, drawing rights. And then we went down the scale and got to poor old Marx who, when put into a capitalistic organisation today, had nothing to say and said so [*laughs*]. So the report would say zero, so zero results is quite a possible one [. . .] Now with the electronic material and the electronic apparatus which we've got now it's bound to be possible to do such things.[24]

How did the APG work in practice? In Latham's description of the pioneering video artist David Hall's 1970 placement with British European Airways, he sounds unconcerned by the achievement of 'zero results' for the airline:

> He made movies with the airline. I don't think it had a great effect on the airline [. . .] but he was more concerned with making an interesting movie and that was as it was. But he was very strong, David was very strong about the principles entailed of not allowing the circumstances of the exigencies of the moment and the requirements of the host body to get in the way of the art, the making of a significant work. One of his things was a cloud off Gibraltar which he got, it was a video of a cloud which doesn't ever move, it starts at one point and ends at another and is always a cloud, so it's a

> sort of a formative cloud one side and the other side is disappearing and evaporating. Well that was quite interesting because it changes shape the whole time, very modern.[25]

You imagine that Latham's view would have been, if BEA couldn't make anything of 'a video of a cloud which doesn't ever move' – well, that was their loss. Steveni, on the other hand, expresses palpable satisfaction at the outcome of Garth Evans' placement in 1969. In this case, the joke turns out to be on the art world, not the industrial host.

> I talked to this person in the Iron and Steel Federation and he said, 'Well I think there could be a case for taking this further,' although I was pushing all the time not for a person to come and do sculpture, which they could understand – 'We could have a great big steel sculpture' – but that there was this wider role. And it was an interesting placement, because the guy that we eventually put forward was a guy who is very into psychology and everything like that, a rather quiet little guy called Garth Evans, Welsh I suppose, and – but he was very, very articulate and wrote very well. And he was actually making plastic sculptures at the time, as many of the artists were at St Martin's – they were using the plastic and the fibreglass. And so I negotiated that there would be a fellowship for a year with the British Steel Corporation in conjunction with St Martin's School of Art, but that it would be wider than just making sculpture. They said, 'Well, as long as we get a sculpture out of it,' most of them always used to say that. But once he was inside, Garth was very good, because he wrote a paper when he was there. He went and looked at Port Talbot and the steel-making process, and he saw what the apprentices were doing, the steel apprentices, and he took lots of photographs of fabrications that the steel workers' apprentices did to teach, you know, to be taught welding. And he took these great big photographs of them, and he brought them back to St Martin's, and everybody thought it was a fantastic new sculpture, and actually it was just the guys' exercises in welding.[26]

The notion of performance: Paul Neagu

Paul Neagu (1938–2004) was born in Bucharest and brought up in Timisoara, where his father ran a shoemaking business and taught Neagu the craft. As a student at Bucharest Institute of Fine Arts, he secretly made abstract art, proscribed by the official dogma of social realism. Much of Neagu's early work combined sculpture and performance. Using his shoemaking skills and materials such as leather and wood, he made boxes and perishable objects, which he encouraged audiences to touch and physically explore, documenting these

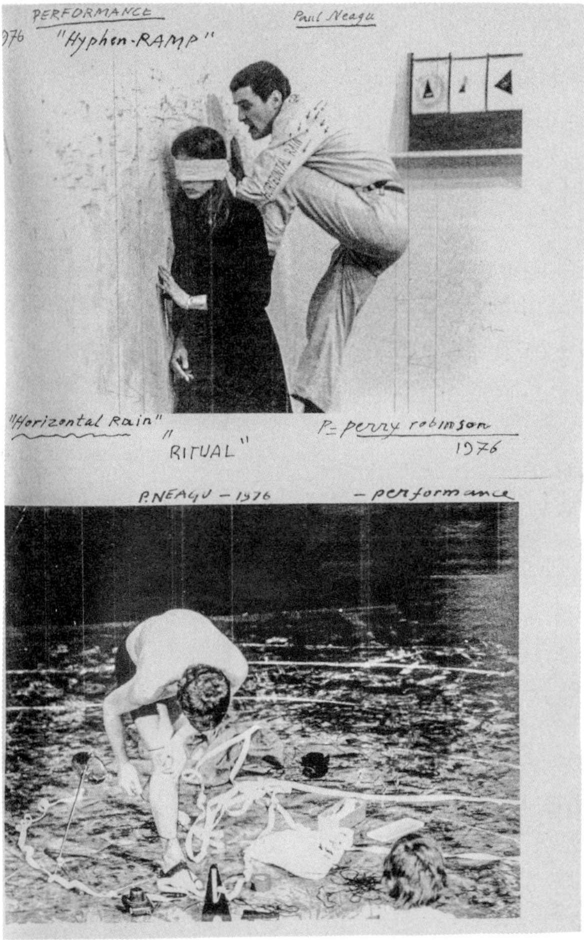

Paul Neagu, page from 'Performance' scrapbook , 1958–2003. Photographer unknown.

events in texts and photographs. Neagu's 'tactile objects' were often also edible, being made from foodstuffs like gingerbread or *mamaliga* (Romanian maize porridge). His work has a strong philosophical basis, reflecting his interest in Rudolf Steiner, George Gurdjieff and other esoteric thinkers.

> The first film I made of my tactile objects was made in '68 in Bucharest, part of which my wife contributed to, as being an animator of some of the objects. We together did what I could call my first performance, street performance in Bucharest, with my tactile iconic secretive objects. I used to place them in awkward corners in the street, sometimes in a very public street, see if the cars will smash it, or will it avoid it. And I have these on film. Actually it was a very exciting time. At the same time I knew I am preparing myself to get out of Romania to exhibit in Hamburg, and then in Edinburgh [. . .] They were like I said, tactile objects, created in rapport with the human measurement, in other words to manipulate for whole body, for one arm, or for just fingers [. . .] My performance was made just by placing them in such a way as the people who would happen to pass by would imagine that they just found something. And secretly I was watching over and even filmed them, photographed some of this behaviour, to see what people would do if they find an object which they don't know what it is but it looks awkward or interesting or attractive. So they couldn't – knowing that the Romanians on the streets of Bucharest are basically curious people, I couldn't imagine that anyone would pass by, seeing them, and ignoring them. And it's true, these performances, most of them were with offering unusual intriguing objects to see what happens. So there I was collecting a lot of psychological data, people finding something and then looking left, looking right to see if anybody sees them before they touch it. And then they very curiously open the door of that to see if it's anything they might be interested further. When they discover just empty boxes inside or maybe a certain material, which looked like a glutinous gold, then they might start smelling it. All that was part of the performance. Or rearranging or kicking it with a foot to see if it is moving, or something strange hidden behind.[27]

After exhibiting at the 1969 Edinburgh Festival, Neagu lived and worked mainly in Britain. His 1971 *Cake Man* performance at Sigi Krauss Gallery in London involved waffles stuck together with cream and crafted into a life-size human figure. In 1972 Neagu founded the Generative Art Group, whose five fictitious members each represented an aspect of his own psyche.

> I also put together the *Manifesto of Palpable Art*, which contained in seven articles everything I wanted to do, stressing and emphasising the elements of texture, materials, tactility, rather than just seeing. In fact to a degree I was going against the visual things. These were essential things for me, planning also at some later stage to take up the idea of eating, the consumption of the art object, which, soon after that – by that I mean '70, '71 – I started making gingerbread objects in order to cover that area as well, which is the completion of that group of ideas. So one of the things was this 'Cake Men', so-called, which was 13 layers of palpable and tactile life-size men. Later in London in '71 I managed to exhibit it in parallel with my first life-size waffle event, which was a laying down waffle man, which was consumed by several participants in Sigi Krauss's gallery.[28]
>
> [. . .] Well they [visitors to the exhibition] had a free choice: they either ate it [the waffle] on the premises, which some did, as we see in the films. Others took it home – you could preserve them. Particularly the first layers were tougher, because they must have been older, and I think we took care to put a bit more sugar in them so the preservation was easier. The ones on top were fresher, therefore more for eating. But the number – because each portion had an attachment, a label, [. . .] describing the event in brief terms. It could have been an art item for a while. Mind you, I was aware at the same time, there were other artists dealing with such things, for instance there was a German bloke who was doing suitcases full of cheese.[29] He would leave them in the galleries and it would smell. So smell, foodstuff and similar stuff were used by Fluxus people. I am saying this so that everybody knows that I wasn't a perfect naïve or innocent Eastern European. I was very well informed what was going on.[30]
>
> [. . . The exhibition] is dismantled to show that it's not about possessing something, but it's rather being part of something [. . .] The notion of performance whereby the actual work is something that exists in time for a moment and is then gone, and it's the documentation and the memory and so on which is important in relation to that work.[31]

It was cathartic: Stuart Brisley

Stuart Brisley was involved with APG from its early days and undertook two placements, in 1970 and 1975. He recalls his unexpected initiation into performance art a few years earlier, at a time when he felt that his practice as a painter and constructor of assemblages had reached a dead end or crisis. From this point onwards, performance combined with installation would become the focus of much of Brisley's work.

> There were some students at Hornsey who wanted to organise a night of activities at a nightclub called the Middle Earth in Covent Garden,[32] and they obviously had numbers of contacts and so forth, and they invited me to do something. And [. . .] this crisis that I'd, what I call a crisis, maybe it wasn't – this sort of coming to a stop as an artist, or coming to a stop in terms of making objects as an artist – when I got that invitation, I had to think, well what am I going to do with it? What am I going to do? I don't quite remember how this worked, but at some point, either after this first performance or before it, was the idea that [. . .] either I gave up or else I had to recognise that I was in the world, I was not outside it. I was in it, and therefore I had to start thinking about what that meant for me [. . .] And so, what I decided to do was to do a performance which was like a demonstration. It wasn't a performance in my mind, because performance wasn't the term that was used. At that point they were called 'events', I seem to remember, and in Germany I guess they were called 'actions'. I wanted to demonstrate, as it were, the act of eating. And in order to do this I thought that – I got another person, so there was going to be a meal between two people. So in order to try to concentrate on eating itself, I wanted to make everything the same, have the same consistency as it were visually. So everything was white, the food was white – there were three courses, and they were white food. I can't remember what it was, but it was almost white, like chicken I guess, which I hate. And we were dressed in white and we had white faces, like an archetypal beginners' sort of performance really. And this was part of an evening of events in which there were something like 40 different things taking place in this huge sort of underground warehouse place in Covent Garden [. . .] And I remember this particular occasion this thing took place. I was very frightened of the whole thing. Anyway, sat down at the table with Deborah and we proceeded to have this meal [. . .] It was perfectly,

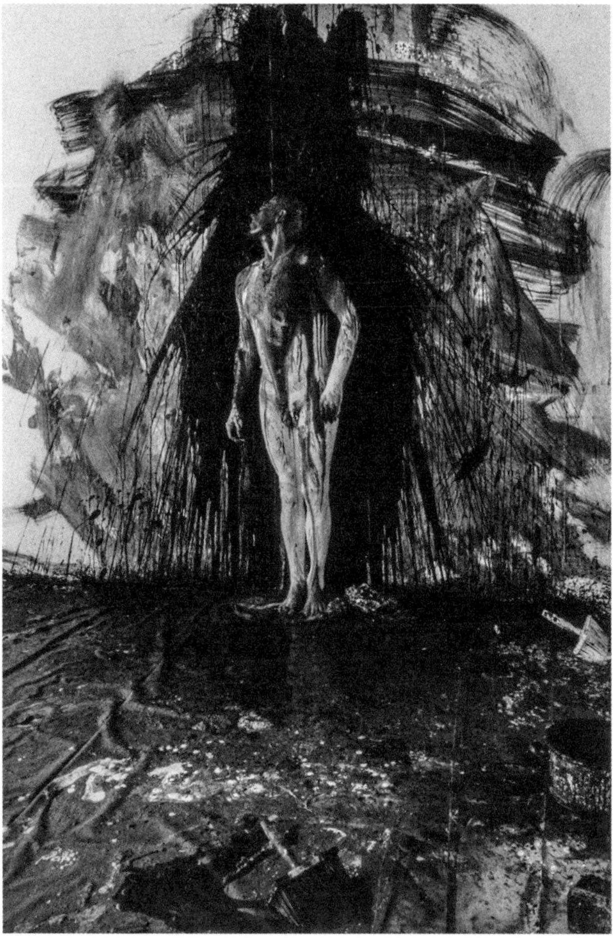

Stuart Brisley in his performance *Moments of Decision/Indecision*, 1975. Photographer unknown.

it went quite well, except some people stole some of the food, and I guess it worked in its own terms. And then, I had a cigarette at the end of the meal. I was smoking Gauloises at the time, I remember, had a Gauloise, put the match down, set fire to the table, and everything went up in flames.

And it was – everything about that work was in retrospect so exhilarating and liberating, that I realised that this was the start of something new, this was actually like the phoenix, like, out [*laughs*]. Having reached this terribly dour point of, you know, stasis – and all that, this kind of, the impossibility of the ideal, and then suddenly this. It had a tremendous – it was so liberating, I guess it was cathartic. And it led me on. From then I just – that was it, the whole thing started. And at that point I had those views that if this is not art, I don't give a damn. I really had no idea what it was – I had no interest in what it was. I was really interested in the fact of doing it, as it were. It was a sort of release from all kinds of – I suppose preconceptions about what art should be and how one operated as an artist, and the complexity of all of that. More connected to the act of making art and being not so much related to the context, i.e. what happens to it afterwards and all the rest of it [. . .] I mean it was just like, it doesn't matter what this is, you know? It's of no consequence to me, because this is what I'm going to do [. . .] I mean, you could look at it now and say, well yes, it was a rather boring piece of performance [. . .] But at the time I had literally no idea. I mean, was it theatre? Was it –? I had no need to try to conceptualise it, right at the beginning. And then slowly the whole thing became a lot more complex.

And so after about the second or third thing, I'd done it all, everything started to open up and become a lot more difficult [. . .] because I was being confronted with aspects of it that I hadn't expected, I hadn't realised, you know, would occur. So, you know, it was a bit like jumping in the deep end on something, and then having to start to learn to swim, and eventually, when you're swimming you realise [. . .] there's all kinds of aspects to what keeps you going as a swimmer, you know, what keeps you going [. . .] So it was like being born again.[33]

[. . .] People invite me to, so I say yes [. . .] they say, 'Would you like to do a performance?' And somebody said to me, 'Would you like to do a performance in my house?' And I said yes. And somebody else said, 'Would you like to do a performance at the Museum of Modern Art in Helsinki?' And I said yes. You know, I've never actually said, 'I want to do a performance' [. . .] So if something comes up – and I'll usually say yes, if I think it's interesting, because it usually is interesting.[34]

All those things were interwoven: Mary Kelly

Mary Kelly (b.1941) was born in Fort Dodge, Iowa. After studying painting in Italy and the USA, she taught at the American University in Beirut. In 1968 she moved to London for postgraduate study at St Martin's. Here she became deeply involved in the political and critical-theoretical debates of the time, especially the newly energised women's movement. In 1975, as a member of the Berwick Street Film Collective, she made *The Nightcleaners*. The film was part of a campaign to unionise the exploited, underpaid women who spent their nights cleaning office blocks. Filmed in real time, lasting 'hours and hours', *The Nightcleaners* was 'like an answer to Andy Warhol [. . .] eight hours of cleaning the toilet!'[35] Kelly recalls the moment of her arrival in London for the start of the autumn term in 1968, the year of widespread labour unrest and student demonstrations, including a general strike in France and violent confrontations between protestors and police on the streets of Paris.

> You can imagine the mood in this historic year, which was only a few months after the events in Paris, in May of '68, which went on, right, into June, and then the Chicago Convention in the US, which was in August. So the political events of the time were absolutely explosive. But the atmosphere in London, too, was extremely electric. There was this style, right, everyone was growing their hair, of course, very, very long. Men had long hair, and I had long hair, with a scarf that I wore [*laughs*] [. . .] Everyone was looking, at sort of vintage old, old clothes, recycling them [. . .] And I was now right here, in the centre, and at St Martin's, where I had read that Charles Harrison, who was the editor of *Studio International* at that time, was publishing work on conceptual art. He was teaching there, and it was the period right after Anthony Caro, and people were challenging this kind of object-making.[36]
>
> [. . .] My memory of it [the atmosphere in 1968] was, you know, not only that it was about doing something to change the situation, being primarily the war in Vietnam, but secondly to do with the way the institutions, you know, like the schools and universities, conducted their business, but even more importantly the sort of division between intellectuals and the so-called working class [. . .] You know, there was a feeling that sort of prevailed that you – of youthful omnipotence [*laughs*], that you *would* prevail, right [. . .] The age, we're all in our early and late 20s, and I suppose there were a few people in their 30s, so you can't underestimate the sort of moment that you're kind of intensely sexually active, as well, and just the way that all that kind of comes together [. . .] I know that when people look back at that time, they often want to insist on the political description of it, or on

> the lifestyle description of it, that is to say, either the sexual revolution, the cultural revolution, the political revolution, but all those things were very interwoven, in my memory of it.[37]

Much of Kelly's work focuses on the particular circumstances and challenges of women's lives: 'I'm of a generation that had to make the very difficult transition in the 60s and 70s, after being brought up in that kind of rather rigid culture–gender role that was the post-war situation.'[38] Her best-known work is *Post-partum Document* (1973–9), a six-year project through which Kelly explored the mother-child relationship. Each of the six parts focuses on an aspect of her infant son's acquisition of language and the maternal process of simultaneously nurturing and letting go. When *Post-partum Document* was first exhibited at the ICA in 1976, Kelly's use of stained nappy liners sparked outrage in the press.

> Moving from the film project [. . .] to *Post-partum Document*, it was a matter of trying to treat, initially in a kind of documentary way, the daily life and the subjective investment in what I had seen as the motive for women's relation to the workplace. [In the *Women and Work* project] the men described in detail what they did at work and not much about what they did at home. They just kind of went home, had supper, went to bed, right. The women didn't describe anything about being at work. They described everything about before, how they'd gotten the children ready, made breakfast [. . .] and went to work. And then they went home and they did all of this. So the descriptions were consistently inverted.[39]
>
> [. . .] The first parts of the *Document* were made in the top floor of Alderney Street, which I used as a studio, and Ray[40] and I lived on the ground floor [. . .] and when I was just saving these things, like the stained nappy liners, and of course everybody must have thought I was mad [*laughs*], and Barry Barker[41] came to the studio and said – he said, 'Yeah, this is the sort of thing people think about but they never do.' And I would always – I would, you know, try to keep the things that I thought were, as we would say 'cathected', in psychoanalytic terms,[42] that had emotional resonance, but I didn't know exactly why. So the process would be about two years from the saving of the thing to the working on it, and sort of analysing what it had meant. But I never considered it to be analysis in terms of explanation, but I considered this to be part of the process. And I was really surprised that later on, the second section

> of the *Document*, about learning to speak, that it was considered a rather useful and serious document of the mother's intervention in the child's acquisition of language, because there weren't a lot of studies [. . .] The University of Chicago did use that as an example.[43]

You have to allow it to occur: Michael Craig-Martin

Michael Craig-Martin (b.1941) was born in Dublin and grew up in Washington, DC, later studying in Bogotá, Colombia, Paris, France, and at Yale University, CT, where he absorbed the minimalist aesthetic and colour theories of Josef Albers. Since his move to Britain in the mid-1960s, much of Craig-Martin's work has involved ordinary domestic objects. *An Oak Tree* (1973), for example, consists of a small glass of water on a glass shelf, with an accompanying text explaining that an oak tree 'is physically present but in the form of the glass of water'. Through his teaching at Goldsmiths' College in the 1980s, Craig-Martin would influence and encourage a new generation who became known as the Young British Artists. He recalls the moment in the early 1970s when conceptual art first moved from the fringes of British artistic practice and public awareness to the main stage, citing the exhibition 'The New Art' at the Hayward Gallery in August 1972:

> I still think of it as one of the great exhibitions there's ever been in London of contemporary art, possibly the best. So that was obviously very useful, very nice thing to be in [. . .] Well, it was really the first conceptual exhibition – of what came to be called conceptual, although it wasn't entirely – but it certainly was – was not what people thought of as painting and sculpture. And it had Gilbert and George, Richard Long, Barry Flanagan, myself, Art & Language, John Stezaker, John Hilliard – lots of things to do with photo – using photography. Kind of installation things. I showed things using mirrors and clipboards, and I did a video thing. It was [. . .] conceptually a brilliant exhibition, because it was very, very uncompromising [. . .] It took various people working differently and said, there is a commonality here that is something very strange or very contemporary – this is something – and put all that stuff together. The exhibition occurred in 1972, and that really defined the generation of the 70s [. . .] I don't have any idea how many people actually went to this

exhibition. I remember it was very controversial, and I certainly know, even with the people who I taught with – those people who made painting and sculpture, some of them were really very, very upset. Some of them were angry, and some of them were panic-stricken about whether everything had been swept aside by this exhibition. Really, I mean, it didn't include any of these things. There was nothing that you would have previously called sculpture, in the British sculptural sense. There certainly was none of the heavy metal sculpture of the Caro school of sculpture, and I don't think there was any painting in the exhibition at all, so it was the first time that people started talking about the death of painting, or the first time I remember people talking about the death of painting. And so – and I think it was quite traumatising for people who were not part of that dialogue, who did suddenly see themselves as very marginal and also rather old-fashioned. And, to a certain extent, all the people from – all the artists who already had a position prior to 'The New Art' seem to me, with one or two exceptions, to have never recovered, in the sense that they are artists of the period. They will always be seen as artists of the period previous to that.[44]

[. . .] One of the main functions of art that people of my generation – that generation – wanted to do was to demystify art, to make it more accessible, to make it so that it was used, ideas and materials that were easily identifiable, that took away a lot of the pretension of art. The thing that upset people was the lack of the familiar guidelines. But if people could forget about the guidelines and look at what was actually presented to them, it was actually wonderfully available to them [. . .] There is a sense in which, with art, you always have to allow it to occur. It's like poetry, you know. If you don't let a poem be a poem, it's just a lot of stupid words, just doesn't really make any sense at all. You have to give it a little bit. And I think people, certainly at that time, found that very difficult. But then, on the other hand, if you're doing something which is unfamiliar, you can hardly expect people to welcome it [. . .] People are not born knowing how to understand, or how to evaluate things. I think today [1998], certainly people of the younger generation don't find any problem with this in general at all.[45]

[. . .] These were very liberating things that happened at that period with conceptual art, because art became so ephemeral and so disparate in its manifestations, you could have people with extraordinarily interesting imaginations participating without having to learn vast skills. So that, whereas skills could be a national tradition – so that you could have a

> country where there was a tradition of painting, and they had schools where people learned how to paint, and where there's another country, Third World country or country where there had been very little history of painting, they'd always be inevitably second-rate in terms of painting, but they might have somebody who was very imaginative in some way that was much looser in terms of how you manifested something. And suddenly it equalised a lot of places, it de-centred the art world.[46]

Ideas for future things: Hamish Fulton

Hamish Fulton (b.1946) describes himself as a walking artist. Since 1972 all his work has related to the experience of walking, translated into photographs, texts and other media, and through the shared responses of participants on group walks. Unlike Richard Long, whose practice of recording long walks is often compared to his, Fulton does not modify or harvest the landscape in any way. He thinks of his walks as 'invisible objects' that exist as experiences rather than physical trails. At art school, says Fulton:

> it happened in my mind that there was this growing sense of a kind of division between art which is either painting, sketching or photography and – we would say that the subject of the paintings and so on is the landscape. But it's not what I was seeing. What I was seeing is that the subject really is photography, the subject really is painting, the subject really is the artist's ability to sketch, and it's not the landscape at all. And so the way to get *at* the landscape is actually to live in it, to walk in it, you know, to spend a night in it, to get wet in it, to cross it, because – very often I would look at a landscape photograph, and I didn't have the feeling that the person actually went into the place that they photographed – that they maybe, they came up in a pickup truck and they walked up to the side of the road, and they got a tripod, and they took a photograph – fantastic photograph, no doubt – that's not my point. But they didn't actually go into it. So that you could have a beautiful photo, but the circumstances under which the photograph was taken were not part of the work.[47]
>
> [. . .] The galleries that I've worked with have always thought of art as a kind of beautiful, collectible object, whereas, even though I'm what I call a 'walking artist', I would be – I think I should really be categorised as a kind

> of permutation of conceptual art or *arte povera*[48] [. . .] not in the world of art which has this sort of, a collectible, tradeable, valuable objectness [. . .] One way of thinking of it is that walking itself is not an art medium. It's a completely – a separate entity, a separate activity, and that when you want to then transform – not quite the right word but, you know, make something from a walk, that it has to become – this other medium has to become this other thing. So it's really important to see it as two separate activities – two separate worlds: the world of walking, and the world of art-making. Whereas you could argue that, if someone is a painter, then their total activity is painting. They don't then have like another activity.[49]
>
> [. . .] The activity, reality of doing different things itself breeds more ideas, as opposed to the notebook ideas, which are just ideas piling up, which are not – they're like dormant, they're not activated. So I really like the idea of every day trying to really struggle, like on the train coming here [to the interview], I had a diary or a notebook, have an idea about what I want to make, what I want to do, how to redefine my work, and so on. I think that's also part of the 'no studio' idea [. . .] I think that ideas for future things, you know, they're – they're all – piles of ideas for that, but then you have to activate them.[50]

Returning briefly to John Latham, who cites a classic example of a simple, activated idea – John Cage's composition 4'33", which was premiered in August 1952. This consists of four minutes, thirty-three seconds of silence, or at least the absence of musical sounds, since the acoustic ambience of the performance venue – the audience rustling, coughing, complaining, getting out of their seats to leave – is an integral part of the piece.

> John Cage, I spoke to him – he didn't analyse, he couldn't think what it meant. He was just concerned that that was a true statement, and when asked, didn't he get bored with it? He said, 'No, I play it all the time.' Which is a wonderful remark. He wants to be by himself and not listening to anything, having quietness.[51]

Or, as Michael Craig-Martin puts it, 'you have to allow it to occur.'

The Work Completes

Being an Artist

Now and again in Artists' Lives interviews, artists will momentarily step aside from the immediate thread of conversation and reflect on what it's all about, this business of being an artist. These reflections are sometimes, though not often, a response to direct questions, and they almost never develop further – into a coherent theory, say, or a personal manifesto. Set beside all the attempts by non-artists, from Plato onwards, to define art, the subjective wisdom tends to be more contingent and less definitive. 'What is it somebody said about being an artist?' asks Jack Smith. 'It's a heavenly curse. Which presumes that there is something about it which, to deal with the imagination, that one doesn't understand. Where that comes from I don't know. Why one has that in the beginning, I don't know.'[1]

I have to make the work

> I mean that is slightly the trouble with me is that I am always incredibly in love with making work and the being an artist, and finding time to do that, and making sure I *do* do that has always come first. And the people I've known have always had to kind of work round that. If I can't do that, then I'm not interested, you know. I have to make the work.[2]
>
> [. . .] I want to be the kind of artist that shifts the way things are, perhaps the way systems are. I'd be sad if I got to the end of my life and I'd only made fantastic pieces of art and I hadn't ever managed to do any of the other things, you know? And I've kind of, as years have gone by, realised that, if

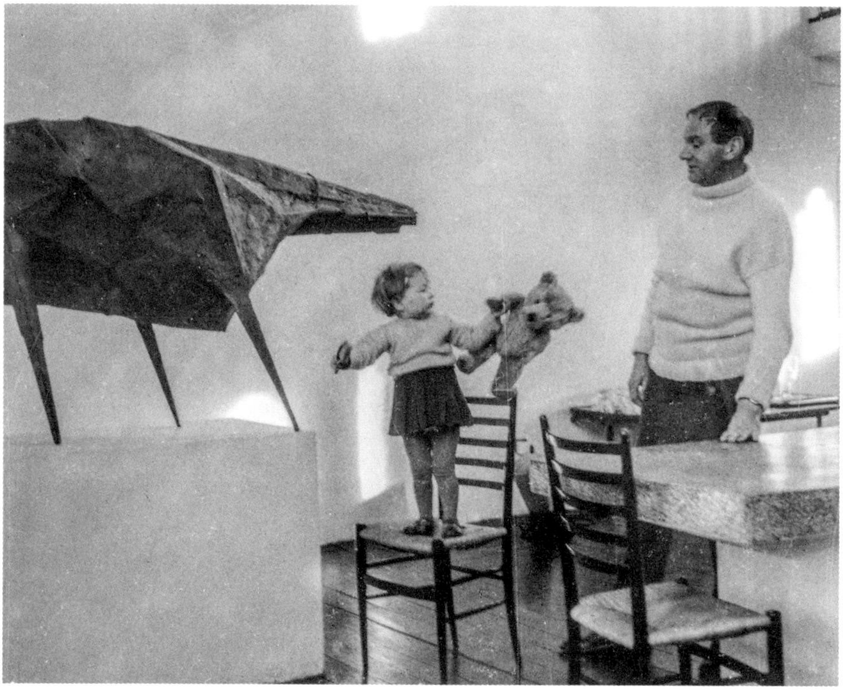

Lynn Chadwick, his daughter Sarah and teddy, with *Black Beast* (1960), at home at Lypiatt Park, *c.*1961. Photographer unknown.

you're gonna do some of those shaking and moving things, then you can't prioritise the art in quite the way you have to. I think. We'll see, you know. There's maybe another 30 years left to disprove that, but so far that's what I think.[3]

LUBAINA HIMID

I think it's a way of life and it's a compulsion to do it, and it's something I've always done. But the reason for doing it is, it has a rather thrilling excitement to the pictures I haven't yet painted but sometimes think of doing. There's something very thrilling about the thought of making them, or what they're going to do or be – an experience in them and in working on them, and also of [. . .] pulling them off, you know, in getting them to work properly, of what they will look like. And I do think that it is a kind of – it sounds awful but it is really, I think these things about art for healing, whatever, it does enhance being alive. And I think that it's a way of experiencing life and being alive that is shown in a kind of beautiful, strong and balanced effect that makes one better for seeing it in some way.[4]

SANDRA BLOW

I don't believe that one ever achieves anything better by doing it better – doing it more, or doing it with intelligence, as opposed to foolishness. I think that whatever one does, has to have a driving force behind it which is a testing ground to see whether you can do it the same way and equally well. And that's how I have lived for many years. And it is for that reason that I don't ever spend a lot of time thinking as to what I can do next, and feeling obliged to having to do something. It's just an automatic way of dealing with my daily life.[5]

PAUL FEILER

At war with myself

I consider my life to be one of conflict. I'm always at war with myself, and obviously if I wasn't I would not be an artist, or at least I certainly would be a different sort of artist. I would not be the sort of artist I am. It would be much easier to be a formulaic artist that just churns the work out, instead of being very involved and very neurotic. No, I would say that life would be much easier if there wasn't this conflict or continuous self-doubt. But in my scheme of things I think the self-doubt is very important. Life would be much easier if I was absolutely convinced all of the time that what I was doing was the right thing and didn't have that – but I would be a different artist, and I think probably the work would have less depth. And I cling to that as a rationale.[6]

MICHAEL SANDLE

I think if you're an artist you don't feel at all confident, and I think you're subject to enormous depressions really that you keep secret. I think you're terribly on your own. But I – I don't know what it is, there's some strange energy that you feel enthusiastic to, which is a sort of driving force, and I don't know how to say about this. I don't know whether it's confidence at all, but I think there's a sort of funny 'must' thing. And maybe sometimes you make mistakes [. . .] but maybe you have to resist so many things from what everybody else does that maybe – so yes, you're open to mistakes of course. But yes, I think it's a funny mixture that's going on all the time within yourself. So you can collapse but you can also be very enthusiastic [. . .] I don't think you are ever confident, secretly.[7]

GILLIAN AYRES

Stripping off one's clothes

One of the problems with performance is that you can never meditate upon it, as it were. You do it. You may think about it before and afterwards, and you may actually have secondary information through reproductive processes, but actually the thing itself is the thing itself and just lives in that time, in a way. And is limited to that, you know. So there's a great frustration in performance it seems to me. And the other thing is, it's also deeply embarrassing as well, because performance – well for me it is, because it often breaks certain sorts of taboos, and so it's very uncomfortable to be in it and do it. And so it's limiting and it's uncomfortable, and it's very elusive as to what its value is as well, it seems to me, at any given point in time. Now the value of something may be equally elusive with painting or sculpture, but at least there's something you can meditate upon. There it is, you can see it, and you can see it actually taking place time and again before your eyes as you look at it, if you see what I mean. But you can't with performance at all. And any reproduction is something else, it's not it. It is taken from it, but it is not it at all. And I just don't believe that the idea of documentation has any real value, because if it's just documentation it always drops to a low level. In order to raise it you have to make it into another fiction, and therefore it's not what it was before in any way. So there's all these ironic difficulties with performance, and this essential limitation of having to be in it and never being able to see it from the outside. At least with these other activities you can actually be inside and outside. You can be inside in its internal sense in the process, and as part of that process you can step out and have a look at it, which is really important, you know, to see what's going on.[8]

STUART BRISLEY

I think inevitably when you're making art you do – I mean in a sense you expose yourself to a – oh you do. I mean having a public exhibition of work does feel like stripping off one's clothes a bit. I mean it is – could be embarrassing. Well I mean, you certainly could, because sometimes you don't know if your ideas are really tenable, you know. I mean they could be ripped apart, or what you put on the wall. No, it's an anxious moment having an exhibition.[9]

MICHAEL KIDNER

Metaphysical facts

I want to say that metaphysical facts in my work are becoming a result, not something I started off with, not something I determined, I want to get at. It is true that if I look at my very early works of painting, for instance, when I was a student even, there was something which displeased me when it came to the world of simply imitating what you see or are trying to be, mimic reality. This wasn't ever satisfying for me. So there was this desire within me always to see an angle which wasn't visible to everybody. So I think that tiny desire which somehow, I think, I inherited from my birth and from my education, if you like, it's grown into a resulting metaphysics. But meanwhile, of course, I have been watering it. I helped that growth by nourishing it with my readings, because I've been interested in poetry and philosophy all my life, psychology at the same time. So it is a metaphysic which is somewhat detached from religious thinking that is related to philosophy, which pure metaphysic is anyway.[10]

PAUL NEAGU

Some people say that they're more inspired by the moon, because it's night-time and it's dark, and you're more likely to be alone. And other people say, 'No, it's the sun that inspires me. The sun and walking in the fields and woods,' and that sort of thing. I feel the same. With me, it's the sun. It's the sun that inspires one to, well, you see everything. And with the moon, it's night, and you can dream.[11]

EILEEN AGAR

Later in my work and research and thoughts, it occurred to me that if you look into the face of God – and this is a sort of metaphor here – you're blinded by pure light, everything is one light, you can't see any colours, you can't see any shapes, you just have total experience. But if you turn your back on God, and therefore the submission, what happens is the light illuminates the world and all its detail and all its colours. I think the role of the artist and anyone who seeks to try to get close to these truths, or this notion of essence, has to have the confidence to turn their back on the known, in order to be surprised, and in fact the gifts [ability] one has to recognise what's there, illuminated by something that you had just faced and challenged. I think there's something powerful about that, the kind of thing that is bigger than individuals themselves, that throughout history has engaged people's imaginations and beliefs. Of course, that's an epic vision, but within all that, they're all the little things that happen in life, and how you make your journey through that is fascinating, knowing at the same time everything you do is part of the history in the making, and nothing is fixed and nothing remains the same, it's all change from moment to moment. So the idea of trying to be comprehensive, theoretically in charge and justifiable is an illusion which one has to sort of go with.[12]

ROLAND PICHÉ

I think art took the place of religion right from the beginning. I mean art is your religion – well, certainly was and still is to me. To me the idea of what someone, a great artist can do – what Michelangelo could achieve or Rembrandt or all the people who, you know, it becomes irrelevant. You look at an Etruscan bronze or a Roman mosaic or a pot, God knows what, and the spirit, the human spirit is there. Or an African carving. That's my religion. I have great belief in the creativity of the human being. It's what makes me want to continue to be an artist. To try and keep up. And if you produce bad art – I've produced a lot of rubbish, good things, bad things – but you know, all artists I think are very conscious of what they're up to. It's a private dialogue with one's own spirit. And all the other sides of it, the acclaim or lack of acclaim, is an extra. The true thing is coming up against yourself when you're making something and recognising your own weaknesses and strengths and knowing yourself. And you know a lot about yourself if you make art. It's a private business.[13]

BRYAN KNEALE

I suppose whenever I'm asked to fill a form, I usually put nothing, but sometimes when I'm in a mood I'll put Buddhist, because if anything it would be the philosophy of Buddhism that would be something that would guide me more than anything else – not the religion, the philosophy of it.[14]

KIM LIM

I am aware of being Jewish, and it is interesting that several of my closest friends actually come from very similar backgrounds. I have had two or three friends in my life who have the same history as I do, who were born in Vienna and came over here, although we didn't meet until our early 20s, but we could well have lived exactly the same life had there never been a war or any of that happening [. . .] There is, you know, a call from the deep, as it were, that speaks occasionally. So I am aware of that [. . .] I think it is an outlook on life. I think it is a way of looking at things. It is even possibly a particular kind of humour [. . .] Perhaps not wanting to take things at face value, perhaps always believing that there'll be a loser somewhere, there will be a disaster, you know, don't take anything for granted, don't ever get complacent. Perhaps wanting to laugh at oneself a little bit, which is a sort of safety valve. A touch of cynicism? Not always believing what you are told. Actually I say that, I'm not like that really, I'm much more naive, I do tend to believe what I'm told until proof has been given that this is not the case [. . .] I think there is a restlessness, a bit of an inability to be satisfied. I mean I certainly, in my work, am very aware of searching for a kind of tranquillity within the work itself, that I want to – I've always wanted my paintings, and I want the places that I'm involved in making to promote a feeling of being a haven, a calmness, a sense of well-being, a kind of – a profound feeling of calm. Now those are not feelings that I have myself. So perhaps lots of artists I think want – they do things in their work that they are not themselves. They are often very thoughtful, highly intellectual people that make tremendously expressionist works, and then you get the opposite, you get people making very calm-looking works who are very exuberant and expressive themselves. So that it's like making a totality, that the work completes the person.[15]

TESS JARAY

A lifetime's job

You see that's a difficult thing for any artist to develop, a language through which he can speak. It takes usually a long time. It took me 20 years to develop a language through which I could speak. And now when I say develop a language, I mean a language which can give you a freedom to express imaginative ideas. Maybe we even have to invent a new language, not a language that belongs to the past [. . .] I think if you concentrate on, shall we say, drawing every day for a year or two years, you will at the end of that time know something about it. I mean we try and paint every day. I mean, one never questions a concert pianist who plays the piano every day, because one knows he has to be proficient. He has to be able to play without thinking, how am I doing it? And it's the same with an artist. I know when I go upstairs to bed, I don't think, 'how am I going to do it?' any longer. I just do it.[16]

[. . .] People have this romantic idea about being an artist, and it's just not like that at all, it's – it's so difficult getting the whole thing right, and I mean, it's a lifetime's job, it's not this idea that you get up and be inspired, and do a painting and then off to the pub and all this kind of thing.[17]

[. . .] Artists are classless, I think, that's what I'd like to say, they're classless, they're without class. I've met artists from all kinds of parts of society, and they're not aware of where they came from, I mean they're just immersed in what they're doing and they expect you to be the same.[18]

JACK SMITH

Somebody called me an artist of the periphery, and I didn't realise this was actually a negative term. At the time I thought, yes, that's rather good, I live in Blaenau and I never really feel that I belong in the middle there, so I thought, yes, I thought that was a very accurate observation.[19]

DAVID NASH

You were asking over lunch how many pieces of sculpture I've made. About a hundred, maybe. But it doesn't matter. I mean, if I could have left three or four that I thought were good – and I occasionally flip through my mind and, you know, leaf through and think, which ones do I really rate? It wouldn't be more than half a dozen. And I don't think more than half a dozen for anybody either, actually, really. I've some good drawings, I mean, a few good drawings, a few good, amusing-enough small pieces of sculpture. But I mean like important sculptures, wow! I mean, to have made half a dozen, that's something.[20]

RALPH BROWN

I was very taken with the still-ongoing cultural clashes that there seemed to be, where politicians who run small states consistently behave like old-time tyrants and, you know, a lot of judicial open killing, people being hung in public and stuff, and my work was very involved with all that in the beginning, once I learnt how to handle drawing and painting. What drew me as an artist was these world dilemma type things. It's only after I went through all of that, and then tackled the basic concerns – geometry, colour – once I'd managed to apply myself to study what the business of making paintings was all about, the rules, if you like, of governing the art of making pictures, right? It's only going through that that I began to realise that my real concern was more to do with the activity itself and not with the social peripheral concerns, like with politics and sociology. I felt that, the real substance that fed me, what made me feel good inside, was the rules within the activity itself, which I felt was a challenge that had to be moved along [. . .] and the rules built in and, deep, you know, thousands of years of reaffirming, and that what the artist, the ambitious artist should be doing is to add another link to that chain.[21]

FRANK BOWLING

I hate obscurity in the sense of art being totally engaged with itself, and with its own values. I think art, the art I like, is about things that concern people, that concern human life, that may not always be readily readable, but that is their concern, and ultimately, of course, one must feel the weight of that importance. If, on the one hand, one thinks of a world without music, without art, without architecture, it seems to me a terrible world, and what the artist adds, what the musician, the poet adds, is something so important. In the end, it seems to me that art is of supreme importance. Without the vision offered by great artists, or the music offered by great composers, it seems to me that the world would be, really, a terrible place, because however awful the things that go on, however frightful Pol Pot may go on in Vietnam or Cambodia, I think the moment one can think of a marvellous building, or something like that, there's a process of retrieval, without which, I think, life would be a nightmare. As regards one's own role, as far as one can see it, I like to do things which mean something to people of sense and sensitivity [. . .] I really hate movements in art, which are concerned with art as a closed room. I only like art that has windows and doors open.[22]

MICHAEL ROTHENSTEIN

If anyone asks me to give an item of advice I would say, to heed the faint whisper, a hunch that can cut right across intended or conscious activities. I wanted to say that the art industry, now I think of it, is enormous; the National Gallery, the Tate Gallery, the South Bank gallery – the Hayward, Whitechapel, the numerous civic galleries right through the country stuffed with paintings and very little sculpture. The auction houses, Sotheby's, Christie's, Bonhams, Phillips; the hundreds of commercial galleries dealing with current art production. The art writers, critics, *et cetera*, the magazines, the paint, frame and paper manufacturers; the bronze foundries; the hundred or so art schools giving employment. Underneath this activity, involving an annual turnover of millions, are many tiny dots. These, the artists, are mainly anonymous, but a few reach star status, mostly for excellence of work but not always so. Individual artists are of course vastly important, but can be lost in the mass of activity we call art. This is all like a benevolent goddess, fading or emerging with circumstance, but always there, indestructible, and continuing for all time. This strange activity occurs only in the human species and nowhere else in life. One might refer to the Australian bowerbird, that builds a kind of ramshackle little wigwam for his lady, and collects mainly blue things to put in front of the door to entice his mate, and it seems to work. But I hardly call that art – at least one doesn't know the mind of the bowerbird but I don't think it is.[23]

KENNETH ARMITAGE

Art is a focused thing, and it's a clarifying thing, and it's a revealing thing. It tells you something about life and about yourself, or it reveals something more. And every living moment doesn't do that. Everything you say isn't poetry. Poetry is something that puts it into a special box. And I think that sculpture is the same [. . .] It's a focusing of something, a focusing of experience, yes, focusing of life.[24]

ANTHONY CARO

Short Biographies

Artists whose interviews are quoted in chapters 1–8 are listed in alphabetical order, with dates of selected exhibitions, awards and honours, and details of their Artists' Lives recordings and key publications. Unless otherwise stated, galleries are located in London.

EILEEN AGAR (b. 1 Dec. 1899, Quinta la Lila, Flores, Argentina; d. 17 Nov. 1991, London). Moved to England, 1911. *Studied*: with Leon Underwood, 1924; Slade School of Fine Art, 1925–6; in Paris with František Foltyn, 1928–30. Member of London Group from 1933. *Exhibitions*: Bloomsbury Gallery, 1933; New Burlington Galleries, 1936; Museum of Modern Art, New York, 1937; Commonwealth Art Gallery, 1971.

Interviewed by Cathy Courtney, Apr.–Aug. 1990, Artists' Lives, British Library reference C466/01.

Agar, Eileen and Lambirth, Andrew. *A Look at My Life* (Methuen, London: 1988).
Remy, Michel. *Eileen Agar: Dreaming Oneself Awake* (Reaktion Books, London: 2017).

KENNETH ARMITAGE (b. 18 Jul. 1916, Leeds; d. 22 Jan. 2002, London). *Studied*: Leeds College of Art, 1934–7; Slade School of Fine Art, 1937–9. Served in Royal Artillery, 1939–46. *Teaching*: head of sculpture, Bath Academy of Art, 1946–56; Gregory Fellow, Leeds University, 1953–5; residency in Berlin, 1967–9; visiting tutor, Royal College of Art, 1974–9. *Exhibitions*: Gimpel Fils, 1952–62; Venice Biennale, 1952, 1958 (David E. Bright Sculpture Prize); Museum of Modern Art, New York, 1955; Marlborough Gallery, 1962–72. Retrospectives: Whitechapel Art Gallery, 1959; Arts Council of Great Britain, 1972; Yorkshire Sculpture Park, Wakefield, 1996. Awarded CBE, 1969; elected RA, 1994.

Interviewed by Tamsyn Woollcombe, Jun.–Dec. 1991, Artists' Lives, British Library reference C466/08.

Elliott, Ann and Woollcombe, Tamsyn. *Kenneth Armitage, Sculptor: A Centenary Celebration* (Sansom & Co., Bristol: 2016).

Scott, James with Milburn, Claudia. *The Sculpture of Kenneth Armitage: With a Complete Inventory of Works* (Lund Humphries, London: 2017).

GILLIAN AYRES (b. 3 Feb. 1930, London; d. 11 Apr. 2018, Barnstaple). *Studied*: Camberwell School of Art, 1946–50. *Teaching*: Bath Academy of Arts, 1959–65; head of painting, Winchester School of Art, 1978–81. *Exhibitions*: Gallery One, 1956; Redfern Gallery, 1958; Kasmin Gallery, 1965–9; Knoedler Gallery, New York, 1979–87; Alan Cristea Gallery, 2007–17. Retrospectives: Serpentine Gallery, 1983; Royal Academy of Arts, Sacker Gallery, 1997; Yale Center for British Art, 1997; Iowa University Museum, 1997. Elected RA, 1991.

Interviewed by Mel Gooding, Jun. 1999, Artists' Lives, British Library reference C466/91.

Gooding, Mel. *Gillian Ayres* (Lund Humphries, Aldershot: 2001).
Gayford, Martin and Cleaton-Roberts, David. *Gillian Ayres* (Art/Books, London: 2017).

PHYLLIDA BARLOW (b. 4 Apr. 1944, Newcastle upon Tyne). *Studied*: Chelsea College of Art and Design, 1960–3; Slade School of Fine Art, 1963–6. *Exhibitions*: Museum of Installation, 1991, 1995; Baltic Centre for Contemporary Art, Gateshead, 2004; Southbank Centre, 2008; Hauser & Wirth, 2011; New Museum, New York, 2012; Henry Moore Institute, Leeds, 2012; Des Moines Art Center, 2013; Norton Museum of Art, West Palm Beach, 2013; Tate Britain, 2014; Kunsthalle Zurich, 2016; Venice Biennale, 2017. Elected RA, 2011; awarded CBE, 2016.

Interviewed by Kirstie Gregory, interview in progress, 2018, Artists' Lives, British Library reference C466/355.

Morris, Frances and Barlow, Phyllida. *Phyllida Barlow: Set* (Hatje Cantz, Berlin: 2015).
Dexter, Emma. *Phyllida Barlow: Folly* (Black Dog, London: 2017).

WILHELMINA BARNS-GRAHAM (b. 8 Jun. 1912, St Andrews, Fife; d. 26 Jan. 2004, Dundee). *Studied*: Edinburgh College of Art, 1931–7. Moved to St Ives, 1940. *Exhibitions*: Redfern Gallery, 1952; Scottish Gallery, Edinburgh, 1956, 1960, 1981; Park Square Gallery, Leeds, 1970; New Art Centre, 1978; Pier Arts Centre, Stromness, 1982; Gillian Jason Gallery, 1987; William Jackson Gallery, 1992. Retrospectives: Scottish National Gallery of Modern Art, Edinburgh, 1996–7; Tate St Ives, 1999–2000.

Interviewed by Tamsyn Woollcombe, Jun. 1994, Artists' Lives, British Library reference C466/34.

Green, Lynne. *W. Barns-Graham: A Studio Life* (Lund Humphries, Aldershot: 2001, rev. 2011).
Gunn, Ann V. *Prints of Wilhelmina Barns-Graham: A Complete Catalogue* (Lund Humphries, Aldershot: 2007).

BASIL BEATTIE (b. 9 Jan. 1935, West Hartlepool). *Studied*: West Hartlepool College of Art, 1950–55; Royal Academy Schools, 1957–61. *Exhibitions*: Mayfair Gallery, 1971; Goldsmiths'

Gallery, 1982; Curwen Gallery, 1987; IKON Gallery, Birmingham, 1994; Todd Gallery, 1995–8; Galerie Renate Bender, Munich, 1997; Tate Britain, 2007; James Hyman, 2011; Jerwood Gallery, Hastings, 2013; Middlesborough Institute of Modern Art, 2016. Elected RA, 2006.

Interviewed by Mel Gooding, Aug. 1996–May 2007, Artists' Lives, British Library reference C466/59.

Moorhouse, Paul *et al. Basil Beattie: Taking Steps, Large Works 1986–2009* (lithoartnew, Turin: 2011).
Gooding, Mel *et al. Basil Beattie, When Now Becomes Then: Three Decades* (Hales Gallery, London: 2016).

PETER BLAKE (b. 25 Jun. 1932, Dartford, Kent). *Studied*: Gravesend Technical College and School of Art, 1946–9; Gravesend School of Art, 1949–51; Royal College of Art, 1953–6. *Teaching*: professor of drawing, Royal Academy, 2002–4. *Exhibitions*: Waddington Galleries, 1970–90; Stedelijk Museum, Amsterdam, 1973; Kunstverein, Hamburg, 1973; Palais des Beaux Arts, Brussels, 1974. Retrospectives: Tate Gallery, 1983; Galerie Claude Bernard, Paris, 1984, 2009; Nishimura Gallery, Tokyo, 1988; National Gallery, 1996; Tate Liverpool, 2007; Galerie Thomas Levy, Hamburg, 2008. Elected RA, 1981 (resigned, 2005); awarded CBE, 1983; knighted 2002.

Interviewed by Linda Sandino, Apr. 2003, Artists' Lives, British Library reference C466/168.

Rudd, Natalie. *Peter Blake* (Tate, London: 2003).
Livingstone, Marco. *Peter Blake: One Man Show* (Lund Humphries, Aldershot: 2011).

SANDRA BLOW (b. 14 Sept. 1925, London; d. 22 Aug. 2006, Truro). *Studied*: St Martin's School of Art, 1941–6; Royal Academy Schools, 1946–7; Accademia di Belle Arti, Rome, 1947. *Exhibitions*: Gimpel Fils, 1952–62; Saidenberg Gallery, New York, 1957; New Art Centre, 1966–73; Francis Graham-Dixon Gallery, 1991; Newlyn Art Gallery; 1995. Retrospectives: Royal Academy of Art Sacker Gallery, 1994; Tate St Ives, 2001–2. Elected RA, 1978.

Interviewed by Andrew Lambirth, Jul. 1996, Artists' Lives, British Library reference C466/42.

Gooding, Mel. *Sandra Blow: Space and Matter* (exhib. cat., Tate St Ives, 2001).
Bird, Michael. *Sandra Blow* (Lund Humphries, Aldershot: 2005).

FRANK BOWLING (b. 29 Feb. 1936, Bartica, Guyana). Moved to Britain, 1950. *Studied*: Regent Street Polytechnic, Chelsea College of Art and Design, 1957–9; Royal College of Art, 1959–60, 1961–2; Slade School of Fine Art, 1960–61. *Teaching*: Camberwell School of Arts and Crafts, 1963–83. Residencies: Rhode Island School of Design, 1974–5; Skowhegan School of Sculpture and Painting, Maine, 1984. *Exhibitions*: Grabowski Gallery, 1962, 1963; Whitney Museum of American Art, New York, 1971; Serpentine Gallery, 1986; De La Warr Pavilion, Bexhill-on-Sea, 1997; Center for Art and Culture, Brooklyn, 1997; Tate Britain, 2012; Dallas Museum of Arts, 2015; Haus der Kunst, Munich, 2017. Elected RA, 2005; awarded OBE, 2008.

Interviewed by Mel Gooding, Mar. 2001–Mar. 2007, Artists' Lives, British Library reference C466/127.

Gooding, Mel. *Frank Bowling* (Royal Academy of Arts, London: 2011).
Enwezor, Okwui. *Frank Bowling: Mappa Mundi* (Prestel, Munich: 2017).

STUART BRISLEY (b. 19 Oct. 1933, Grayswood, Surrey). *Studied*: Guildford School of Art, 1949–54; Royal College of Art, 1956–9; Akademie der Bildenden Künste, Munich, 1959–60; Florida State University, Tallahassee, 1960–62. *Teaching*: head of media fine art, Slade School of Fine Art, 1985. *Exhibitions and performances*: Studio F, Ulm, 1961; New Vision Centre, 1965; Tate Gallery, 1968; Hille Fellowship, Suffolk, 1970; Battersea Arts Centre, 1976; Acme Gallery, 1978; Chantal Crousel Gallery, Paris, 1982; Cenotaph Project, 1987–90, various locations; Museum of Modern Art, Oxford, 1993; South London Gallery, 1996; Freud Museum, 2002; England & Co., 2006, 2009; Mummery+Schnelle, 2013; Royal Academy of Arts, 2014; MAC, Belfast, 2015; Hales Gallery, 2016. Retrospectives: Institute of Contemporary Art, 1981; Serpentine Gallery, 1996.

Interviewed by Melanie Roberts, Sept.–Nov. 1996, Artists' Lives, British Library reference C466/43.

Stuart Brisley: Crossings (exhib. cat., John Hansard Gallery, Southampton, 2008).
Newman, Michael. *Stuart Brisley: Performing the Political Body and Eating Shit* (MAC, Belfast: 2015).

RALPH BROWN (b. 24 Apr. 1928, Leeds; d. 3 April, 2013). *Studied*: Leeds College of Art, 1948–51; Royal College of Art, 1952–6; in Paris with Ossip Zadkine, 1954. *Teaching*: head of sculpture, Bournemouth College of Art, 1956–8; Bristol College of Art and Royal College of Art, 1958–73. *Exhibitions*: Leicester Galleries, 1961, 1963; Taranman Gallery, 1976; Browse & Darby, 1979; Beaux Arts, Bath, 1983, 1987; Leeds City Art Gallery, 1988; Bruton Gallery, Leeds, 1999; Pangolin London, 2009–16. Elected RA, 1972.

Interviewed by Gillian Whiteley, Sept. 1999–Jun. 2000, Artists' Lives, British Library reference C466/93.

Ralph Brown: Sculpture and Drawings (exhib. cat., Henry Moore Sculpture Trust, Leeds, 1988).
Whiteley, Gillian *et al. Social, Savage, Sensual: The Sculpture of Ralph Brown* (Sansom and Co., Bristol: 2009).

ANTHONY CARO (b. 8 Mar. 1924, New Malden, Surrey; d. 24 Oct. 2013, London). *Studied*: Christ's College, Cambridge (engineering), 1942–44; Regent Street Polytechnic (sculpture), 1946; Royal Academy Schools, 1947–52. Served in Fleet Air Arm, 1944–6. Assistant to Henry Moore, 1951–3. *Teaching*: St Martin's School of Art, 1952–3, 1964–73; Bennington College, Vermont, 1963–4. *Exhibitions*: Galleria del Naviglio, Milan, 1956; Gimpel Fils, 1957; Whitechapel Art Gallery, 1963; Andre Emmerich Gallery, New York, 1964–89; Kasmin Gallery, 1965–72; Richard

Gray Gallery, Chicago, 1976–89; Waddington Galleries, 1983, 1986; Knoedler Gallery, 1978–91; Gallery One, Toronto, 1982–90; Leeds City Art Gallery, 1984; Annely Juda Fine Art, 1989–2010; Yorkshire Sculpture Park, Wakefield, 1994, 2001; Chatsworth, Derbyshire, 2012. Retrospectives: Hayward Gallery, 1969; Museum of Modern Art, New York, 1975; Kunstverein Braunschweig, 1979; Whitworth Art Gallery, Manchester, 1994; Museum of Contemporary Art, Tokyo, 1995; Tate Britain, 2005. Awarded CBE, 1969; knighted, 1987; awarded Order of Merit, 2000; elected RA, 2004.

Interviewed by Paul Moorhouse, Oct. 1993, Artists' Lives, British Library reference C466/016.

Reid, Mary *et al. Anthony Caro: The Definitive Series on the Sculpture of Anthony Caro*, 5 vols (Lund Humphries, Aldershot: 2010).
Glanville, Toby *et al. Caro* (Phaidon, London: 2014).

LYNN CHADWICK (b. Nov. 1914, Barnes, London; d. 2003, Lypiatt Park, Glos.). Trained as a draughtsman; served in Fleet Air Arm, 1941–4. *Exhibitions*: Gimpel Fils, 1950, 1996; Venice Biennale, 1952; International Prize for Sculpture, Venice Biennale, 1956 (followed by British Council touring exhibition); Galerie Charles Lienhard, Zurich, 1959; Marlborough Fine Art, 1961–89; Knoedler Galleries, New York, 1965; Galleria Blu, Milan, 1968–2003; Berman Museum of Art, Ursinus, PA, 1991; Museum of Modern Art, Toyama and touring, 1991. Retrospectives: Yorkshire Sculpture Park, Wakefield, 1991; Tate Britain, 2003. Awarded CBE, 1964.

Interviewed by Cathy Courtney, Apr.–May 1995, Artists' Lives, British Library reference C466/28.

Farr, Dennis. *Lynn Chadwick* (Tate, London: 2003).
Bird, Michael. *Lynn Chadwick* (Lund Humphries, London: 2014).

MICHAEL CRAIG-MARTIN (b. 28 Aug. 1941, Dublin). *Studied*: Yale University, 1961–3; Yale School of Arts and Architecture, 1964–6. Moved to Britain, 1966. *Teaching*: Bath Academy of Art, Corsham, 1966–69; Canterbury College of Art, 1966–70; Goldsmiths' College, 1974–2000 (professor of fine art, 1994–2000). Artist in residence: King's College, Cambridge, 1970–72. *Exhibitions*: Hayward Gallery, 1972; Tate Gallery, 1972; Sydney Biennale, 1976, 1990; Whitechapel Art Gallery, 1995; Museum of Modern Art, New York, 1991; Centre Pompidou, Paris, 1994; São Paulo Bienal, 1998; Waddington Galleries, 2000; National Art Centre, Tokyo, 2007; Alan Cristea Gallery, 2008, 2014; New Art Centre, Salisbury, 2011; Serpentine Gallery, 2015. Retrospective: Irish Museum of Modern Art, Dublin, 2006–07. Elected RA, 2006; awarded CBE, 2001; knighted 2016.

Interviewed by Melanie Roberts, Jul. 1998–Feb. 2002, Artists' Lives, British Library reference C466/109.

Michael Craig-Martin: Works 1964–2006 (exhib. cat., Irish Museum of Modern Art, Dublin, 2006).
Craig-Martin, Michael. *On Being an Artist* (Art/Books, London: 2015).

PAUL FEILER (b. 30 Apr. 1918, Frankfurt-am-Mein; d. 8 Jul. 2013, Paul, nr. Penzance). Moved to Britain, 1933. *Studied*: Slade School of Fine Art, 1936–9. *Teaching*: West of England College of Art, 1946–1980s (head of painting from 1960). *Exhibitions*: Redfern Gallery, 1953–7; Richard Demarco Gallery, Edinburgh, 1968; Wills Lane Gallery, St Ives, 1977; Le Cadre Gallery, Hong Kong, 1986; Galerie 20, Paris, 1987; Austin/Desmond Fine Art, 1990; Redfern Gallery, 1993–2013. Retrospectives: Arnolfini Gallery, Bristol, 1961; Tate St Ives, 2005.

Interviewed by Cathy Courtney, Dec. 1999–Jun. 2000, Artists' Lives, British Library reference C466/95.

Paul Feiler: The Near and the Far (exhib. cat., Tate St Ives, 2005).
Raeburn, Michael. *Paul Feiler* (Lund Humphries, London: 2018).

ELISABETH FRINK (b. 14 Nov. 1930, Thurlow, Suffolk; d. 18 Apr. 1993, Woolland, Dorset). *Studied*: Guildford School of Art, 1947–9; Chelsea School of Art, 1949–53. *Teaching*: Chelsea School of Art, 1953–60; St Martin's School of Art, 1955–7. *Exhibitions*: St George's Gallery, 1955; Waddington Galleries, 1959–81; Royal Academy of Arts, 1985; Fischer Fine Art, 1989; National Museum of Women in the Arts, Washington, DC, 1990. Retrospective: Hong Kong, 1989. Awarded CBE, 1969; elected RA, 1977; awarded DBE, 1982; appointed Companion of Honour, 1992.

Interviewed by Sarah Kent, Dec. 1992, Artists' Lives, British Library reference C466/12.

Gardiner, Stephen. *Frink: The Official Biography of Elisabeth Frink* (Harper Collins, London: 1999).
Ratuszniak, Annette. *Elisabeth Frink: Catalogue Raisonné of Sculpture, 1947–93* (Lund Humphries, London: 2013).

TERRY FROST (b. 13 Oct. 1915, Leamington Spa; d. 1 Sept. 2003, Hayle, Cornwall). *Studied*: Camberwell School of Arts and Crafts, 1947–9; Gregory Fellow, University of Leeds, 1954–6. *Teaching*: Bath Academy of Art, 1952–4; University of Reading, 1965–74 (professor emeritus, 1981). *Exhibitions*: Leicester Galleries, 1952–8; Bertha Schaeffer Gallery, New York, 1960; Waddington Galleries, 1961–78; Arnolfini Gallery, Oxford, 1965; Queen Square Gallery, Leeds, 1967; Institute of Contemporary Arts, 1971; Peter Scott Gallery, Lancaster University, 1994; Newlyn Art Gallery, 1995. Retrospectives: Arts Council and South West Arts, touring, 1975; Royal Academy of Arts, 2000; Tate St Ives, 2015. Elected RA, 1992; knighted 1998.

Interviewed by Tamsyn Woollcombe, Nov.–Dec. 1994, Artists' Lives, British Library reference C466/022.

Lewis, David *et al. Terry Frost* (Scolar, Aldershot: 1994).
Bristow, Roger. *Terry Frost: A Painter's Life* (Sansom & Co., Bristol: 2013).

HAMISH FULTON (b. 21 Jul. 1946, London). *Studied*: Hammersmith College of Art, 1965–6; St Martin's School of Art, 1966–8; Royal College of Art, 1968–9. *Exhibitions*: Richard Demarco

Gallery, Edinburgh, 1971; Museum of Modern Art, Oxford, 1974; Kunstmuseum, Basel, 1975; Whitechapel Art Gallery, 1979; Centre Georges Pompidou, Paris, 1981; Waddington Galleries, 1980, 1982; Victoria Miro, 1987, 1989; Serpentine Gallery, 1991; Museum of Modern Art, Wakayama, Japan, 1996; Palais Thurn und Taxis, Bregenz, 1999; Sainsbury Centre for the Visual Arts, Norwich, 2001; Tate Britain, 2002; IKON Gallery, Birmingham, 2012; Turner Contemporary, Margate, 2012; Galleri Riis, Oslo, 2016; Fine Art Society, Edinburgh, 2017. Retrospectives: Stedelijk van Abbemuseum, Eindhoven, and touring, 1985; Albright-Knox Art Gallery, Buffalo, NY, and touring, 1990.

Interviewed by Stephen Bury, Dec. 2002, Artists' Lives, British Library reference C466/158.

Vettese, Angela *et al. Hamish Fulton: Walking Artist* (Richter, Düsseldorf: 2002).
Baur, Andrea *et al. Hamish Fulton: Walking Transformation* (Snoek, Cologne: 2015).

WILLIAM GEAR (b. 2 Aug. 1915, Methil, Fife; d. 12 Mar. 1997, Birmingham). *Studied*: Edinburgh College of Art, 1932–6. Curator, Towner Art Gallery, Eastbourne, 1958–64. *Teaching*: head of fine art, Birmingham College of Art and Design, 1964–75. *Exhibitions*: Gimpel Fils, 1948; South London Art Gallery, 1954; Edinburgh Festival, 1966; Royal Birmingham Society of Artists, 1976; IKON Gallery, Birmingham, 1982; Redfern Gallery, 1987–96; Karl & Faber, Munich, 1988–9; Scottish Arts Club, Edinburgh, 1995.

Interviewed by Tessa Sidey, Jul.–Aug. 1995, Artists' Lives, British Library reference C466/33.

McEwen, John. *William Gear* (Lund Humphries, Aldershot: 2003).
Lambirth, Andrew. *William Gear* (Sansom & Co., Bristol: 2016).

SHEILA GIRLING (b. 1 Jul. 1924, Birmingham; d. 14 Feb. 2015, London). *Studied*: Birmingham School of Art; Royal Academy Schools. *Exhibitions*: Edmonton Art Gallery, Alberta, 1978; Acquavella Contemporary Art, New York, 1980–85; Warwick Arts Trust, 1986; Francis Graham-Dixon Gallery, 1989–93; Churchill College, Cambridge, 1999; Pilgrim Gallery, 2003; Art First, 2007. Retrospectives: Institut Valencià d'Art Modern, Valencia, 2006; Annely Juda, 2015.

Interviewed by Hester Westley, Aug. 2009, Artists' Lives, British Library reference C466/296.

Sheila Girling (exhib. cat., Institut Valencià d'Art Modern, Valencia, 2006).
Westley, Hannah. *Sheila Girling* (Lund Humphries, Farnham: 2008).

JOSEF HERMAN (b. 3 Jan. 1911, Warsaw; d. 19 Feb. 2000, London). Moved to Britain, 1940. *Studied*: Warsaw School of Art and Decoration, 1930–31. *Exhibitions*: Les Grillets, Brussels, 1939; Reid Gallery and Lefevre, 1943; Roland, Browse and Delbanco, 1946–76; Arts Council, Glynn Vivian Gallery, Swansea and touring, 1948; Southampton Art Gallery, 1952; Ferens Art Gallery, Hull, 1953; Whitechapel Art Gallery, 1956; Kunstkabinett, Frankfurt, 1958; Aberdeen Art Gallery, 1962; Helene C. Seiferheld Gallery, New York, 1963; Towner Art Gallery, Eastbourne, 1966; Gardner Art Centre, University of Sussex, 1972; Glasgow Art Gallery and Museum, and touring, 1975; Bernard Jacobson,

1984; Third Eye Centre, Glasgow, 1985; Pier Arts Centre, Stromness, 1987; Boundary Gallery, 1987–94; Wakefield Art Gallery and Museum, 1991; Flowers East, 1991–8. Retrospectives: Camden Arts Centre, 1980; Boundary Gallery, 1998. Awarded OBE, 1981; elected RA, 1990.

Interviewed by Paul Thompson, Apr.–May 1991, Artists' Lives, British Library reference C466/004.

Davies, Peter. *Josef Herman's Drawings and Studies* (Redcliffe Press, Bristol: 1989).
Bohm-Duchen, Monica. *The Art and Life of Josef Herman* (Lund Humphries, Farnham: 2009).

PATRICK HERON (b. 30 Jan. 1920, Leeds; d. 20 Mar. 1999, Zennor, Cornwall). *Studied*: Slade School of Fine Art, 1937–9. *Exhibitions*: Redfern Gallery, 1947–58; Waddington Galleries, 1959–87; Bertha Schaefer Gallery, New York, 1960–65; São Paulo Bienal, 1965; Rudy Komon Gallery, Sydney, 1970; Whitechapel Art Gallery, 1972. Retrospectives: Wakefield City Art Gallery, and touring, 1952; Richard Demarco Gallery, Edinburgh, 1967; Kunstnernes Hus, Oslo, 1967; Museum of Modern Art, Oxford, 1968; University of Texas at Austin Art Museum, 1978; Oriel Gallery, Cardiff, 1979; Barbican Art Gallery, 1985; Tate Gallery, 1998.

Interviewed by Mel Gooding, Apr. 1996, Artists' Lives, British Library reference C466/049.

McNay, Michael. *Patrick Heron* (Tate, London: 1992).
Gooding, Mel. *Patrick Heron* (Phaidon, London: 1995).

LUBAINA HIMID (b. 25 Jul. 1954, Zanzibar). *Studied*: Wimbledon College of Art; Royal College of Art. *Teaching*: professor of contemporary art, University of Central Lancashire, from 2001. *Exhibitions*: Pentonville Gallery, 1986; Chisenhale Gallery, 1989; Rochdale Art Gallery and South Bank Centre, 1992; Black Art Gallery, 1993; Peg Alston Gallery, New York, 1996, 2008; Harris Museum and Art Gallery, Preston, 1997, 2007, 2012; Tate St Ives, 1999; St Jorgens Museum, Bergen, 2001; Hatton Gallery, Newcastle upon Tyne, 2004; Sudley House and Liverpool Museums, 2010; Platt Hall Museum of Costume, Manchester, 2011; Tate Britain, 2011, 2012; International Institute for Visual Art, 2013; Spike Island, Bristol, 2017; Modern Art Oxford, 2017. Awarded MBE, 2010; Turner Prize, 2017.

Interviewed by Anna Dyke, Sept.–Nov. 2006, Artists' Lives, British Library reference C466/249.

Lubaina Himid: Naming the Money (exhib. cat., Hatton Gallery, University of Newcastle upon Tyne, 2004).
Orlando, Sophie. *British Black Art Works: Debates on the Western Art History* (Dis Voir, Paris: 2016).

TESS JARAY (b. 31 Dec. 1937, Vienna). *Studied*: St Martin's School of Art, 1954–7; Slade School of Fine Art, 1957–60. *Teaching*: Hornsey College of Arts and Crafts, 1964–8; Slade School of Fine Art, 1968–99. *Exhibitions*: Grabowski Gallery, 1963; Richard Demarco Gallery, Edinburgh, 1967; City Art Gallery, Bristol, 1972; Angela Flowers Gallery, 1976; Adelaide Festival Centre, Adelaide, 1980; Whitworth Art Gallery, Manchester, 1984; Ashmolean Museum, Oxford, 1984; Serpentine

Gallery, 1988; Todd Gallery, 1993; Purdy Hicks Gallery, 2001, 2003; Clifford Chance, 2001; Lyon & Turnbull, 2008; Piper Gallery, 2012; Djanogly Art Gallery, Nottingham, 2013. Elected RA, 2010.

Interviewed by Judith Bumpus, Mar.–Jul. 1996, Artists' Lives, British Library reference C466/045.

Davey, Richard. *Tess Jaray: Thresholds* (Royal Academy of Arts, London: 2012).
Davey, Richard, *et al. The Art of Tess Jaray* (Ridinghouse, London: 2013).

MARY KELLY (b. 7 Jun. 1941, Fort Dodge, Iowa). *Studied*: College of Saint Teresa, Winona, Minnesota, 1963; Pius XII Institute, Florence, 1965; St Martin's School of Art, 1968–70. *Teaching*: American University, Beirut, 1965–8; Camberwell School of Arts and Crafts, 1974–7; University of California, Los Angeles, 1996–present (professor of art and critical theory). *Exhibitions*: Institute of Contemporary Art, 1976; Museum of Modern Art, Oxford, 1977; Riverside Studios, 1986; Vancouver Art Gallery, 1990; New Museum of Contemporary Art, New York, 1990; Power Plant, Toronto, 1991; Institute of Contemporary Art, 1993; Helsinki City Art Museum, 1994; Konstmuseet Malmø, 1996; Generali Foundation, Vienna, 1998; Santa Monica Museum of Art, 2001; Espacio AV, Murcia, 2006; Ujazdowski Castle Centre for Contemporary Art, Warsaw, 2008; Moderna Museet, Stockholm, 2010; Whitworth Art Gallery, Manchester, 2011; Postmasters Gallery, New York, 2012; Pippy Houldsworth Gallery, 2014.

Interviewed by Lydia O'Ryan, Sept. 2004, Artists' Lives, British Library reference C466/194.

Kelly, Mary. *Post-Partum Document* (Routledge & Kegan Paul, London: 1983).
Crimp, Douglas *et al. Mary Kelly* (Phaidon, London: 1997).

MICHAEL KIDNER (b. 11 Sept. 1917, Kettering; d. 29 Nov. 2009, London). *Studied*: University of Cambridge (history and anthropology); Ohio State University (landscape architecture); Goldsmiths' College (art and design); in André Lhote's atelier, Paris. Served in Canadian army, 1941–6. *Exhibitions*: St Hilda's College, Oxford, 1959; Grabowski Gallery, 1964; Gardner Centre Gallery, University of Sussex, 1967; Axiom Gallery, 1967; Lucy Milton Gallery, 1974; Kunstfackskolan, Stockholm, 1981; Air Gallery, 1983; Victoria Art Gallery, Bath, 1985; Museum of Contemporary Art, Lodz, 1985; Hatton Gallery, Newcastle upon Tyne, 1985; Escola de Artes Visuales, Rio de Janeiro, 1988; Galerie Hubert Winter, Vienna, 1990–2010; Center for International Contemporary Arts, New York, 1990; Henry Moore Institute, Leeds, 1997; Flowers East, 2003, 2007; Flowers Central, 2004; Royal Academy of Arts, 2009; Royal West of England Academy, 2011; Flowers Gallery, 2012; Flowers Gallery, New York, 2016. Elected RA, 2004.

Interviewed by Penelope Curtis and Cathy Courtney, Aug. 2005–Feb. 2006, Artists' Lives, British Library reference C466/040.

Michael Kidner: At-tension to the Wave (exhib. cat., Center for International Contemporary Arts, New York, 1990).
Michael Kidner (exhib. cat., Flowers East, London, 2008).

BRYAN KNEALE (b. 13 Jun. 1930, Douglas, Isle of Man). *Studied*: Douglas School of Art, 1947; Royal Academy Schools, 1948–52. *Teaching*: Royal College of Art, tutor (1963–85), head of sculpture (1985–90), professor of drawing (1990–95); head of sculpture; Hornsey College of Arts and Crafts, 1968; professor of sculpture, Royal Academy Schools, 1980–87. *Exhibitions*: Redfern Gallery, 1954–69; Dartington Hall, Devon, 1972; Taranman Gallery, 1977–81; 51 Gallery, Edinburgh, 1981; Chelsea Harbour, 1993; Goodwood Sculpture Park, Chichester, 1996; Lewes Festival, 1997; New Art Centre, Salisbury, 2000; Hart Gallery, 2004, 2007, 2012; Cass Sculpture Foundation, 2005; Royal Academy of Arts, 2011. Retrospectives: Whitechapel Art Gallery, 1966; Serpentine Gallery, 1978; Royal College of Art, 1986; Natural History Museum, 1991; Royal West of England Academy, 1995; Pangolin London, 2015. Elected RA, 1974.

Interviewed by Andrew Lambirth, Dec. 1997–Sept. 1998, Artists' Lives, British Library reference C466/113.

Bryan Kneale: Phoenix (exhib. cat., Beaux Arts Gallery, London, 2011).
Bryan Kneale: Five Decades (exhib. cat., Pangolin London, 2015).

BRUCE LACEY (b. 1927, Lewisham, London; d. 18 Feb. 2016, Norfolk). Served in the Royal Navy, 1945–6. *Studied*: Hornsey College of Arts and Crafts, 1948–51; Royal College of Art, 1951–4. *Exhibitions*: Gallery One, 1963; Marlborough New London Gallery, 1965; Fairfield Hall, Croydon, 1965; Arts Council Gallery, Cardiff, 1967; Retrospective: Whitechapel Art Gallery, 1975; Fruitmarket Gallery, Edinburgh, 1975; Camden Arts Centre, 2012.

Interviewed by Gillian Whiteley, May–Jul. 2000, Artists' Lives, British Library reference C466/099.

Bruce Lacey: 40 Years of Assemblages, Environments and Robots (exhib. cat., Whitechapel Art Gallery, London, 1975).
Mellor, David Alan *et al. The Bruce Lacey Experience: Paintings, Sculptures, Installations, Performances* (London: Camden Arts Centre, 2012).

JOHN LATHAM (b. 23 Feb. 1921, Livingstone, Zambia; d. 1 Jan. 2006, Peckham, London). *Studied*: Regent Street Polytechnic, 1946; Chelsea College of Art and Design, 1947–51. *Exhibitions*: Kingly Gallery, 1948, 1951; Obelisk Gallery, 1955, 1957; Galerie Schmela, Düsseldorf, 1960; Galerie Internationale d'Art Contemporain, Paris, 1962; Kasmin Gallery, 1963; Alan Gallery, New York, 1964; Bangor City Art Gallery, 1965; Bluecoat Gallery, Liverpool, 1969; Lisson Gallery, 1970–2016; Gallery House, 1972; Städtische Kunsthalle, Düsseldorf, 1975; Tate Gallery, 1976; Fruitmarket Gallery, Edinburgh, 1976; Riverside Studios, 1982; Van Abbemuseum, Eindhoven, 1983; Museum of Modern Art, Oxford, 1991; Tate Britain, 2005; John Hansard Gallery, University of Southampton, 2006; Richard Saltoun/Karsten Schubert, 2010; Henry Moore Institute, Leeds, 2016; Serpentine Gallery, 2017; Lisson Gallery, New York, 2018.

Interviewed by Melanie Roberts, Mar. 1998–Jul. 2000, Artists' Lives, British Library reference C466/069.

Hill, John *et al. A Lesson in Sculpture with John Latham* (Henry Moore Institute, Leeds: 2016).
Donagh, Rita *et al. A World View: John Latham* (Walter König, Berlin: 2017).

KIM LIM (b. 1 Feb. 1936, Singapore; d. 23 Oct. 1997, London). *Studied*: St Martin's School of Art, 1954–6; Slade School of Fine Art, 1956–9. *Exhibitions*: Axiom Gallery, 1966, 1968; Waddington Galleries, 1973, 1990; Alpha Gallery, Singapore, 1974; Museum of Modern Art, Oxford, 1975; Tate Gallery, 1977; Roundhouse Gallery, 1979; Southampton Museum and Art Gallery, 1981; Nicola Jacobs Gallery, 1984, 1985; New Art Centre, Salisbury, 1993, 2014; Flowers East, 1993; Yorkshire Sculpture Park, Wakefield, 1995; Camden Arts Centre, 1999.

Interviewed by Cathy Courtney, Oct. 1995, Artists' Lives, British Library reference C466/051.

Kim Lim (exhib. cat., Waddington Galleries, London, 1990).
Kim Lim: Sculpture and Works on Paper (exhib. cat., Yorkshire Sculpture Park, Wakefield, 1995).

FRANK MARTIN (b. 27 Dec. 1914, Portsmouth; d. 19 Jan. 2004, Clacton-on-Sea). *Studied*: Portsmouth Art School; assistant to William McMillan; Royal Academy Schools, 1947–50. *Teaching*: St Martin's School of Art, 1947–79 (head of sculpture, 1952–79).

Interviewed by Melanie Roberts, Aug. 1997, Artists' Lives, British Library reference C466/058.

Caro, Anthony. 'Frank Martin' (obituary), *Independent* (11 Feb. 2004).
McLean, Bruce. 'Frank Martin' (obituary), *Guardian* (2 Mar. 2004).

ROBERT MEDLEY (b. 19 Dec. 1905, London; d. 20 Oct. 1994, London). *Studied*: Byam Shaw School of Art, 1921; Royal Academy Schools, 1921; Slade School of Fine Art, 1923–6. Served in army, 1941–5. *Teaching*: Chelsea School of Art and Design, 1932–41, 1945–51; Slade School of Fine Art, 1951–8; head of painting, Camberwell School of Arts and Crafts, 1958–65. *Exhibitions*: Cooling Galleries, 1931; Lefevre Gallery, 1948; Leicester Galleries, 1960; Lisson Gallery, 1972; Coram Gallery, 1994; James Hyman Gallery, 2005–7; Retrospectives: Whitechapel Art Gallery, 1963; Museum of Modern Art, Oxford, 1984.

Interviewed by Andrew Lambirth, May.–Aug. 1994, Artists' Lives, British Library reference C466/019.

Robert Medley: Paintings, Drawings and Sculpture, 1928–1963 (exhib. cat., Whitechapel Art Gallery, London, 1963).
Medley, Robert. *Drawn from the Life: A Memoir* (Faber and Faber, London: 1983).

DAVID NASH (b. 14 Nov. 1945, Esher, Surrey). *Studied*: Kingston College of Art, 1963–5; Chelsea School of Art and Design, 1969–70. *Exhibitions*: Oriel, Bangor, 1973, 1976; Arnolfini Gallery, Bristol, 1979; Yorkshire Sculpture Park, Wakefield, 1982; Third Eye Centre, Glasgow, and touring, 1983; Rijksmuseum Kröller-Müller, Otterlo, 1985; Juda Rowan Gallery, 1986; Galerij S65, Aalst, 1988; Annely Juda, 1989–2018; Musée des Beaux-Arts, Calais, 1990; Mappin Art Gallery, Sheffield,

1991; Louver Gallery, New York, 1992; Asahikawa Museum of Art, Hokkaido, and touring, 1994; Henry Moore Institute, Leeds, 1996; Parc Régional Tournay–Solvay, Brussels, 1998; Galerie Lelong, Paris, 2000–16; Galerie Lelong, New York, 2002; New Art Centre, Salisbury, 2003; Gerhard Marcks Haus, Bremen, 2003; Tate St Ives, 2004; Royal Academy of Arts, 2004; Musée d'Angers, Angers, 2005; Konstructiv Tendens, Stockholm, 2006; Kunsthalle, Emden, 2008; Abbot Hall, Kendal, 2009; Royal Botanic Gardens, Kew, 2012; Kukje Gallery, Seoul, 2014; Plas Glyn-y-Weddw, Gwynedd, 2017. Retrospectives: Serpentine Gallery, 1990; Yorkshire Sculpture Park, Wakefield, 2010. Elected RA, 1999; awarded OBE, 2004.

Interviewed by Denise Hooker, Jun. 1995, Artists' Lives, British Library reference C466/032.

Lynton, Norbert. *David Nash* (Thames & Hudson, London: 2007).
Payne, Michelle. *David Nash: A Natural Gallery* (Royal Botanic Gardens, Kew, London: 2013).

PAUL NEAGU (b. 22 Feb. 1938, Bucharest; d. 16 Jun. 2004, London). *Studied*: Bucharest Institute of Fine Arts, 1959–65. Moved to Britain, 1970. *Teaching*: Chelsea School of Art; Middlesex Polytechnic. *Exhibitions*: Amphora Gallery, Bucharest, 1969; Richard Demarco Gallery, Edinburgh, 1969–76; Compass Gallery, Glasgow, 1970; Sigi Krauss Gallery, 1971; Serpentine Gallery, 1973; Museum of Modern Art, Oxford, 1975; Whitechapel Gallery, 1975; Institute of Contemporary Arts, 1979; Third Eye Centre, Glasgow, 1979; Norwich Arts Centre, 1980; Rivolta Gallery, Lausanne, 1981, 1984; Sunderland Arts Centre, 1981; Gallery K, Tokyo, 1983, 1990; Kamakura Gallery, Tokyo, 1983; Liverpool University, 1983; London Business School, 1985; British School at Rome, 1992; Flowers East, 1993–99; Tochigi Prefectural Museum of Fine Art, Tochigi, 1995; Retrospectives: Brukenthal Museum, Sibiu, 1994; National Museum of Romania, 1997; Muzeul de Arta Contemporana, Bucharest, 2004; Henry Moore Institute, Leeds, 2015.

Interviewed by Mel Gooding, Oct. 1994–Mar. 1995, Artists' Lives, British Library reference C466/027.

Simionescu, Cristian. *A Derridean Tornado: Paul Neagu, 1965–2000* (Generative Art Trust, London: 2000).
Gooding, Mel *et al. Paul Neagu: Palpable Sculpture* (Henry Moore Institute, Leeds: 2015).

BREON O'CASEY (b. 30 Apr. 1928, London; d. 22 May 2011, Penzance). *Studied*: Anglo-French Art Centre, London. *Exhibitions*: Somerville College, Oxford, 1954; Arnolfini Gallery, Bristol, 1960; Marjorie Parr Gallery, 1969, 1973; British Crafts Centre, 1976, 1985; Oxford Gallery, London, 1979–96; Kruger Gallery, New York, 1983; Helen Drutt Gallery, Philidelphia, 1989–2000; Oriel, Cardiff, 1995; St James's Gallery, Bath, 1995; Brewery Arts, Cirencester, 1997; Royal Hibernian Academy, Dublin, 2000; Mullan Gallery, Belfast, 2004, 2006; Somerset House, London, 2010; Newlyn Art Gallery, 2012; Pangolin, 2014.

Interviewed by Christopher Reid, Aug. 2001, Crafts' Lives, British Library reference C960/10.

Fallon, Brian and O'Casey, Breon. *Breon O'Casey* (Ashgate, Aldershot: 1999).
O'Sullivan, Jack and Bowness, Sophie. *Breon O'Casey: Celtic Artist* (Lund Humphries, Aldershot: 2003).

EDUARDO PAOLOZZI (b. 7 Mar. 1924, Leith; d. 22 Apr. 2005, London). *Studied*: Edinburgh College of Art, 1943–4; St Martin's School of Art, 1944–5; Slade School of Fine Art, 1945–7. *Teaching*: Central School of Arts and Crafts, 1955–6; Royal College of Art, 1968–89; Fachhochschule, Cologne, 1977–81; Akademie der Bildenden Künste, 1981–91. *Exhibitions*: Mayor Gallery, 1947; Betty Parsons Gallery, New York, 1960, 1962; Tate Gallery, 1971, 1996; Victoria & Albert Museum, 1973; Nationalgalerie, West Berlin, 1975; Fruitmarket Gallery, Edinburgh, 1976; Glasgow League of Artists, 1979; Museum für Künste und Gewerbe, Hamburg, 1982; Architectural Association, 1984; Contemporary Art Centre, Lyon, 1985; Ivan Dougherty Gallery, Sydney, 1985; Royal Academy of Arts, 1986; Serpentine Gallery, 1987; Fitzwilliam Museum, Cambridge, 1992, 1996; Yorkshire Sculpture Park, Wakefield, 1994; Hayward Gallery, 1996; Dean Gallery, Edinburgh, 1999. Retrospectives: Victoria & Albert Museum, 1977; Dean Gallery, Edinburgh, 2004. Awarded CBE, 1968; elected RA, 1979; knighted 1989.

Interviewed by Frank Whitford, Jun. 1993–May 1994, Artists' Lives, British Library reference C466/017.

Collins, Judith. *Eduardo Paolozzi* (Lund Humphries, London: 2014).
Foster, Hal *et al. Eduardo Paolozzi* (exhib. cat., Whitechapel Gallery, London, 2017).

ROLAND PICHÉ (b. 21 Nov. 1938, Hackney, London). *Studied*: Hornsey College of Arts and Crafts, 1956–60; Royal College of Art, 1960–64. *Teaching*: Maidstone Collge of Art, 1964–89. *Exhibitions*: Marlborough New London Gallery, 1967; Gallery Ad Libitum, Antwerp, 1969; Canon Park, Birmingham, 1975; IKON Gallery, Birmingham, 1980; Kopp-Bardellini Gallery, Zurich, 1993; Glaxo Smith Kline, Harlow Research Centre, 2001; Chappel Galleries, Colchester, 2005; Time & Life Building, 2010; Chapter House, Canterbury Cathedral, 2013.

Interviewed by Matthew Withey, Feb. 2004, Artists' Lives, British Library reference C466/183.

Roland Piché (exhib. cat., Marlborough New London Gallery, London, 1967).
Roland Piché (exhib. cat., Hay Hill Gallery, London, 2010).

MICHAEL ROTHENSTEIN (b. 19 Mar. 1908, Hampstead, London; 6 Jul. 1993, Stisted, Essex). *Studied*: School of Art and Woodcarving, London, 1922–3; Chelsea Polytechnic School of Art, 1923–4; Central School of Art and Crafts, 1924–6. *Teaching*: Camberwell School of Arts and Crafts; Hornsey College of Arts and Crafts; *Exhibitions*: The Minories, Colchester, 1974; Redfern Gallery, 1986–92; Angela Flowers Gallery, 1988; Royal Academy of Arts, 1992; Flowers East, 1992. Retrospective: Stoke-on-Trent City Museum and Art Gallery, 1989. Elected RA, 1983.

Interviewed by Mel Gooding, Jul. 1990, Artists' Lives, British Library reference C466/002.

Rothenstein, Michael. *Frontiers of Printmaking: New Aspects of Relief Printing* (Reinhold, New York: 1966).
Mel Gooding *et al. Michael Rothenstein: The Retrospective* (exhib. cat., Stoke-on-Trent City Museum and Art Gallery, 1989).

MICHAEL SANDLE (b. 18 May 1936, Weymouth). *Studied*: Douglas School of Art, 1951–4; Slade School of Fine Art, 1956–9. *Teaching*: Coventry College of Art, 1964–8; University of Calgary, Alberta, 1970–71; University of Victoria, BC, 1972–3; Fachhochschule für Gestaltung, Pforzheim, 1973–80; professor of sculpture, Akademie der Bildenden Künste, Karlsruhe, 1980–99. *Exhibitions*: Jason and Rhodes, 1995; Manx Museum, Isle of Man, 1998; Centenary Art Gallery, Leeds, 2007; Tate Britain, 2008; Flowers Gallery, Pforzheim, 2012. Retrospectives: DLI Gallery, Durham, 2005; Ludlow Castle, 2007. Elected RA, 1989, resigned 1997, rejoined 2004.

Interviewed by Melanie Roberts, Apr. 1994, Artists' Lives, British Library reference C466/103.

McEwen, John. *The Sculpture of Michael Sandle* (Henry Moore Foundation/Lund Humphries, London: 2002).
Sandle, Michael. *Time, Transition and Dissent* (exhib. cat., Flowers Gallery, London, 2016).

JACK SMITH (b. 18 Jun. 1928, Sheffield; d. 11 Jun. 2011, Hove). *Studied*: Sheffield College of Art, 1944–6; St Martin's School of Art, 1948–50; Royal College of Art, 1950–3. *Exhibitions*: Beaux Arts Gallery, 1952–8; Catherine Viviano Gallery, New York, 1958, 1962; Whitchapel Art Gallery, 1959, 1971; Matthiesen Gallery, 1960, 1963; Pittsburgh International, 1955–64; Grosvenor Gallery, 1965; Marlborough Fine Art, 1968; Konsthallen, Gothenburg, 1968; Bear Lane Gallery, Oxford, 1970; Redfern Gallery, 1973, 1976; Serpentine Gallery, 1978; Fischer Fine Art, 1981, 1983; Museo Municipal, Madrid, 1983; Flowers East, 1990–2000. Flowers Central, 2003, 2007. Retrospective: Flowers East, 2009.

Interviewed by Cathy Courtney, Nov. 1999–May 2001, Artists' Lives, British Library reference C466/096.

Lynton, Norbert. *Jack Smith: A Painter in Pursuit of Marvels* (Momentum, London: 2000).
Heller, Robert. *The Art of Jack Smith* (Flowers East, London: 2007).

BARBARA STEVENI (b. 21 Aug. 1928, Mashhad, Iran). *Studied*: Chelsea School of Art and Design. Founded Artist Placement Group, 1966; 'inn70' Hayward Gallery, 1971; APG at Whitechapel Art Gallery, 1977; founded Organisation and Imagination, 1989; established 'Art in Context' at the London Institute, 1991.

Interviewed by Melanie Roberts, Jun.–Oct. 1998, Artists' Lives, British Library reference C466/080.

Latham, Barbara and Hills, Joan. *Artist Placement Group* (APG, London: 1966).
Steveni, Barbara, 'Repositioning Art in the Decision-making Processes of Society', presentation at the *Artist as Educator* symposium at the Ikon Gallery, Birmingham (2003).

WILLI SOUKOP (b. 5 Jan. 1907, Vienna; d. 8 Feb. 1995, Glasgow). *Studied*: Academy of Fine Art, Vienna, 1928–34. *Teaching*: Dartington Hall, Totnes, 1935–45; Bromley School of Art, 1945–6; Guildford School of Art, 1945–47; Chelsea School of Art, 1947–72; master of sculpture, Royal

Academy Schools, 1969–82. *Exhibitions*: Royal Academy of Arts, from 1935; Battersea Park, 1949, 1950; Yehudi Menuhin School, Cobham, 1979; Belgrave Gallery, 1991. Elected RA, 1969.

Willi Soukop, interviewed by Andrew Lambirth, November 1994, Artists' Lives, British Library reference C466/29.

Soukop, Willi. 'Modelling for Beginners', *The Artist* (winter 1953).
Willi Soukop RA (exhib. cat., Belgrave Gallery, London, 1991).

ROSEMARY YOUNG (Butler) (b. 1930, Esher, Surrey). *Studied*: Camberwell School of Arts and Crafts, 1947–8; Wimbledon School of Art, 1948–9; Slade School of Fine Art, 1949–53. *Exhibitions*: Hanover Gallery, 1955; Pangolin London, 2014, 2016; The Lightbox, Woking, 2017.

Interviewed by Gillian Whiteley, Sept. 1999–Jun. 2000, Artists' Lives, British Library reference C466/094.

Rosemary Young, Robert Clatworthy, Tikis Vassilakis (exhib. cat., Hanover Gallery, London, 1955)
Sculpture in the Home (exhib. cat., Pangolin London, 2014).

Notes

Full details of Artists' Lives interviews, including the interviewer's name and the month and year the interview was started and concluded, are given in the first instance. Subsequent citations give only the British Library sound catalogue reference. Where a full transcript of an interview is available, I have given page references; where there is no transcript, and I have transcribed extracts from digital audio, track numbers and time-spans are cited.

INTRODUCTION

1 Bruce Lacey, interviewed by Gillian Whiteley, May–Jul. 2000, Artists' Lives, British Library reference C466/99, transcript, p.291.

2 Thompson, Paul, *The Voice of the Past: Oral History* (Oxford University Press, Oxford: 1978; 4th edn, 2017), p.23.

3 Barthes, Roland and Heath, Stephen (trans.), 'The Grain of the Voice', *Image Music Text*, (Fontana, London: 1977), pp 179–89. Writing of vocal music, Barthes defines the 'grain of the voice' as 'the materiality of the body speaking its mother tongue' (p.182).

4 Paul Thompson's *The Voice of the Past* provides an excellent introduction to the development, scope and methodology of oral history.

5 Auden, W.H., 'Making, Knowing and Judging', *The Dyer's Hand and Other Essays* (Random House, New York: 1962), p.49.

6 Derrick Greaves, interviewed by Cathy Courtney, Jul. 1999–Jun. 2000, Artists' Lives, British Library reference C466/83, track 12 of 22, 2'59"–4'02".

7 See www.bl.uk/projects/national-life-stories.

8 Sylvester, David, 'The Kitchen Sink', *Encounter* (Dec 1954), p.62.

9 ibid.

10 *The Forgotten Fifties* (exhib. cat. Graves Art Gallery, Sheffield, 1984), p.49.

11 Jack Smith, interviewed by Cathy Courtney, Nov. 1999–May 2001, Artists' Lives, British Library reference C466/96, transcript, p.83.

12 ibid., pp 248–9.
13 Quoted in Gayford, Martin, *Modernists and Mavericks: Bacon, Freud, Hockney and the London Painters* (Thames & Hudson, London: 2018), p.262.
14 Phyllida Barlow, interviewed by Kirstie Gregory, interview in progress, 2018, Artists' Lives, British Library reference C466/355, track 17, clip 1, 19'21"–19'56.
15 Pliny the Elder and Healy, John F (trans.), *Natural History: A Selection* (Penguin, London: 1991), p.331.
16 Vasari, Giorgio and Bull, George (trans.), *Lives of the Artists* (Penguin, Harmondsworth: 1965; repr. 1974), p.216.
17 Vasari includes four female artists in the *Lives*: the Bolognese sculptor Properzia de' Rossi (c.1490–1530); the painter and prioress of the convent of S. Caterina di Siena in Florence, Sister Plautilla Nelli (1524–88); the painter Madonna Lucrezia (fl. c.1560); and Sofonisba Anguissola (c.1532–1625), the most celebrated of six sisters, all painters, from a noble family in Cremona.
18 Berenson, Bernard, *The Italian Painters of the Renaissance* (Phaidon, London: 1952), pp 56–7.
19 David Nash, interviewed by Denise Hooker, Jun. 1995, Artist's Lives, British Library reference C466/32, transcript, p.182.
20 ibid.
21 Samuel, Raphael, 'Perils of the Transcript', *Oral History*, vol.1, no.2 (1972), p.19.
22 ibid.
23 ibid., p.21.
24 ibid.
25 The option for interviewees to close their recordings, or parts of their recordings, for a set term of years is an important provision, allowing people to speak freely about sensitive subjects.
26 C466/355, track 8, clip 1, 22'49"–23'09".
27 Tess Jaray, interviewed by Judith Bumpus, Mar.–Aug. 1996, Artists' Lives, British Library reference C466/45, transcript, p.134.

CHAPTER 1

1 Winnicott, D.W. and Winnicott, Clare (ed.), Shepherd, Ray (ed.), Davis, Madeleine (ed.), *Home Is Where We Start From: Essays by a Psychoanalyst* (Penguin, London: 1990), p.40.
2 C466/32, transcript, pp 244–5.
3 William Rothenstein (1872–1945) had studied in Paris, where he was encouraged by Edgar Degas and Camille Pissarro and was influenced by James Abbott McNeill Whistler. Principal of the Royal College of Art between 1920 and 1935, he was knighted in 1931. He served as a war artist in both world wars.
4 Michael Rothenstein, interviewed by Mel Gooding, Jul. 1990, Artists' Lives, British Library reference C466/02, transcript, p.5.
5 John Rothenstein (1901–92) became an eminent art historian and director of the Tate Gallery (1938–64).
6 C466/02, transcript, pp 6–7.
7 ibid., p.9.
8 ibid., p.3

9 ibid., p.4.

10 Leon Underwood (1890–1975) was a sculptor, painter and writer, who studied at the Slade before opening his own radical art school in 1921. In the 1940s he published a series of books on African sculpture.

11 Quoted in *Illustrated Catalogue of Acquisitions 1986–88* (Tate Gallery, London: 1996), p.239.

12 Eileen Agar, interviewed by Cathy Courtney, Apr.–Aug. 1990, Artists' Lives, British Library reference C466/01, transcript, pp 1–2.

13 ibid., pp 4–5.

14 ibid., p.11.

15 Josef Herman, interviewed by Paul Thompson, Apr.–May 1991, Artists' Lives, British Library reference C466/04, transcript, p.56.

16 ibid., p.7.

17 ibid., p.56.

18 ibid., p.1.

19 Michael Sandle, interviewed by Melanie Roberts, Apr. 1999, Artists' Lives, British Library reference C466/103, transcript, p.2.

20 ibid., p.10.

21 Quoted in Johnston, Chris, 'Farewell Bruce Lacey, multifaceted artist who was one of a kind', *Guardian* (20 Feb, 2016).

22 Lacey, Bruce, 'A Statement', typescript, Tate Gallery Archive 8714/3/3.

23 C466/99, transcript, p.1.

24 ibid., pp 14–15.

25 ibid.

26 ibid., pp 12–13.

27 C466/01, transcript, p.38.

28 Reg Butler (1913–81) trained as an architect, then turned to sculpture after learning blacksmithing as a conscientious objector during the Second World War. His welded metal sculptures attracted attention at the 1951 Festival of Britain; in 1953 he won the international sculpture competition to design a monument to the Unknown Political Prisoner. He taught at the Slade between 1951 and 1980.

29 Butler's virulent disparagement of women artists is independently confirmed by other former students, such as Elisabeth Frink: 'There was this idea being circulated that the students at the Slade who were serious were the men, and that the women were really there to entertain the men, to be their girlfriends [. . .] This was an idea circulating within the institution itself, so it was the staff within the institution, who [. . .] definitely didn't treat the women seriously [. . .] I can remember Philip Sutton was very dismissive of female students, for instance. And Reg Butler argued that a woman couldn't really be a sculptor, it was impossible for a woman to be a sculptor. If she was a good sculptor, she wasn't a good woman! You know, you had the choice of either being one or the other, really.' Elisabeth Frink, interviewed by Sarah Kent, Dec. 1992, Artists' Lives, British Library reference C466/12 transcript, p.16.

30 Rosemary Butler (Young), interviewed by Gillian Whiteley, Sept. 1999–Jun. 2000, Artists' Lives, British Library reference C466/94, transcript, p.138.

31 ibid., p.146.

32 ibid., pp 147–8.

33 Sheila Girling, interviewed by Hester Westley, Aug. 2009, Artists' Lives, British Library reference C466/296, transcript, p.42.
34 ibid., pp 177–8.
35 ibid., pp 115–16.
36 ibid., p.180.
37 C466/45, transcript, p.225.
38 ibid., pp 221–2.
39 ibid., p.225.
40 ibid., p.227.
41 Barlow, Phyllida, 'My Teacher: Phyllida Barlow on George Fullard', *Tate Etc*, no.38 (Autumn 2016).
42 Richard Wentworth (b.1947). British artist and curator; tutor at Goldsmiths' College, London, 1971–87. Interviewed for Artists' Lives by Hester Westley, Apr. 2008–Nov. 2013, British Library reference C466/282.
43 C466/355, track 17, clip 1, 18'35"–21'49".
44 Terry Frost, interviewed by Tamsyn Woolcombe, Nov.–Dec. 1994. Artists' Lives, British Library reference C466/22 transcript, p.135.
45 ibid., pp 141–2.
46 C466/32, transcript, pp 244–5.
47 Richard Hughes (1900–75). British novelist and poet; Hughes' best-known novels include *A High Wind in Jamaica* (1929) and *The Fox in the Attic* (1961).
48 C466/32, transcript, p.246.
49 ibid., p.12.

CHAPTER 2

1 C466/32, transcript, p.12.
2 C466/96, transcript, p.7.
3 Quoted in Roditi, Edouard. *Dialogues on Art* (Secker and Warburg, London: 1960), p.160.
4 Eduardo Paolozzi, interviewed by Frank Whitford, Jun. 1993–May 1994, Artists' Lives, British Library reference C466/17, transcript, p.285.
5 Quoted in Kirkpatrick, Diane. *Eduardo Paolozzi* (Studio Vista, London: 1970), p.31.
6 Popular in the 1930s, though little read today, Arthur Conan Doyle's novel *The White Company* (1891) is set in the fourteenth century, during the Hundred Years' War. As a member of the White Company of archers, its young hero, Alleyne, survives successive perilous adventures to be reunited with his true love, Maude.
7 C466/17, transcript, pp 16–17.
8 ibid., p.17.
9 ibid., p.8.
10 Kenneth Armitage, interviewed by Tamsyn Woollcombe, Jun.–Dec. 1991, Artists' Lives, British Library reference C466/08, transcript, pp 12–13.
11 ibid., p.15.
12 Wilhelmina Barns-Graham, interviewed by Tamsyn Woollcombe, Jun. 1994, Artists' Lives, British Library reference C466/34, transcript, p.1.

13 ibid., pp 7–8.

14 ibid., pp 3–4.

15 ibid., p.11.

16 ibid., p.15.

17 William Gear, interviewed by Tessa Sidey, Jul.–Aug. 1995, Artists' Lives, British Library reference C466/33, transcript, p.17.

18 William George Gillies (1898–1973) was a Scottish painter. As a student at Edinburgh College of Art in 1922 he co-founded the 1922 Group with William MacTaggart (they would both later teach Gear and Barns-Graham). In 1924 Gillies won a scholarship to study in Paris with André Lhote.

19 C466/33, transcript, pp 18–19.

20 ibid., p.19.

21 Paul Feiler, interviewed by Cathy Courtney, Dec. 1999–Jun. 2000, Artists' Lives, British Library reference C466/95, transcript, p.151.

22 Tilman Riemenschneider (*c.*1460–1531) was a celebrated medieval German sculptor. The sculpture Feiler refers to is probably a grey sandstone *Virgin Mary*, in the Liebieghaus sculpture collection, Frankfurt-am-Main.

23 C466/95, transcript, p.16.

24 ibid., p.12.

25 C466/04, transcript, p.18.

26 A tenter is a wooden frame used for drying new woollen cloth that has been washed clean of oil and dirt in a fulling mill. Hooks in the tenter frame hold the cloth taut so that it does not lose its shape. From O'Casey's description, it sounds as if the orchard at Dartington doubled as a tenter field, full of long tenter frames.

27 Breon O'Casey, interviewed by Christopher Reid, 2001, Crafts Lives, British Library reference C960/10, track 1 of 10, 16'51"–20'45". O'Casey's recording for National Life Stories' Crafts Lives archive is the only interview included in this book from a source other than Artists' Lives. There's no question that O'Casey – a painter, printmaker and sculptor – was (and considered himself to be) an artist. For much of his career, however, he earned a living from making jewellery and, to a lesser extent, hand-woven textiles, which led to his identification as a craftsman. O'Casey himself had no time for such categorical distinctions. At Dartington School he had learned 'to think with my hands as well as my head', and he believed in the artist's capacity to think in any medium that came to hand, however utilitarian. 'To make a piece of weaving into a work of art,' he noted, 'it is necessary to adapt the process of weaving, not the function of the woven.'

28 ibid., 22'31"–25'12".

29 Patrick Heron, interviewed by Mel Gooding, Apr. 1996, Artists' Lives, British Library reference C466/49, transcript, p.102.

30 ibid., tape 5.

31 ibid.

32 Bryan Kneale, interviewed by Andrew Lambirth, Dec. 1997–Sept. 1998, Artists' Lives, British Library reference C466/113, transcript, pp 57–8.

33 ibid.

34 ibid., p.58.

35 C466/103, transcript, pp 13–14.

36 John Sell Cotman (1782–1842) was an English landscape and marine painter, and member of the Norwich School of Artists, known for the almost abstract effects he achieved with flat watercolour washes.

37 Albert Pinkham Ryder (1847–1917) was an American painter of imaginative and allegorical landscape scenes. Jackson Pollock (1912–56) was just five years old when Ryder died but would later admire his work.

38 John Tunnard (1900–71). English modernist artist and designer.

39 C466/103, transcript, pp 19–20.

40 C466/32, transcript, p.78.

41 ibid., p.53.

42 *The Famous Five* is a series of 21 adventure stories published by the English children's author Enid Blyton (1897–1968) between 1942 and 1962.

43 Tom Kitten, Peter Rabbit and the rabbit-hunting gardener Mr McGregor are all characters in the tales for children written and illustrated by Beatrix Potter (1866–1943).

44 C466/32, transcript, pp 47–8.

45 Nash could be referring either to his grandparents' house, where he regularly stayed as a boy, or his own, much later home in Wales.

46 C466/32, transcript, pp 11–12.

47 Nash recounts the purchase by his father of Oaklands Park Hotel, a late-eighteenth- or early-nineteenth-century mansion in Weybridge, which was then demolished and the grounds divided into building plots for sale.

48 C466/32, transcript, pp 35–6.

49 ibid., pp 29–30.

50 Nash's reference to geometrical drawing and the holistic art and design ethos of the Bauhaus suggests that Gordon Taylor was interested in the innovatory Basic Design programme for teaching art.

51 C466/32, transcript, p.70.

52 C466/355, interview in progress.

53 ibid.

54 Lubaina Himid, interviewed by Anna Dyke, Sept. 2006–Jan. 2007, Artists' Lives, British Library reference C466/249, transcript, pp 86–8.

CHAPTER 3

1 C466/95, transcript, p.5.

2 Terry Frost, interviewed by Tamsyn Woollcombe, Nov.–Dec. 1994, Artists' Lives, British Library reference C466/22, transcript, p.2.

3 ibid., p.17.

4 This would have been the BBC documentary series *The Great War*, first broadcast in 1963–4, for which the military historian John Terraine wrote the script.

5 Ralph Brown, interviewed by Gillian Whiteley, Sept. 1999–Jun. 2000, Artists' Lives, British Library reference C466/93, transcript, p.3.

6 C466/296, transcript, pp 34–5.

7 C466/04, transcript, p.5.

8 ibid., pp 71–2.

9 In 1925 Leonard and Dorothy Elmhirst acquired the Dartington Estate in Devon, at the centre of which was a medieval great hall and imposing courtyard. Leonard had worked with the Indian poet Rabindranath Tagore on the latter's Institute of Rural Reconstruction in West Bengal and wanted to establish a similar idealistic rural community in England. By the early 1930s the Elmhirsts had established a progressive school at Dartington and were inviting artists and craftspeople to teach there. Before and during the Second World War, as Soukop explains, Dartington welcomed many refugees from Nazi Europe.

10 Willi Soukop, interviewed by Andrew Lambirth, Nov. 1994, Artists' Lives, British Library reference C466/29, transcript, p.16.

11 Mark Tobey (1890–1975). American painter. In 1931 he became the resident artist at the progressive school established at Dartington by Dorothy and Leonard Elmhirst.

12 Hein Heckroth (1901–70). German stage designer and movie art director.

13 C466/29, transcript, pp 16–17. In 1945 Soukop married the dancer Simon Moser (Michelle), who had come to Dartington as a member of Ballets Jooss.

14 C466/95, transcript, p.136.

15 C466/296, transcript, p.34.

16 C466/96, transcript, pp 110–11.

17 Basil Beattie, interviewed by Mel Gooding, Aug. 1996–May 2007, Artists' Lives, British Library reference C466/59, transcript, p.12.

18 Stuart Brisley, interviewed by Melanie Roberts, Sept.–Nov. 1996, Artists' Lives, British Library reference C466/43, transcript, pp 10–11.

19 ibid., p.13.

20 C466/103, transcript, p.3.

21 ibid., pp 90–1.

22 C466/22, transcript, p.65.

23 ibid., p.68.

24 ibid., p.72.

25 ibid., p.80.

26 ibid., p.73.

27 John Latham, interviewed by Melanie Roberts, Mar. 1998–Jul. 2000, Artists' Lives, British Library reference C466/69, transcript, p.16.

28 ibid., pp 16–17.

29 Michael Kidner, interviewed by Penelope Curtis and Cathy Courtney, Aug. 2005–Feb. 2006, Artists' Lives, British Library reference C466/40, transcript, p.47.

30 ibid., p.55.

31 The Savoia-Marchetti SM79 was a three-engine Italian torpedo bomber.

32 C466/69, transcript, p.22.

33 C466/59, transcript, pp 19–20.

34 Between June 1948 and May 1949 the Soviet Union blocked all land access to West Berlin, so that the Allied-controlled sector of the city had to be supplied by air.

35 C466/96, transcript, pp 8–9.

36 The glasshouse is a term for a military prison, named after a Victorian army prison in Aldershot that had a glazed roof.

37 C466/96, transcript, pp 98–9.
38 C466/17, transcript, p.183.
39 Ho Chi Minh (1890–1969). Vietnamese Communist leader.
40 Roland Piché, interviewed by Matthew Withy, Feb. 2004, Artists' Lives, British Library reference C466/183, transcript, pp 51–2.
41 C466/103, transcript, p.78.
42 C466/99, transcript, pp 112–15.

CHAPTER 4

1 C466/01, transcript, p.36.
2 Henry Tonks (1862–1937) trained and practised as a surgeon before taking evening classes in art, exhibiting with the New English Art Club and, in 1892, starting to teach at the Slade. He returned to medicine during the First World War, and from 1918 served as an official war artist. From 1918 to 1930 he was Slade Professor of Fine Art.
3 C466/01, transcript, p.54.
4 ibid., pp 37–8.
5 ibid., p.38.
6 ibid.
7 Philip Wilson Steer (1860–1942) trained in Paris and was a founder member of the New English Art Club. Steer's seascapes and beach scenes are as close as British artists of the period came to French Impressionism.
8 Robert Medley, interviewed by Andrew Lambirth, May–Aug. 1994, Artists' Lives, British Library reference C466/19, transcript, pp 31–2.
9 ibid., p.54.
10 ibid., p.31.
12 ibid., p.51.
12 *Les Bergers d'Arcadie* (The Arcadian Shepherds) (*c.*1637–9), also known as *'Et in Arcadia Ego'* ('I too [Death] Am in Arcadia'), a painting by Nicolas Poussin.
13 C466/19, transcript, p.52.
14 Sandra Blow, interviewed by Andrew Lambirth, Jul. 1996, Artists' Lives, British Library reference C466/42, transcript, p.35.
15 ibid., p.36.
16 Myra Hess (1890–1965) was a British concert pianist. In the inter-war years she toured Britain, Europe and America, where she was especially popular. During the Second World War, Hess organised almost 2,000 lunchtime concerts in the National Gallery, Trafalgar Square, playing in about 150 of them. Against a background of night-time bombing raids (which closed London's concert halls) and the war's effect on public morale, Hess's concerts lifted people's spirits.
17 C466/42, transcript, pp 38–9.
18 ibid., p.44.
19 ibid., pp 90–1.
20 Peter Blake, interviewed by Linda Sandino, Apr. 2003, Artists' Lives, British Library reference C466/168, track 4 of 28, 6'15"–6'46".

21 ibid., 6'15"–6'54", 14'40"–15'20".
22 ibid., 3'49"–4'57".
23 ibid., 19'00"–20'00".
24 ibid., 22'24"–24'27".
25 C466/59, transcript, pp 169–70.
26 ibid., p.23.
27 Barbara Steveni, interviewed by Melanie Roberts, Jun.–Oct. 1998, Artists' Lives, British Library reference C466/80, transcript, pp 33–4.
28 ibid., pp 34–5.
29 ibid., p.41.
30 ibid., pp 35–6.
31 ibid., p.40.
32 C466/69, transcript, p.29.
33 Frank Martin, interviewed by Melanie Roberts, Aug. 1997, Artists' Lives, British Library reference C466/58, transcript, p.7.
34 ibid., pp 7–8.
35 ibid., pp 64–5.
36 Anthony Caro, interviewed by Paul Moorhouse, Oct. 1993, Artists' Lives, British Library reference C466/016, recording closed, partial transcript, p.3.
37 ibid.
38 Barry Flanagan (1941–2009) was a sculptor and printmaker who studied at St Martin's between 1964 and 1966. Flanagan's approach to sculpture was always ironic. In the late 1960s he created ambiguous biomorphic forms out of sewn hessian containers filled with plaster and sand. In the 1980s he began making bronze sculptures of hares and other animals.
39 C466/016, partial transcript, p.5.
40 ibid., p.3.
41 Kim Lim, interviewed by Cathy Courtney, Oct. 1995, Artists' Lives, British Library reference C466/51, transcript, p.93.
42 ibid., p.97.
43 ibid., p.105.
44 ibid., p.97.
45 F. E. (Frederick Edward) McWilliam (1909–92) taught at the Slade from 1946 to 1968. He was a leading figure sculptor of the post-war era, whose many public commissions included *The Four Seasons* at the 1951 Festival of Britain and *Women of Belfast* (1972).
46 C466/51, transcript, p.92.
47 ibid., p.96.
48 ibid., pp 97–8.
49 C466/45, transcript, p.74.
50 ibid., p.104.
51 ibid., pp 141–2.
52 ibid., p.161.
53 ibid., p.172.
54 ibid., p.141.
55 ibid., p.92.

56 ibid.

57 William Townsend (1909–73) was a landscape painter. He had been a pupil of Henry Tonks at the Slade and an associate of William Coldstream and the Euston Road realist painters. In 1968 he was appointed professor at the Slade, with a brief to develop the postgraduate fine art course.

58 C466/45, transcript, pp 204–5.

59 C466/355, track 7.

60 ibid.

61 C466/43, transcript, pp 32–3.

62 ibid., p.112.

63 ibid.

64 ibid., pp 168–9.

65 ibid., p.173.

66 Euan Uglow (1932–2000) studied at Camberwell under William Coldstream, Claude Rogers and Victor Pasmore in the late 1940s. He became the most thorough exponent of Coldstream's methods, painting nudes and occasionally other subjects with the aid of painstakingly precise measurements and markers.

67 C466/43, transcript, p.174.

CHAPTER 5

1 C466/95, transcript, p.19.

2 C466/19, transcript, p.149.

3 Honoré Daumier (1808–79) was a French painter, sculptor and caricaturist. He is much better known as a maker of topical and satirical prints, and for his satirical busts of contemporary political figures, than as a portrait painter.

4 C466/19, transcript, pp 150–1.

5 ibid., p.156.

6 ibid., p.96.

7 C466/33, transcript, pp 97–8.

8 ibid., pp 227–8.

9 ibid., pp 37–8.

10 C466/95, transcript, pp 125–6.

11 ibid., p.199.

12 ibid., p.68.

13 ibid., p.19.

14 C466/34, transcript, pp 94–5.

15 ibid., pp 97–8.

16 C466/22, transcript, pp 142–3.

17 The golden section is a system for dividing a line or a rectangle into two unequal parts so that the ratio of the smaller part to the greater is the same as the ratio of the greater part to the whole. It can be applied to any picture, abstract or figurative. Frost was fascinated by the golden section, finding it both logical and mysterious as a means of organising pictorial space.

18 C466/22, transcript, pp 142–3.

19 ibid., p.207.

20 ibid., p.210.

21 Ceri Richards (1903–71), British painter, printer and maker of reliefs.

22 C466/69, transcript, p.28.

23 ibid., pp 20–1.

24 Frank Bowling, interviewed by Mel Gooding, Mar. 2001–Mar. 2007, Artists' Lives, British Library reference C466/127C466/127, transcript, p.462.

25 ibid., pp 160–1.

26 ibid., pp 573–5.

27 C466/59, transcript, pp 179–80.

28 Gillian Ayres, interviewed by Mel Gooding, Jun. 1999, Artists' Lives, British Library reference C466/91, transcript, pp 203–7.

29 ibid., p.244.

30 C466/296, transcript, p.122.

31 ibid., p.117.

32 ibid., p.169.

33 ibid., pp 163–4.

34 ibid., p.176.

35 C466/42, transcript, pp 109–10.

36 ibid., pp 155–7.

37 C466/45, transcript, pp 316–7.

38 ibid., p.144.

39 ibid., p.193.

40 ibid., p.249.

41 ibid., pp 267–8.

42 Peter Blake, interviewed in *Art Quarterly* (winter 2015) on the occasion of the first public exhibition of his portraits at Waddington Custot Galleries, London, Jan. 2016.

43 C466/168, track 13 of 28, 17'20"–19'19".

44 ibid., 7'56"–9'16".

45 C466/249, transcript, p.133.

46 ibid., pp 316–18.

CHAPTER 6

1 Lynn Chadwick, interviewed by Cathy Courtney, Apr.–May 1995, Artists' Lives, British Library reference C466/28, transcript, p.112.

2 ibid., pp 261–2.

3 ibid., p.277.

4 ibid., p.259.

5 ibid., p.277.

6 This phrase was used by Herbert Read in the exhibition catalogue to characterise and connect the work of Lynn Chadwick, Kenneth Armitage, Reg Butler, Geoffrey Clarke, F.E. McWilliam, Bernard Meadows, Eduardo Paolozzi and William Turnbull.

7 Alexander Calder (1898–1976). American sculptor who, in the early 1930s, began constructing

sculptures with movable parts, for which Marcel Duchamp invented the term 'mobiles'.

8 In 1952 the Institute of Contemporary Arts ran an international competition to create a monument to the Unknown Political Prisoner. The shortlisted sculptures were exhibited at the Tate Gallery in March–April 1953.

9 A reference to the burnished sunglasses on the 'Goggle Head' series of sculptures by Elisabeth Frink.

10 C466/08, transcript, pp 107–8.

11 C466/28, transcript, p.164

12 Charles-Edouard Jeanneret, known as Le Corbusier (1887–1965). Swiss-French modernist architect, who pioneered the use of stilt-like concrete columns ('pilotis') to raise buildings off the ground.

13 C466/08, transcript, pp 96–7.

14 Armitage is referring to the 1960s, and to Anthony Caro and his students and associates, such as Phillip King, Tim Scott and William Tucker.

15 C466/08, transcript, pp 199–200.

16 C466/93, transcript, p.63.

17 ibid., transcript, p.100.

18 In an article titled 'Social Realism and the Young', published in *The New Statesman and Nation* in July 1955, the critic John Berger identified Ralph Brown as one of a group of young social realist artists (also including the painters Derrick Greaves, Edward Middleditch and Jack Smith, and sculptor George Fullard). Berger championed what he saw as their spirit of social commitment, describing their work as 'famously unacceptable' to the British art establishment. He characterised Brown and Fullard's sculpture admiringly as 'cumbersomely large, totally lacking in charm, raw, nearly always proletarian in subject matter and possibly somewhat aggressive.'

19 C466/93, transcript, p.137.

20 ibid., p.173.

21 Smithfield Meat Market, on the northern edge of the City of London.

22 André Malraux (1901–76) was a French novelist and writer on art who served as Minister of Cultural Affairs under President Charles de Gaulle between 1959 and 1969. His three-volume work *The Psychology of Art* (1947–9) was reissued in a single volume titled *The Voices of Silence: Man and His Art*, which appeared in English translation in 1953.

23 C466/93, transcript, pp 145–6.

24 ibid., pp 230–1.

25 Elisabeth Frink, interviewed by Sarah Kent, Dec. 1992, Artists' Lives, British Library reference C466/12, transcript, p.9.

26 ibid., pp 12–13.

27 ibid., p.13.

28 ibid., p.30.

29 The pioneer British aviators John Alcock and Arthur Brown made the first non-stop Atlantic crossing in an adapted Vickers Vimy bomber from Newfoundland to Ireland in June 1919.

30 C466/12, transcript, pp 44–5.

31 ibid., pp 75–6.

32 ibid., p.77.

33 C466/40, transcript, p.187.

34 The Henry Art Gallery forms part of the University of Washington, Seattle, WA.

35 Family nickname of Kidner's son, Simon.

36 Kidner taught at Bath Academy of Art, Corsham, Wiltshire, from 1962 to 1982.

37 Commercial fibreglass resin filler.

38 C466/40, transcript, pp 128–9.

39 Phillip King (b.1934) studied with Anthony Caro at St Martin's School of Art and was one of a group of younger British sculptors to come to prominence following the exhibition 'New Generation Sculpture' at the Whitechapel Gallery in 1965.

40 The Russian sculptor and thinker Naum Gabo (1890–1977) lived in Britain between 1936 and 1946. His ideas about the spatial nature of sculpture broke with the traditional view of sculpture in terms of (apparently) solid mass: 'We [Constructivist sculptors] consider space from an entirely different point of view. We consider it as an absolute sculptural element, released from any closed volume.' ('Sculpture: Carving and Construction in Space', *Circle: International Survey of Constructive Art* [Faber and Faber, London: 1937], pp 106–7).

41 C466/40, transcript, pp 147–8.

42 ibid., p.131.

43 C466/113, transcript, p.17.

44 George Fullard (1923–73) began as a realist figurative sculptor in the 1950s; by the 1960s he was making large-scale junk assemblages. Hubert Dalwood (1924–76) similarly moved from figurative sculpture to more abstract, ambiguously biomorphic or totemic forms.

45 Probably a reference to a recording made by Garth Evans of people in Cardiff talking about his sculpture, included in the Peter Stuyvesant Foundation's City Sculpture Project 1972. A typical extract runs:

> *Man in butcher's shop: 'What's it supposed to be? Tell me, what is it? What's the idea of putting it there? It's a sculpture, and I suppose that's modern art, is it? Well, isn't art supposed to represent a thing, I always understood art was, it represented something. Well, what is that supposed to represent? [. . .] Well, I don't know, I can't see what it represents, I can't see [. . .] It's just angles and that's it to me, I can't see any form of anything in it. I can't see what it represents.'* (Quoted in 'City Sculpture Projects 1972', Studio International, accessed at http://www.studiointernational.com/index.php/city-sculpture-projects-1972-henry-moore-institute-leeds)

46 C466/113, transcript, p.34.

47 Kneale is referring to the Manx runestones, thought to date from between the fifth and twelfth centuries. These monuments are carved with both Christian symbols and Norse runes.

48 Oakeley Quarry near Blaenau Ffestiniog, at one time the largest underground slate quarry in the world, closed in March 2010.

49 C466/113, transcript, p.20.

50 C466/51, transcript, pp 78–9.

51 ibid., p.68.

52 ibid., p.100.

53 Site of a large ancient settlement near present-day Konya in Turkey. Çatalhöyük was occupied between about 7500 and 5700 BCE.

54 C466/51, transcript, pp 99–101.

55 C466/183, transcript, p.7.

56 Oliffe Richmond (1919–77), often described as a New Zealander by former students and colleagues, was in fact born in Hobart, Tasmania. After war service in the Australian army, he won a travelling scholarship to Europe. He was employed as an assistant by Henry Moore and in 1951 became a sculpture tutor at Chelsea School of Art. During the 1960s his work changed from figurative bronze sculpture to aluminium assemblage.

57 C466/183, transcript, p.8.

58 ibid., p.51.

59 ibid., pp 45–6.

60 C466/32, transcript, pp 158–9.

61 ibid., pp 223–5.

62 C466/355, track 8, clip 1, 29'43"–33'09".

63 In late August 2005 Hurricane Katrina caused widespread destruction in and around New Orleans. After a storm surge breached the flood defences in more than 20 places, around 80 per cent of the city was flooded for up to three weeks.

64 C466/355, track 8, clip 2, 1'03"–5'47".

CHAPTER 7

1 C466/69, transcript, p.20.

2 ibid., p.117.

3 Hamish Fulton, interviewed by Stephen Bury, Dec. 2002, Artists' Lives, British Library reference C466/158, track 4 of 4, 3'41"–3'45".

4 Michael Craig-Martin, interviewed by Melanie Roberts, Jul. 1998–Feb. 2002, Artists' Lives, British Library reference C466/109, track 9 of 33, 12'36"–12'53".

5 C466/58, transcript, pp 70–1.

6 A reference to the social class categories U (for upper class) and non-U (for middle-class pretensions to higher social status) first used by the social linguist Alan Ross in 1954 and popularised by the writer Nancy Mitford. In Latham's analogy, the sculpture department saw itself as the aristocracy of St Martin's.

7 'Barry Flanagan and John Latham', University College North Wales Art Festival, Bangor Art Gallery, 5–25 March 1966.

8 C466/69, transcript, p.60.

9 The magazine *Studio International* was the post-war incarnation of an art magazine that had first been published in 1893. Under Peter Townsend's editorship in the 1960s and 1970s, it became the leading British journal of contemporary art.

10 The event at Galerie Aachen took place in December 1966.

11 C466/69, transcript, pp 86–7.

12 Carlyle Reedy (b.1938) is an American poet and performance artist who has been based in Britain since the 1960s.

13 C466/80, transcript, p.85.

14 Alongside Steveni and Latham, other early members of APG included Stuart Brisley, David Hall, Barry Flanagan, Anna Ridley and Jeffrey Shaw. It would be more than two years before

the first industrial placement was agreed, involving the sculptor Garth Evans. In 1971 APG staged an exhibition at the Hayward Gallery, London. In 1975–6 Latham's own placement at the Scottish Office in Edinburgh resulted in proposals to designate the region's vast industrial spoil as works of art and mark them with beacons. The group continued until 1989, when it was reconstituted as O+I (Organisation and Imagination). In 2004 Tate acquired the APG archives.

15 Daniel Spoerri (b.1930) is a Romanian-born Swiss artist, known for his 'snare picture' assemblages of the remnants of meals and his book *An Anecdoted Topography of Chance* (1966).

16 Robert Filliou (1926–87) was a French artist and political scientist, much of whose work involved audience participation. On 17 January 1973 he initiated Art's Birthday, an annual celebration of the hypothetical birth of art 1 million years ago.

17 Run by the art dealer Victor Musgrave between 1953 and 1963, Gallery One was one of the most experimental British galleries of its time, showing a wide range of British and international contemporary practice, including conceptual art.

18 C466/80, transcript, pp 72–3.

19 ibid., pp 95–6.

20 Col. Sir Robert Adeane (1905–79). Trustee of the Tate Gallery and businessman whose numerous directorships included the record label Decca and building-materials supplier Ruberoid.

21 Roland Penrose (1900–84) was an artist, collector, and co-founder and chairman of the Institute of Contemporary Arts in London.

22 Michael Compton (1927–2013) was Keeper of Museum Services at the Tate Gallery (1970–87) and wrote on Op, Pop and kinetic art. Interviewed by Lydia O'Ryan, Jul.–Aug. 2005, Artists' Lives, British Library reference C466/198.

23 C466/80, transcript, pp 72–3.

24 C466/69, transcript, pp 81–2.

25 ibid., pp 67–8.

26 C466/80, transcript, pp 97–8.

27 Paul Neagu, interviewed by Mel Gooding, Oct. 1994–Mar. 1995, Artists' Lives, British Library reference C466/27, transcript, pp 84–5.

28 ibid., p.98.

29 For his exhibition 'Staple Cheese (A Race)' (1970) at the Eugenia Butler Gallery, Los Angeles, the Swiss artist Dieter Roth (1930–98) exhibited 37 suitcases full of cheese, together with pictures made of cheese.

30 C466/27, transcript, p.112.

31 ibid., p.112.

32 Middle Earth was a club in King Street, Covent Garden, known for the quality of the bands it hosted in the late 1960s (among them Pink Floyd, The Who and T Rex) and regular police raids.

33 C466/43, transcript, pp 148–51.

34 ibid., p.252.

35 Mary Kelly, interviewed by Lydia O'Ryan, Sept. 2004, Artists' Lives, British Library reference C466/194, track 7 of 10, 10'54"–11'20".

36 ibid., track 6 of 10, 0'33"–3'09".
37 ibid., 11'16"–13'55".
38 ibid., track 1 of 10, 11'14"–11'31".
39 ibid., track 7 of 10, 29'10"–31'12".
40 Kelly's partner, the sculptor Ray Barrie.
41 In 1973 Barry Barker and the artist William Furlong had established *Audio Arts*, a magazine containing interviews with artists and distributed in the form of audio cassettes, which ran until 2006. William Furlong was interviewed for Artists' Lives by Cathy Courtney, Dec. 2004–Jul. 2008, British Library reference C466/215. Also interviewed for Artists' Lives by Cathy Courtney, Jan. 2011–Dec. 2014, British Library reference C466/310.
42 Cathexis, from an Ancient Greek word meaning retention, is the English translation of Sigmund Freud's term *Besetzung*. It means the investment of psychic energy (mental or emotional) in a person, idea or object.
43 C466/194, track 9 of 10, 0'12"–2'15".
44 C466/109, track 9 of 33, 7'30"–11'41".
45 ibid., track 9 of 33, 12'36"–14'27".
46 ibid., track 11 of 33, 7'06"–7'57".
47 C466/158, track 3 of 4, 0'15"–1'26".
48 *Arte povera* is an Italian term meaning 'poor art'. First used by the critic Germano Celant in 1967, it refers to non-art or 'poor' materials like soil, rags and tree branches, used by such artists as Luciano Fabbro, Mario Merz and Michelangelo Pistoletto as a means of subverting what Fulton describes as art's 'collectible, tradeable, valuable objectness'.
49 C466/158, track 4 of 4, 3'19"–5'10".
50 ibid., track 4 of 4, 19'43"–20'40"
51 C466/69, transcript, p.93.

CHAPTER 8

1 C466/96, transcript, p.7.
2 C466/249, transcript, p.16.
3 ibid., p.22.
4 C466/42, transcript, pp 155–7.
5 C466/95, transcript, pp 124–5.
6 C466/103, transcript, p.92.
7 C466/91, transcript, p.59.
8 C466/43, transcript, pp 296–7.
9 C466/40, transcript, p.169.
10 C466/27, transcript, p.191.
11 C466/01, transcript, pp 79–80.
12 C466/183, transcript, p.41.
13 C466/113, transcript, p.68.
14 C466/51, transcript, p.28.
15 C466/45, transcript, pp 132–4.
16 C466/96, transcript, pp 21–2.

17 ibid., p.47.

18 ibid., p.51.

19 C466/32, transcript, p.182.

20 C466/93, transcript, p.165.

21 C466/127, transcript, pp 474–5.

22 C466/02, transcript, p.122.

23 C466/08, transcript, pp 304–5.

24 C466/016, partial transcript, p.9.

Image Credits

The images in this book are courtesy of and (where indicated) copyright of the following individuals and institutions.

Annely Juda Fine Art, London / © David Nash 72
© APG / Tate Archive 182
Barford Sculptures 84, 114
Wilhelmina Barns-Graham Trust 58
Central Saint Martins Museum & Study Collection 100
Estate of Paul Feiler / © Andrew Lanyon 133
Flowers Gallery 91
Estate of Elisabeth Frink 164
Estate of Nigel Henderson 55
Estate of Patrick Heron / © F.E. McWilliam 67
Patricia Holland / Creative Commons licence 121
Tess Jaray 45
Lypiatt Studios 34
Roger Mayne Archive / Mary Evans Picture Library 48, 104, 108, 141, 157
National Portrait Gallery, London 35, 89, 94, 130, 177 (© John Malcolm Couzins)
New Art Centre, Roche Court 117
Estate of Breon O'Casey 65
Osborne Samuel / © David Farrell 154
Pangolin, London 162
Redfern Gallery / © Steve Garvey 19
Julian Rothenstein 30
Science and Society Picture Library / © Lewis Morley Archive 97
Tate Images / © Estate of Paul Neagu. All Rights Reserved, DACS 2018 188
Tate Images / © Stuart Brisley 192
Waddington Custot 148
ZUMA Press, Inc. / Alamy Stock Photo Frontispiece

Index

Page numbers in *italics* refer to illustrations.

Académie Moderne, Paris 103
Ackerman Linkage 57
acrylic paints 140–2, 143, 150
Adams, Robert 169
Adeane, Sir Robert 185, 241
Agar, Eileen *19*
  on being an artist 205
  biography 211
  childhood 29, 33–4
  on parenthood 40
  Slade School of Fine Art 100–1
Aitchison, Craigie 149
Albers, Josef 196
Alcock, John 238
Angry Arts Week 98
Anguissola, Sofonisba 228
Apelles 20–1
APG *see* Artist Placement Group
Armitage, Kenneth *157*
  on being an artist 210
  biography 211–12
  first steps in art 53, 56–8
  People in the Wind 158–9
  on sculpture 153, 156–60
Art and Culture (Greenberg) 181
Art and Culture 1966–69 (Latham) 181
Art & Language 196
art school experience and 'first steps in art'
  Central School of Art and Crafts *108*
  Chelsea School of Art *2*, 110–12, 122–3
  Feiler, Paul 61–3
  Gravesend Technical College and School of Art 99, 106–9
  Guildford School of Art 123–4
  Herman, Josef 63–4
  Heron, Patrick 53–4, 66–8
  Himid, Lubaina 75–6
  Hornsey College of Arts and Crafts 120, 124–5, 173
  Kneale, Bryan 68–9
  Nash, David 71–3
  O'Casey, Breon 53, 64–6
  Paolozzi, Eduardo 53, 54–6
  Portsmouth School of Art 112–13
  Rothenstein, Michael 53–4
  Royal Academy Schools 99, 106
  Royal College of Art 99, 106
  St Martin's School of Art 25, 99, 103–6, 113–16, 180–1, 185
    sculpture teaching studio *100*

Sandle, Michael 53, 69–70
Slade School of Fine Art 99, 100–2, 105, 116–22, 119–20, 122, 125–6
Smith, Jack 54
West Hartlepool College of Art 109–10
arte povera 199, 242
Artist, The (magazine) 70
Artist Placement Group (APG) 25, 112, 183–7, 191, 240–1
Artists' International Association 102
Art's Birthday 241
Ascott, Roy 180
Auden, W.H. 16
Audio Arts (magazine) 242
Auerbach, Frank 20, 148–9
Ayres, Gillian *141*
on being an artist 203–4
biography 212
on painting 127, 141–2

Bacon, Francis 17, 26, 105, 129
Bailey, David 107
Bar-B-Q (Piché) 96
Barker, Barry 195, 242
Barlow, Phyllida *177*
biography 212
Chelsea School of Art 122–3
first steps in art 73–5
on parenthood 20, 47–8
on sculpture 153, 176–8
untitled: upturnedhouse, 2 178
Barns-Graham, Wilhelmina *58*
biography 212
first steps in art 53, 58–60
on painting 127–8, 134
'Things of a Kind in Order and Disorder' 134
Barrie, Ray 195, 242
Barthes, Roland 16
Beatles, the 38
Beattie, Basil
biography 212–13
on painting 140–1
Second World War 83–4, 92–3
West Hartlepool College of Art 109–10
Beerbohm, Max 32
Bell, Clive 102
Bell, Vanessa 102
Berenson, Bernard: *The Italian Painters of the Renaissance* 22
Berger, John 161, 238
Bergers d'Arcadie, Les (Poussin) 103, 234
Berwick Street Film Collective 194
Better Books, London 97
Biba 183
Bird (Frink) 163
Black Beast (Chadwick) *202*
Blake, Peter *148*
biography 213
Gravesend Technical College and School of Art 99, 106–9
on painting 127, 148–9
Royal College of Art 106
Bloomsbury Group 102
Blow, Sandra *104*
on being an artist 202–3
biography 213
Green and White 106
on painting 127–8, 144–5
Royal Academy Schools 106
Royal College of Art 106
St Martin's School of Art 103–6
Vivace 144–5
Blythe, Ronald 24
Blyton, Enid 71, 232
Bowling, Dan 139
Bowling, Frank
on being an artist 209
biography 213–14
national service 94–5
on painting 138–9
Brancusi, Constantin 116, 165
Braque, Georges 54, 66
Bratby, John 17
Brill, Frederick 111
Brisley, Deborah 182–3, 191
Brisley, Stuart
Artist Placement Group (APG) 191, 240

- on being an artist 204
- biography 214
- Guildford School of Art 123–4
- Hornsey College of Arts and Crafts 124–5
- *Moments of Decision/Indecision 192*
- performance art 182–3, 191–3
- Second World War 84–5
- Slade School of Fine Art 125–6

British European Airways 186–7
Brown, Arthur 238
Brown, Ralph 238
- on being an artist 208–9
- biography 214
- First World War 79
- *The Meat Porters* 161–3, *162*
- on sculpture 153, 160–3, 169

Buenos Aires 33
Buhler, Robert: photograph of Peter Blake *148*
Bumpus, Judith 219
Burial of Count Orgaz (Latham) 180
Burke, Thomas: *Limehouse Nights* 54–5
Burri, Alberto 106
Burroughs, William 125
Bury, Stephen 217
Butler, Cortina 41
Butler, Creon 41–2
Butler, Reg 29, 40–2, 158, 169, 173, 229
Butler, Rosemary *see* Young, Rosemary

Cage, John: *4'33"* 199
Cake Man (Neagu) 189, 190
Calder, Alexander 154, 157, 237–8
Caro, Anthony 26, 153
- on being an artist 210
- biography 214–15
- *Early One Morning* 43
- family life 42, 43, 44
- *Month of May* 43
- St Martin's School of Art 69, 113–15, 116
- *Woman in Pregnancy 114*

Çatalhöyük, Turkey 172, 239
cathexis 242
Celant, Germano 242
Central School of Art and Crafts *108*
Cézanne, Paul 61, 66, 74, 102, 136
Chadwick, Lynn *202*
- biography 215
- *Black Beast 202*
- on sculpture 153–8, 169
- *The Watchers 154*, 156

Chagall, Marc 109
Chamberlain, Neville 82
Chelsea School of Art 2, 110–12, 122–3
childhood
- Agar, Eileen 29, 33–4
- Beattie, Basil 83–4, 92–3
- Brisley, Stuart 84–5
- Herman, Josef 34–7
- Lacey, Bruce 38–40
- Rothenstein, Michael 29, 30–3
- Sandle, Michael 37–8, 85–6

Ciobotaru, Gillian Wise 46
Clatworthy, Robert 122–3, 169
Coldstream, William 120, 125–6, 148, 185, 236
Compton, Michael 185, 186, 241
Cornwall 62, 67
- St Ives 49, 59, 134–6

Cotman, John Sell 70
Courtney, Cathy 211, 215, 216, 219, 221, 224
Couzins, John Malcolm (photograph of Phyllida Barlow) *177*
Craig-Martin, Michael 179, 196–8, 199, 215
- *An Oak Tree* 196

Craxton, John 105
Crisp, Quentin 107
Crucifix in 4 Parts (Piché) 174
Cruikshank, Robert 75
cubism 103
Curtis, Penelope 219
Cut Piece (Ono) 183

Dalwood, Hubert 169, 239
Dartington Hall 64, 65, 81–2, 233
Daumier, Honoré 128, 236
de Kooning, Willem 140
Deacon, Richard 180
Degas, Edgar 128, 228
Delacroix, Eugène 103

Destroyed City, The (Zadkine) 160
Destruction in Art Symposium (1966) 181–3
Dobson, Frank 160
Donovan, Terence 107
Doone, Rupert 101
Doyle, Arthur Conan: *The White Company* 55, 230
Dring, William 106
Duchamp, Marcel 21, 179
Dyke, Anna 218

Early One Morning (Caro) 43
Elder, Nicholas (photograph of Breon O'Casey) *65*
Elmhirst, Dorothy 64, 233
Elmhirst, Leonard 64, 233
Emin, Tracey 42
Evans, Garth 169, 187, 239, 241
Evans, George Ewart 24

Fabbro, Luciano 242
Famous Five, The (Blyton) 71, 232
Farrell, David (photograph of Lynn Chadwick) *154*
fatherhood
  Frost, Terry 48–9
  Nash, David 29, 48, 50–1, 53
Fedden, Mary 156
Feiler, Paul *133*
  on being an artist 203
  biography 216
  first steps in art 61–3
  First World War 77–8
  Nazi persecutions 62, 82
  on painting 127, 132–3
Fenwick Place, Lambeth, London 169–70
Filliou, Robert 184, 241
First (magazine) 114
First World War (1914--18) 77–80
Flanagan, Barry 115, 180, 181, 196, 235, 240
Flayed Ox (Rembrandt) 163
Fluxus 179, 184, 190
Forge, Andrew 119
4'33" (Cage) 199
Frankenthaler, Helen 140, 142, 143
Freud, Lucian 21, 26, 105
Freud, Sigmund 242
Frink, Elisabeth 41, 153, 158, *164*, 169, 229, 238
  biography 216
  Bird 163
  on sculpture 163–6
  St Martin's School of Art 116, 122–3
Frost, Adrian 49
Frost, Matthew *48*
Frost, Stephen *48*
Frost, Terry *48*
  biography 216
  First World War 78–9
  on painting 134–6
  on parenthood 48–9
  Second World War 86–8
  Walk Along the Quay 49
  Walking Along the Quay, Blue Movement 135
Fry, Roger 102, 103
Fullard, George 47, 161, 169, 238, 239
Fulton, Hamish 198–9, 216–17
Furlong, William 242

Gabo, Naum 59, 168, 179, 239
Gallery One, London 181, 241
Gargoyle Club, London 105
Garvey, Steve (photograph of Eileen Agar) *19*
Gear, William *130*
  biography 217
  first steps in art 60–1
  Landscape Image No.1 129–32
  on painting 129–32
Generative Art Group 190
Gertler, Mark 102
Giacometti, Alberto 116, 155, 165
Gilbert & George 180, 185, 196
Gillies, Sir William 61, 231
Gillray, James 75
Girling, Sheila *84*
  biography 217
  First World War 79–80

on painting 142–4
on parenthood 40, 42–4
Second World War 82–3
glasshouses 233
golden section 236
Gombrich, Ernst 16, 37
Gooding, Mel 212, 213, 218, 222, 223
Gore, Frederick 115–16, 120
Gowing, Lawrence 122
Goya, Francisco 128
Gozzoli, Benozzo 22
Grant, Duncan 102
Gravesend Technical College and School of Art 99, 106–9
Great War, The (BBC documentary series) 232
Greaves, Derrick 16–17, 18, 22, 120, 161, 238
Greco, El 92, 180
Green and White (Blow) 106
Greenberg, Clement: *Art and Culture* 181
Gregory, Clive and Anita 137
Gregory, Kirstie 212
Group Theatre, London 101
Guildford School of Art 123–4
Gurdjieff, George 189

Hall, David 186–7, 240
Hamilton, Richard 180
Harrison, Charles 194
Harrison, George 38
Haven (Jaray) 147
'Hayward Annual '78' (exhibition) 46–7
Hebblethwaite, Miss 59
Heckroth, Hein 81, 233
Help! (film) 38
Henderson, Nigel (photograph of Eduardo Paolozzi) *55*
Hepworth, Barbara 41, 49, 56, 59, 134, 136, 160
Herman, David 36
Herman, Josef *35*
biography 217–18
childhood 34–7
first steps in art 63–4
Nazi persecutions 34, 80–1
Herodotus: *Histories* 20
Heron, Delia 66, *67*
Heron, Patrick *67*
biography 218
first steps in art 53–4, 66–8
Hess, Myra 105, 234
Hilliard, John 196
Himid, Lubaina 26
on being an artist 201–2
biography 218
first steps in art 75–6
on painting 149–51
Hockney, David 21, 106, 107, 138
Hogarth, William 75
Holden-White, Vere 111
Holland, Patricia: stills from *The Hornsey Film 121*
Hooker, Denise 222
Hornsey College of Arts and Crafts 120, 124–5, 173
The Hornsey Film 121
Hoyland, John 120
Hughes, Richard 51
Hurricane Katrina 240

Ingres, Jean-Auguste-Dominique: *Odalisque* 103
Institute of Contemporary Arts (ICA) 238
Iron and Steel Federation 187
Isle of Man 70–1
Italian Painters of the Renaissance, The (Berenson) 22

Jaray, Anna 44, *45*
Jaray, Georgia *45*
Jaray, Tess *45*
on being an artist 207
biography 218–19
Haven 147
Hornsey College of Arts and Crafts 120–2
on painting 127–8, 146–7
on parenthood 44–7
Slade School of Fine Art 119–20, 122
Jeanneret, Charles-Edouard 238 *see* Le Corbusier

John, Augustus 32
Jooss Ballet 81

Kar, Ida (photographs by)
Gear, William *130*
Herman, Joseph *35*
Latham, John *89*
Smith, Jack *94*
Kelly, Mary 193–6, 219
The Nightcleaners 194
Post-partum Document 195–6
Women and Work Project 195
Kent, Sarah 216
Kidner, Michael *91*, 239
on being an artist 205
biography 219
on sculpture 153, 166–8
Second World War 90–2
King, Phillip 168, 169, 239
Kitaj, R.B. 106
Kitchen, Paddy 139
Kitchen Sink School 17–19
Kneale, Bryan 70
on being an artist 206
biography 220
first steps in art 68–9
on sculpture 153, 168–70

Lacey, Bruce 5, *97*
biography 220
childhood 38–40
Vietnam War protest 97–8
Lambirth, Andrew *19*, 213, 220, 221, 225
Landscape Image No.1 (Gear) 129–32
Lanyon, Andrew
photograph of Paul and Catharine Feiler *133*
Lanyon, Peter 68
Latham, John *89*
Art and Culture 1966–69 181
Artist Placement Group (APG) 183, 185–7
biography 220–1
Burial of Count Orgaz 180
Chelsea School of Art 110–11, 112, 136–7
on conceptual art 179, 199
Second World War 88–9, 92
St Martin's School of Art 180–1
Lawson, Julie 185
Le Corbusier (Charles-Edouard Jeanneret) 159, 238
Léger, Fernand 60, 103
Lhote, André 167, 231
Lijn, Liliane 46
Lim, Kim 46, *117*, 207, 221
on sculpture 153, 170–2
Slade School of Fine Art 116–18
St Martin's School of Art 115–16
Limehouse Nights (Burke) 54–5
Lippi, Fra Filippo 21–2
Lives of the Most Excellent Architects, Painters and Sculptors (Vasari) 20, 21–2, 228
London Labour and the London Poor (Mayhew) 15–16
Long, Richard 180, 196, 198
Louis, Morris 140, 143
Lucrezia, Madonna 228

McCullin, Don 107
MacTaggart, William 231
McWilliam, F.E. 116, 235
photograph of Patrick and Delia Heron *67*
Malraux, André: *The Voices of Silence* 163, 238
Manchester Airport, Frink sculpture at 165–6
Mancini, Frederick and George 113
Mandrake Club, London 105
Manifesto of Palpable Art (Neagu) 190
Manx runestones 239
Manzú, Giacomo 160
Marc, Franz 62
Marchand, Jean 103
Marini, Marino 160
Marowitz, Charles 97
Martin, Frank 181
Artist Placement Group (APG) 184, 185
biography 221
Portsmouth School of Art 112–13
St Martin's School of Art 99, 113, 114, 116, 180

materials
  acrylic paints 140–2, 143, 150
  austerity decade 129
  bronze 54, 86, 160, 163
  clay 122–3, 159
  fibreglass 96, 167, 168, 187
  foodstuffs 189–90, 191–2
  oil paints 119–20, 129
  plaster of Paris 144, 159, 163, 165
  plastic 187
  in POW camps 87–8
  slate 169–70
  steel 155–6, 159, 187
  stone 136, 170–1, 173
  video 186–7
  wood 174–6, 178, 180
Matisse, Henri 54, 66, 110, 136
Mayhew, Henry: *London Labour and the London Poor* 15–16
Mayne, Roger, photographs by
  Armitage, Kenneth *157*
  Ayres, Gillian *141*
  Blow, Sandra *104*
  Central School of Art and Design *108*
  Frost, Terry *48*
Meadows, Bernard 169
Meat Porters, The (Brown) 161–3, *162*
Meccano 53, 54, 56–7
Medici, Cosimo de' 21–2
Medley, Robert
  Académie Moderne, Paris 103
  biography 221
  on painting 127, 128–9
  Slade School of Fine Art 101–2
Mellis, Margaret 59
Merz, Mario 242
Michelangelo 21, 128
Michelet, Jules 15
Middle Earth, London 191, 241
Middleditch, Edward 17, 120, 238
Milligan, Spike 38
Miró, Joan 136
Mitford, Nancy 240
Modern French Painters (Wilenski) 54
Moments of Decision/Indecision (Brisley) *192*
Monet, Claude 62
Month of May (Caro) 43
Moore, Henry 26, 33, 56, 102, 116, 160, 172, 173
Moorhouse, Paul 215
Morley, Lewis (photograph of Bruce Lacey) *97*
Morris, Bob 61
Morris, William 16
Mother Bathing a Child (Smith) 18
motherhood
  Agar, Eileen 40
  Barlow, Phillida 20, 47–8
  Girling, Sheila 40, 42–4
  Jaray, Tess 44–7
  Young, Rosemary 40–2
Musgrave, Victor 241
music 134
Mussolini, Benito 92

Nash, David *72*
  on being an artist 23, 25, 208
  biography 221–2
  first steps in art 71–3
  on parenthood 29, 48, 50–1, 53
  on sculpture 153
  Wooden Boulder 174–6
  Wooden Waterway 174–6
Nash, Jack 50
Nash, William 50
National Life Stories 13, 17
national service 93–5
Nazis 34, 44, 62, 77, 80–2
Neagu, Paul
  on being an artist 205
  biography 222
  Cake Man 189, 190
  Manifesto of Palpable Art 190
  performance art 179, 187–90, *188*
Nelli, Sister Plautilla 228
'New Art, The' (exhibition, 1972) 196–7
'New Generation Sculpture' (exhibition, 1965) 173, 239

Nicholson, Ben 59, 68
Nightcleaners, The (Kelly) 194

Oak Tree, An (Craig-Martin) 196
Oakeley Quarry 170, 239
Oaklands Park Hotel, Weybridge 232
O'Casey, Breon *65*, 222–3, 231
  first steps in art 53, 64–6
O'Casey, Sean 64
Odalisque (Ingres) 103
O+I (Organisation and Imagination) 241
Ono, Yoko 179, 181–3
  Cut Piece 183
  Shadow Piece 182
O'Ryan, Lydia 219
Ozenfant, Amédée 103

painting
  Ayres, Gillian 127, 141–2
  Barns-Graham, Wilhelmina 127–8, 134
  Beattie, Basil 140–1
  Blake, Peter 127, 148–9
  Blow, Sandra 127–8, 144–5
  Bowling, Frank 138–9
  Feiler, Paul 127, 132–3
  Frost, Terry 134–6
  Gear, William 129–32
  Girling, Sheila 142–4
  Himid, Lubaina 149–51
  Jaray, Tess 127–8, 146–7
  Medley, Robert 127, 128–9
Paolozzi, Eduardo *55*
  biography 223
  first steps in art 53, 54–6
  Vietnam War 95
parenthood
  Agar, Eileen 40
  Barlow, Phyllida 20, 47–8
  Frost, Terry 48–9
  Girling, Sheila 40, 42–4
  Jaray, Tess 44–7
  Nash, David 29, 48, 50–1, 53
  Young, Rosemary 40–2
Paris 33–4, 60, 101, 102–3, 108, 124
Parker, Ian (photograph of David Nash) *72*
Pasmore, Victor 236
Penrose, Roland 185, 241
People in the Wind (Armitage) 158–9
'Performance' scrapbook (Neagu) *188*
Picasso, Pablo 29, 54, 110
Piché, Roland
  Bar-B-Q 96
  on being an artist 206
  biography 223
  Crucifix in 4 Parts 174
  on sculpture 153, 172–4
  Vietnam War 96
Piché, Samsone 96
Piper, John 102
Pissarro, Camille 228
Pistoletto, Michelangelo 242
Plato 201
Pliny the Elder 20–1
Plymouth 85–6
Pollock, Jackson 70, 143, 232
Portsmouth School of Art 112–13
Post-partum Document (Kelly) 195–6
Potter, Beatrix 71, 232
Poussin, Nicolas: *Les Bergers d'Arcadie* 103, 234
Protogenes 20–1

Read, Herbert 237
'Recording Britain' project 31
Reedy, Carlyle 183, 240
Reid, Christopher 222
Rembrandt 62, 147
  Flayed Ox 163
Rex, Xavery 63–4
Reynolds, Sir Joshua 99
Rhoikos 20
Riace bronzes 165
Richards, Ceri 237
  Trafalgar Square, London 136
Richmond, Oliffe 173, 240
Ridley, Anna 240
Riemenschneider, Tilman 62, 231
Riley, Bridget 42, 144, 167
Roberts, Melanie 214, 215, 220, 221, 224

Rodin, Auguste 165
Rogers, Claude 236
Ross, Alan 240
Rossetti, Dante Gabriel 16
Rossi, Properzia de' 228
Roth, Dieter 241
Rothenstein, Alice 30, 32
Rothenstein, Betty *30*, 31
Rothenstein, John 31, 228
Rothenstein, Michael *30*
 on being an artist 209–10
 biography 223
 childhood 29, 30–3
 first steps in art 53–4
Rothenstein, Rachel *30*, 31
Rothenstein, William 30, 31, 32, 228
Roundhouse: Angry Arts Week 98
Rover, The (comic) 55
Royal Academy Schools 99, 106
Royal College of Art 99, 106
Ryder, Albert Pinkham 70, 232

Samuel, Raphael 24
Sandino, Linda 213
Sandle, Michael
 on being an artist 203
 biography 224
 childhood 37–8
 first steps in art 53, 69–70
 Second World War 85–6
 A Twentieth Century Memorial 96–7
 Untergang des Dritten Reichs (*The End of the Third Reich*) 86
 Vietnam War 96–7
Savoia-Marchetti SM79 (plane) 92, 233
Scott, Tim 169, 185
sculpture
 Armitage, Kenneth 153, 156–60
 Barlow, Phyllida 153, 176–8
 Brown, Ralph 153, 160–3, 169
 Chadwick, Lynn 153–8, 169
 Frink, Elisabeth 163–6
 Kidner, Michael 153, 166–8
 Kneale, Bryan 153, 168–70
 Lim, Kim 153, 170–2
 Nash, David 153
 Piché, Roland 153, 172–4
Second World War (1939--45) 82–92
 national service 93–5
 'Recording Britain' project 31
 see also Jews, Nazi persecutions of
Sellers, Peter 38
Seurat, Georges 101, 102
Shadow Piece (Ono) *182*
Shaw, George Bernard 64
Shaw, Jeffrey 240
Sheffield 83, 99
Shepp, Alan 96
Sidey, Tessa 217
'significant form' 102
Signorelli, Luca 128
Slade School of Fine Art 99, 100–2, 105, 116–22, 119–20, 122, 125–6
Smith, David 113
Smith, Jack *94*, 238
 on being an artist 201, 208
 biography 224
 first steps in art 54
 and the Kitchen Sink School 17, 18–19
 Mother Bathing a Child 18
 Second World War 83, 93–4
Smith, Matthew 70
Soukop, Willi 81–2, 163, 224–5
Spoerri, Daniel 184, 241
St Ives, Cornwall 49, 59, 66, 67, 134–6
St Martin's School of Art 25, 99, 103–6, 113–16, 180–1, 185
 sculpture teaching studio *100*
Stamp, Terence 107
Steer, Philip Wilson 102, 234
Steiner, Rudolf 50, 175, 189
Steveni, Barbara 179
 Artist Placement Group (APG) 183–5
 biography 224
 Chelsea School of Art 110–12
 Destruction in Art Symposium (1966) 181–3, *182*
Steveni, Leo 111–12

Stezaker, John 196
Stokes, Adrian 59
Stroud Valley 31
Studio International (magazine) 182–3, 240
Sutton, Philip 229
Sylvester, David 17–19

Tagore, Rabindranath 233
Taylor, John Gordon 73, 232
Theodoros 20
'Things of a Kind in Order and Disorder' (Barns-Graham) 134
Thompson, Paul 218
Tobey, Mark 81, 233
Tonks, Henry 101, 102, 234
Townsend, Peter 240
Townsend, William 122, 236
Trafalgar Square, London (Richards) 136
training *see* art schools
Trevelyan, Julian 156
Trix construction sets 56
Tucker, William 169, 181
Tunnard, John 232
Turner, J.M.W. 140
Twentieth Century Memorial, A (Sandle) 96–7

Uglow, Euan 126, 236
Underwood, Leon 33, 229
Untergang des Dritten Reichs (*The End of the Third Reich*) (Sandle) 86
untitled: upturnedhouse, 2 (Barlow) 178

Vasari, Giorgio: *Lives of the Most Excellent Architects, Painters and Sculptors* 20, 21–2, 228
Velázquez, Diego 70
Vietnam War 77, 95–8, 194
Vivace (Blow) 144–5
Voices of Silence, The (Malraux) 163, 238

Waddington, Ferriel (photograph of Kim Lim) *117*
Walk Along the Quay (Frost) 49
Walking Along the Quay, Blue Movement (Frost) 135
Watchers, The (Chadwick) *154*, 156
Wentworth, Richard 47, 230
West Hartlepool College of Art 109–10
Westley, Hester 217
Whistler, James Abbott McNeill 228
White Company, The (Doyle) 55, 230
Whiteley, Gillian 214, 220, 225
Whiteread, Rachel 41
Whitford, Frank 223
Wilenski, R.H.: *Modern French Painters* 54
Williams, D.J.: photograph of Ralph Brown *162*
Williamson, H.S. 111
Winnicott, Donald 29
Withey, Matthew 223
Wizard, The (comic) 55
Woman in Pregnancy (Caro) *114*
women
  disparagement of 41, 46, 101, 122, 229
  and family responsibilities 42–5, 46–7
  Hayward Annual '78 exhibition 46–7
  women's movement 194–6
Women and Work Project (Kelly) 195
Wood, Christopher 70
Wooden Boulder (Nash) 174–6
Wooden Waterway (Nash) 174–6
Woodrow, Bill 180
Woollcombe, Tamsyn 211, 212, 216
World War I (1914–18) *see* First World War
World War II (1939—45) *see* Second WorldWar

Young, Rosemary 40–2, 225
Young British Artists 196

Zadkine, Ossip: *The Destroyed City* 160